10 TOUCHPOINTS TO TRANSITION SMOOTHLY,
STRENGTHEN YOUR FAMILY,
AND CONTINUE BUILDING YOUR CAREER

THE
PARENTAL
LEAVE
PLAYBOOK

AMY BEACOM, EdD

FOUNDER AND CEO OF
THE CENTER FOR PARENTAL LEAVE LEADERSHIP

SUE CAMPBELL

WILEY

Published by John Wiley & Sons, Inc., Hoboken, New Jersey.
Published simultaneously in Canada.

For general information on our other products and services or for technical support, please contact our Customer Care Department within the United States at (800) 762-2974, outside the United States at (317) 572-3993 or fax (317) 572-4002.

Wiley publishes in a variety of print and electronic formats and by print-on-demand. Some material included with standard print versions of this book may not be included in e-books or in print-on-demand. If this book refers to media such as a CD or DVD that is not included in the version you purchased, you may download this material at http://booksupport.wiley.com. For more information about Wiley products, visit www.wiley.com.

Library of Congress Cataloging-in-Publication Data

Names: Beacom, Amy, author. | Campbell, Sue (Freelance writer), author.
Title: The parental leave playbook : 10 touchpoints to transition smoothly, strengthen your family, and continue building your career / Amy Beacom, Sue Campbell.
Description: Hoboken, New Jersey : John Wiley & Sons, Inc., [2021] | Includes bibliographical references and index.
Identifiers: LCCN 2021033913 (print) | LCCN 2021033914 (ebook) | ISBN 9781119789239 (hardback) | ISBN 9781119789116 (adobe pdf) | ISBN 9781119789246 (epub)
Subjects: LCSH: Parental leave.
Classification: LCC HD6065 .B34 2021 (print) | LCC HD6065 (ebook) | DDC 331.25/763—dc23
LC record available at https://lccn.loc.gov/2021033913
LC ebook record available at https://lccn.loc.gov/2021033914

Cover Design: Wiley
Cover image: Inspired by Sorbetto/Getty Images and created using Humaaans.com

SKY10028911_080621

This book is dedicated to:

My children, Luca and Maggie, who transformed me and my world.
My beloved, Mike, who believes in me always.
My mom, Peggy, who taught me how to do it all, with heart first.
—AB

My family and all the families about to form.
—SC

Contents

Author's Note

THIS BOOK WAS written during a global pandemic, social justice protests, climate catastrophes, and extreme political division. At points, our stock market crashed, our hospitals nearly did, our Capitol fell under siege, our loved ones got sick, and unimaginable numbers of them died. Our social safety net was tested and found sorely lacking. Record numbers of people became homeless, and those of us who didn't couldn't safely leave our houses. Our schools and workplaces shut down, and parents had to somehow figure out how to keep working—while also serving as online school navigators or homeschool teachers *and* loving moms and dads.

There wasn't a lot about 2020 and early 2021 that most of us had ever experienced before. It was the definition of a world in transition and often pure chaos. There were genuine moments of dread when we asked ourselves if we would get to the other side intact—as individuals, as a country, and as an interdependent world.

Over a year into it, we are only now beginning to lift our heads to notice that we have also been given some invaluable gifts during this time.

For many, our relationships with our loved ones have moved back into center position after being pushed aside by work for too long. Nurturing our physical and mental health has taken on new significance and priority. Where our careers may have felt off-track, job loss (either from being let go or being forced to quit for caregiving duties) has created an opening to realign our work with our values. Indeed, our guiding values have taken on deeper significance as we search for meaning amid so much trauma.

These gifts that we couldn't have imagined just a year ago now exist and are real. They will alter our perspective of the future as well as how we live each day. We wouldn't have developed our new priorities and enhanced awareness if we hadn't first weathered and persevered through the storm.

As much as the polarization of 2020 tried to force everyone into opposing camps, the aftermath is reminding us a healthy system cannot be *either/or*. You cannot have happiness without sadness, light without shadow, skill without practice, growth without challenge. It is the same with the transition that happens during the parental leave time frame, though on a personal scale.

When it comes to parental leave, our country is also at a historic moment of transition. We see clearly that the system is broken and employers and employees need better support. However, while the transition may be under way, it is far from complete.

We have never had a nationwide paid family leave policy in the United States, and, although some will fight against it, we soon will. We have never had a robust field of parental leave coaching and support, but again, we soon will. We don't yet have a standard parental leave practice or process, but with this book as a start, that too is coming. If the analogy is an employee announcing a pregnancy, then as a country we have just announced to our manager that we are expecting, and they have dropped their head into their hands and promptly responded, "Oh, crap. What am I supposed to do now?" We have a chaotic situation without a clear and shared understanding about how to fix it, and we are not yet to the part where the gifts that come with the chaos are obvious. But we will be there soon.

In the meantime, you're about to welcome a child and you want or need to keep working. It is foundational to your family's future that you feel successful as a parent *and* in your work.

Although (most) everyone has the best of intentions, many companies don't know what good policy and practice need to be, and managers are woefully unprepared to support their new parent employees. Employees, for their part, often have no idea the extent to which their transition to parenthood will cause a major life upheaval for themselves and those around them.

Please don't read this book and think that if your transition is challenging, you're doing it wrong. You are in a broken system. It won't get fixed in time to give you the transition you deserve. But, this book will give you the tools to make it the best transition possible under the circumstances.

Know that there are people working on fixing the system *and* there are things within your personal power that will help you carve out a beautiful parental leave experience.

In a culture that likes to push us into us versus them and either/or thinking, my hope is that this book makes the case and provides the tools that instead lead us down the path of *both/and*. A path that has us asking ourselves: How can employers and employees approach the parental leave transition from a place of partnership and possibility? How can managers and direct reports serve as each other's advocates and allies? How can we support each other to set things up well for companies *and* families within an imperfect system? How can we make sure that together we build a parental leave culture that is not either/or but is exquisitely both/and? If we keep these questions at the forefront, I have no doubt that together we will find transformative solutions along the way.

—Amy Beacom, EdD

Introduction

Congratulations! You are about to enter one of the most transformational periods of your life. By picking up this book, you are acknowledging the joy and challenges that lie ahead of you. Parenting is incredibly rewarding *and* extremely difficult. Habit experts will tell you that big life transitions (graduating, moving, getting married) provide opportunities to reshuffle your routines and establish new norms. Becoming a parent is the fast track to personal growth, a chance to rewrite your entire life. (If you don't want to hear that right now, don't worry; it's not a strict requirement.)

Like most of my clients, you are probably excited *and* a bit anxious. You can't wait to welcome your child *and* you want to be thoughtful about what this means for your working life. Whether you always knew you'd be a parent or you aren't quite sure how you got here, you are at a crossroads moment, and the way you move forward will have lasting implications for your career and your personal life. I will help you transition between, and then integrate, two potentially opposing sides of yourself—your familiar, more career or work-identified self and the other more family-identified self that will be growing with you—so that you can move forward with confidence and clarity to create the next phase of your life, while deepening your commitment to yourself and your career goals.

First, as your coach, I need to level with you.

The culture concerning parental leave in the United States is a mess. We are the only developed country in the world without a national paid leave policy to support families welcoming a child. The "American Dream" that you can achieve anything with enough hard work leaves parents scrambling to make all areas of their life work, with little to no practical or social support. Due in part to the breadwinner/homemaker model we have clung to for generations, we have no federally mandated paid leave or childcare subsidies. Most employers give no thought as to how to build in practical support for new parents. And we certainly do not have a cultural or procedural infrastructure to help you use the transition to parenthood to rewrite your life for the better and align yourself with your highest potential and purpose.

Most new parents expect their manager or human resources representative to give them a company intranet link that will make the whole parental leave process clear and the transition to working parenthood smooth as silk. Most workplaces don't have such an intranet site. Most managers are usually clueless about how to handle an employee about to become a parent.

An expectant mom I worked with recently, a congregational leader named Rachael who was due in three weeks with her third child, shared a perfect example of this kind of institutional shortcoming: "HR told me I have to find the short-term disability forms and submit them, and there is usually a 30-day lag before I'll receive the 60% pay reimbursement. I don't know why they expect this to be my problem. I have a contract that says I have eight weeks of paid leave. I don't care how they figure that out, that's their job. I just need to know I'll be paid when I'm away, and not with a pay cut or 30-day lag. If they need me to sign something, they should send it to me, not make me find it." Her understandable frustration does not factor in the reality that most organizations in our country don't understand (or don't care) that their employees expect parental leave logistics to be the organization's responsibility. In other words, she's right that it shouldn't be her job to sort out a disability claim, but if she wants it done, it *has* to be her job.

Although I envision a world where making the transition from working person to working parent is a fully transparent and supported process that benefits all of society, we are not there yet. Not by a long shot. The burden of learning how to prepare for a child while keeping your career on track falls on you. You will need help, and it will be up to you to organize and ask for that help. To make this a successful transition at work you'll have to do a fair bit of "managing up." Should it be this way? No. But if you take ownership over your leave experience, you'll avoid a lot of frustration and heartache and have a far better chance of carving out a deeply satisfying life going forward.

That's where this book comes in. As the founder and CEO of the Center for Parental Leave Leadership (CPLL), I have spent over a decade working with organizations ranging from small businesses to Fortune 100 companies. While helping guide managers and expectant and new parents, I have seen a pattern emerge. Though the experience of becoming a working parent is a profoundly individual one, there are 10 milestones that everyone must pass through successfully in order to navigate this time frame well. How you and your manager interact with each other in terms of these 10 critical milestones, which I refer to in this book as *touchpoints*, will have an oversized impact on your parental leave experience—for better or for worse. If I've learned anything, it is that the more you are aware of and supported through these touchpoints, the greater the likelihood that you will enjoy one of life's most meaningful events.

I want to help you use this experience to improve not just your home life but your work life, too. Though it may seem inconceivable from where you stand now, becoming a parent changes your identity, not just your day-to-day life. I will show you when to stay alert and use the insight and passion that will ignite as your family expands to develop in the direction you choose. I'm here to shine a spotlight on these moments to help you realize the opportunities inherent in this transition to build a life you love, at work and at home.

This may involve a shift in your thinking, or bucking cultural norms. Too often, we are expected to deprioritize, or even hide, our personal lives to advance at work. I have a friend—let's call her Asha—who was one of the first in our group to get pregnant. Every time I saw her, she would ask me to rate how pregnant she looked. Her goal: to not look pregnant at all. She was young and starting her career in a male-dominated field that required her to give expert advice to senior-level executives all day long. Although she is one of the warmest, kindest, most brilliant people I know, she believed that in order to be taken seriously she couldn't give off even a whiff of vulnerability.

To avoid being seen as a "soft" pregnant woman, she spent real energy contorting herself to fit a very specific image: the competent business-woman. She bought dark suits that fell just right and used layers to hide her growing bump, she changed her tone and cadence to become more direct, she used makeup to hide her changing skin and tired eyes, and she even thought of ways to deflect questions that got too close to uncovering her pregnancy. She solicited friends who could cover for her.

This charade consumed her, and at the time we both believed she was successful at it. She hid her pregnancy from her work world until she was over 5 months along. But what I have come to see is the many ways she failed herself *and* her workplace community. She couldn't share her excitement. She put up false boundaries that felt inauthentic to her and kept her from bringing her *all* to her work. She endured real stress, affecting her health and wellness. Those senior executives she worked with didn't get to see that someone could be brilliant and effective while at the same time being pregnant and, yes, vulnerable. Their bias, unconscious or not, went unchallenged and thus was not given a chance to change.

Another friend I'll call Jarvez told everyone at work early on about his wife being pregnant. Right away he seemed to get more leeway and understanding if he fell behind or didn't meet a goal. His coworkers even admonished him if he stayed too late at the office, telling him to go home because he wasn't going to get much more time alone with his wife. These stories exemplify what researchers call the "fatherhood bonus" and the "motherhood penalty."[1]

Indeed, studies show that parenthood leads to different career outcomes for moms and dads. Compared to women without chil-dren, working moms are penalized in the form of fewer promotions and salary increases. Working dads, by contrast, get a boost in sta-tus and salary compared to childless men. The good news is that this might come down to outdated assumptions employers make about the employee's family role and how parenthood affects them, namely, that a mom's dedication to her career will wane because her attention will be divided with caregiving, but a dad's dedication will increase because he will be responsible for bringing home the bacon. These assump-tions can be challenged and changed in how you talk to your man-ager and colleagues. Researchers found that the fatherhood bonus was more accurately a "breadwinner bonus" that could apply to mothers, too. Simply changing terms and reframing working mothers as breadwinners seems to reduce the motherhood penalty. Sadly, a caregiving penalty remains a reality, whether mom or dad does the caregiving.[2]

Clearly, our culture has prejudices about both moms and dads. One of the most effective ways to change those perceptions is case by case. When a manager experiences a mom who takes charge of her own parental leave and a new dad who makes it a priority to spend time at home bonding with his baby while both are still rocking it at work, those preconceptions are released and new norms have a chance to form.

I will coach you on how to flip the script so you can create the type of transition experience you want. Moms and dads alike, I will show you ways to embrace parenthood while crafting the career path that makes sense for you and your priorities *and* helps level the playing field. Only when men are empowered to be equal caregivers will women experience equality in the workplace and men experience equality at home. The ultimate goal is for *all* new parents to be able to live to the fullest the joys and triumphs of both career and home.

Because our workplaces are largely inept at helping employees through parental leave, many new parents see it as a big, unmanageable process that must be discreet or even hidden for fear of jeopardizing career prospects. It does not have to be that way. A successful parental leave strategy can be broken down into touchpoints to be managed well for the benefit of all. I'll give you the tools and resources to handle anything and everything this transition throws at you. I can't promise it will always be easy. But it will be easier and more enjoyable when you know what to expect, what to watch out for, and how to make the most of what you have working for you.

* * *

Thankfully, times are changing in your favor. We are on the brink (fingers crossed) of a federal paid leave policy. There is far less stigma about the challenges of adoption, pregnancy, miscarriage, and parenting than ever before. One silver lining of the coronavirus pandemic is the growing recognition that working parents pull off amazing feats *every single day* and that it is time our society gave them more support (as evidenced by the aid for parents included in the nearly $2 trillion American

Rescue Plan passed by Congress and signed by President Biden in 2021, as well as Biden's American Families Plan, which he unveiled at his first congressional address in April 2021. That $1.8 trillion proposal was the first to include a plan for paid parental leave and recognized it as a critical component of any successful national caregiving infrastructure).

Still, there is much work to be done, and on an individual level, we all need more support. You are about to undergo exciting changes in all the roles you play in your life. Here is what our path together in this book will look like.

Understanding What You Face: Challenges Are Opportunities in Disguise

First, we will take a brief look at the current state of parental leave in this country. We'll touch on challenges faced by working families, the challenges unique to motherhood and fatherhood, respectively, and the issues that arise in workplaces when employees become parents. Feel free to skim any areas that feel like too much information. You do not need to become overwhelmed with every possibility, but you also do not want the "Why didn't anyone tell me?!" feeling so many new parents experience.

We will go over how you can shape your experience by implementing the actions outlined in this playbook and also what the future could look like for all of us, if we are willing to work toward it. Every parent, every manager, every CEO, every legislator, and every voter has a role to play in creating a future in which families are healthier and more prosperous—and true equity is realized.

Understanding the Framework

While I was finishing my doctorate after my son's birth over a decade ago, I set out to create a field of coaching dedicated to better navigating the transition to parenthood for working people. Drawing on seven academic research streams, I created a model that helps support new and expecting working parents to leverage the profound opportunities of this often overlooked and sometimes purposefully hidden life event. Although you don't need to know all the theoretical underpinnings of this model, called RETAIN (an acronym), a quick walkthrough in Chapter 1 will help you implement what you find in this playbook.

The Playbook in Three Phases

Most people think of parental leave as the time you are absent from work to bond with your new child. I want to encourage you to think more holistically than that. *I have come to see parental leave as a transition period that is best broken into three phases: (1) preparing for leave, (2) during leave, and (3) returning from leave—whether you have an official paid parental leave or not.* I will coach you on how to approach this transition from a position of thoughtfulness instead of being forced into reaction mode. If you let our culture steer your leave, you will likely have many difficult experiences (and that's me putting it nicely). This playbook walks you through the critical moments for each phase so you can lead your own leave and have a successful transition—however *you* define success.

In Phase 1, especially if this is your first child, you are naturally still very much work identified. Now is the time to take practical steps to prepare to be away from work to welcome your child. We will focus on your announcement and on identifying the supports you can draw on to overcome any bumps in the road. Then we will dig into action planning for your leave and find ways to soak in and celebrate as you put work on hold so you can embrace parenthood.

In Phase 2, you are on leave to welcome your child! Here you will focus on diving deep into being a new parent and the role expansion that requires. You will spend time bonding with your new child and family. This is a momentous time. You should have clear boundaries with work and as much support as possible from your friends, family, and community. I will help you to develop a communication plan with work (how/when to be in touch), prepare to advocate for yourself and your child with your support system and health care team, and when it is time, think about what arrangements you will put in place as your leave ends and you return to work.

In Phase 3, you will focus on returning to work and adjusting to your new normal as a working parent. For many, this is the trickiest part of parental leave, bringing up new and unexpected role conflicts. Echoing the preparations you made as you moved into leave, I will walk you through ways to acknowledge this big transition and adjust to your new roles. We will also work on ensuring you have access to ongoing career development opportunities so you can continue to build your career in the ways you want to.

We will wrap up the playbook by naming some of the additional human experiences and circumstances that can make the transition more challenging, such as perinatal mood disorders, single parenthood, and the way oppression and bias compound the difficulties for marginalized and underrepresented individuals, especially those in Black, Indigenous, Asian, Latinx, and other communities of color, as well as for LGBTQ+ parents. We will also look at how to carve out a better future as a working parent and help others do the same by your example.

Appendix 2 will link you to concrete tools and resources to plan and manage your leave, including a leave plan template, checklists, reflection prompts, a perinatal mental health screening tool, books I recommend, and more to help round out your understanding and preparedness.

I am so excited to put this book into your hands. You deserve to enjoy both your family and your career. With the right tools and support, you can do just that. This playbook, based on extensive research and experience with hundreds of parents and managers in organizations around the world, will help you see what's coming so you can navigate this major life and career transition competently and confidently—while having fun along the way!

Chapter
One

Parental Leave Is a Mess—
Let's Fix It!

TAKE A MOMENT and imagine your ideal parental leave experience. What would it be like to have ample time at home with your new child *and* receive your full paycheck the whole time? How would it feel if your manager, HR representatives, and work colleagues were thoroughly trained and given all the resources they might need to guide you? What if there was clarity in how to best hand off your work and to whom, what paperwork you needed and when, and how much time you could take off?

Imagine your team throwing you a celebratory send-off that gave you just the right amount of attention, in ways that remind you that they know and care for *you* as you embark on parental leave to welcome your new child. And what if it didn't stop there? What if when your child arrives, your team sends you a basket full of useful new essentials, and some of those really cute stylish items you had been eyeing but weren't going to splurge on. There is even a matching t-shirt and onesie set with your work logo, and the back of yours reads *Promoted to Parent!*

During your leave, they know just how and when to check in and what news you want to be kept in the loop on so that you can let go of the mental load of work to completely immerse yourself in getting to know your child. When it is time to turn your attention back to work, they reach out to check if any of your return plans need to be adjusted and ask what they can do to make your first week (and beyond) go smoothly.

When you walk through those doors your first day back, you are able to breeze past any security because you have been proactively reactivated in the system. Your manager and colleagues have made a special effort to greet you with big smiles, and everyone wants to see more pictures of your new cutie pie. Your desk and IT access are set up flawlessly. A bouquet or a small plant welcomes you. When you sink into your chair you are able to soak in how much you were missed and how much your team values you. Even if you haven't been completely confident in yourself since you've been away, they are.

Notice how you felt imagining that future. Were your reactions unexpected? Did you feel hopefulness, pessimism, or something else? Did this feel like a possible future for you? Did you laugh at the idea? How did your body feel while you were visualizing this future? Were you tense or relaxed?

Now imagine if every new working parent was supported this way and was able to build their new family on a foundation consciously crafted without stress or shame, whether they were going back to work in an office, a restaurant, construction, their own business, or any kind of workplace. Think how strong our society would be.

This rosy future does not need to be hypothetical. Let's claim it as yours. *Just as expecting parents take birthing classes to understand and handle the challenges of labor, I will help you understand the basics of the parental leave transition so you can better prepare yourself, practically and emotionally, for your transition into life as a working parent.*

In this book we are going to lead you into your exciting new role and help you integrate it with your career plans and ambitions. With the right tools and support, I have seen (and helped) countless people do it well. Following the principles I'll outline in the following chapters, you will be able to maximize the upsides of your transition, sidestep pitfalls, and guide yourself and those around you through the rocky patches. You will have an easier time handing off your work, enjoy better communication with your boss and coworkers, gain more support at home, turn more thoughtful attention to the bonding experience of your family, and enjoy a smoother transition and adjustment back to work.

You will also be well positioned to use what you have learned to educate and inspire those around you on how to approach parental leave, paving the way for parents who come after you to have an even better experience. When working parents are given the support they need to thrive, we improve society and our companies at every level. Making sure *you* get that support lays the foundation for that progress.

Before we continue, let's get clear on some definitions.

Language Matters: Defining Parental Leave

Inclusivity is vital to our workplaces and our society. In this book I am using the broadest definition of family and parenting in order to support *all* parents, across all races, religions, gender identities, and sexual orientations. I'm speaking to you no matter what method you have chosen to form a family, be it birth, adoption, surrogacy, fostering, or another creative way. Notice that the language and imagery customarily used for parental leave issues are still problematically heteronormative and skew toward assuming a traditional birth as the path to parenthood. (Even the terms *mom* and *dad* do not always adequately label trans or nonbinary parents.) My goal is to always be inclusive, but there are places where the language (and even my awareness) has not yet caught up with the evolution of family structure. Using inclusive language is a simple way to show we care for each other. Let's work together to help influence this culture shift, and let's also give each other grace and understanding when we aren't yet able to get it exactly right. *If you are becoming a parent, this book is for you.*

Next, we need to define the term *parental leave*. When most people hear these words, they still think of maternity leave: the time a mother (because let's admit it, dads are still largely ignored) is absent from work to be at home with her new baby and recover from childbirth. This is a very limited view that (unintentionally) reinforces prejudices and inequity and misses the bigger picture and the opportunities inherent in this major life transition. *Parental leave* describes any leave, inclusive of all gender identities, that provides time off from work to bond with a new child.

Using a time-based definition has proven to be holistic and productive for my clients. Therefore, let us define parental leave as an extended period of transition for all new parents in three phases: (1) preparing for leave, (2) during leave, and (3) returning from leave. This transition lasts roughly from the time you announce the upcoming arrival of your child through your return to work, and it also includes an indefinite period of adjustment after your return that can last anywhere from three to six months or longer. Altogether, we are talking about at least nine to 12 months—maybe more—of your life.

Although I have written this book with the idea that your parental leave will last longer than a few weeks, we will discuss aspects of this important transition that affect all expectant and new working parents, even those who are not taking leave at all.

Finally, the language I use in the book is geared toward people who are traditionally employed (those who work for a company or organization and have a boss over them) because that is still the majority of workers in the United States. However, these touchpoints are equally applicable to you if you are a freelancer, an entrepreneur, run a nonprofit, or do any other type of work. Even if you're not formally employed, you will still find value in thinking through how these touchpoints apply to your transition to parenthood. They are universal.

A Broken System: Parental Leave in the United States

At the time of this writing, most people in the United States do not have access to *paid* parental leave (in 2020, just 20% of US employees had access to paid family leave through their employer).[1] It is a common misconception that the Family Medical Leave Act (FMLA) provides paid leave. FMLA only allows for unpaid *job protection* for a specific period of time, if an employee meets certain criteria. It is estimated only 56% of the workforce is eligible for FMLA, which means the other 44% receive neither job protection nor pay.[2] Depending on your state, you may have paid leave through a state and/or local law. You also may be lucky enough to have an employer who voluntarily provides paid parental leave, which is a growing and welcome trend, especially among large companies. The companies I work with are forward-thinking and supportive of their employees, but for most parents in the US, welcoming a child has a serious financial impact.

This is not a policy book and I won't go deeply into policy, but I will cover a few basics in the next section so that you are not caught off guard by anything you run up against. I've been reading the tea leaves on this issue for many years. I believe we are very close to federal legislation that will finally address this grievous oversight in our social safety net and economic infrastructure and help us catch up to almost every other country in the world. However, even with such long-overdue legislation, many challenges will remain—most of them related to perceptions and practices, not policies.

****

Note: Now is not the time for you to feel responsible for fixing our enormously flawed system (or to feel overwhelmed by it). Now is the time for you to focus inward on what *you* and *your family* need and fill your cup. In nourishing yourself in this way, you will ensure you come to the other side of your transition in a position of strength and awareness. Along the way, your success will help make it better for those who come next as, one family at a time, we heal our broken system.

****

When We Get Parental Leave Wrong

When we fail to support working parents with good policies and practices, the detrimental ripple effect is vast, yet we often fail to realize how profound it is because this is simply the way we do things in this country. As depressing as it may be, it is important for you to have a high-level understanding of how this systemic failure to properly support the parental leave transition affects us all.

• *Working Families Suffer*

As if it were not enough that most parents lose wages while staying home to bond with a new child, many families who welcome a child by giving birth face exorbitant health care costs and inadequate health insurance. Big hospital bills hit just when paychecks shrink or temporarily disappear.

New parents are also at risk for mental health challenges during this period, regardless of their path to parenthood (birth, adoption, surrogacy, etc.). Many parents suffer in silence without ever getting proper care, fearing stigma or even that their children will be taken from them if they confess to a serious struggle.

When it is time to go back to work, they often need to seek and pay for infant childcare (and in many cases, care for older children), the *average* costs of which range from $9,000 to $24,000 per child per year for in-center care, depending on where you live.[3] The cost to hire a private nanny can run even higher.

High childcare expenses often drive one parent to leave the workforce—or quit a more formal career in favor of work in the gig economy, which provides more flexibility but fewer (if any) benefits and often lower wages. In two-parent heteronormative relationships, most of the time, it is the mothers who stay home and care for the children, both because of caregiving stereotypes and because they often earn less. As a result, our workplaces and society miss out on their talent, and these women lose out on advancement opportunities, benefits, retirement savings, and more. The coronavirus pandemic that began in 2020 put even more pressure on working families, particularly mothers. In fact, according to the National Women's Law Center, between February 2020 and January 2021, more than 2.3 million women, compared to nearly 1.8 million men, were pushed out of the labor force, meaning they were not working or looking for work.[4] That's over a half million more women than men.

These are tough circumstances by any measure, and many families face additional challenges if fertility, pregnancy, or birth are complicated and if mom or baby end up having medical issues. Some parents who have waited until their late thirties or early forties to have children may also join the "sandwich generation," caring for their aging parents while also caring for young children *and* trying to work.

In Chapter 16 we will cover additional challenges such as those faced by single parents, those who belong to underrepresented and marginalized communities, LGBTQ+ parents, and more.

• *Managers Are Left to Fend for Themselves*

Parents aren't the only ones affected by the policy and practice vacuum concerning parental leave. Managers and supervisors face serious challenges when one of their team members is planning to welcome a new child. Most companies lack a transparent process to let employees know what benefits are available to them, much less a standardized procedure to help them prepare to hand off their duties and pick them back up when they return. Managers are often left without resources to figure out how to juggle the workload and the tools needed to provide support to the new parent and cover team.

Furthermore, managers are not trained in what to say and how to say it. Many are afraid to say anything for fear of saying the wrong thing and sparking hurt feelings—or worse, a gender or pregnancy discrimination lawsuit. This moment could be a powerful opportunity to increase team trust and communication, provide support to new parents (thus boosting employee loyalty and retention), and grow junior staff members' skills during the coverage period. Instead, it is often handled so badly that it has all the opposite effects: communication fails, morale dips, and people quit.

• *Companies Are Expected to Do the Work of Society*

When I decided to dedicate my career to helping parents through this transition, I was very thoughtful about the most efficient way to do it. The truth is that this is not parents' problem to solve. It's a *systemic* problem. One which today's companies are in a unique position to fix—and benefit from its solution. In part because the effort for a paid leave law was already well established and given my area of expertise in organizational development and executive coaching, I decided to focus the bulk of my efforts on companies, managers, and working parents. For many of us, financial stability and even self-esteem depend on gainful employment. A good boss can make or break the parental leave experience. (If you haven't yet heard someone say you've won or lost "the boss lottery," you will.)

I wanted to help companies understand the advantages for them in being supportive during this major life transition: an edge over their competitors when it comes to recruitment, better retention, increased growth of their female leadership pipeline, improved morale and productivity for working parents, and improved risk management, to name a few. Too many companies mistakenly categorize parental leave as a one-way "benefit," when in reality it needs to be seen as a *strategic opportunity* not to be missed for the whole organization.

Increasingly, leaders within organizations are coming around to this perspective. Starting in 2015 we began to see a spate of major US companies announcing generous parental leave benefits that were in line—or even more generous than—what many European countries offer. Microsoft, one of my company's long-time clients, announced in 2015 that they would offer 12 weeks of 100% paid parental leave to all parents, in addition to the 8 weeks of maternity disability offered to birthing mothers. In making their expansion, Microsoft also realized that policy alone is not enough. Supporting practices must be put in place to require—and influence—culture change. We worked with Microsoft to develop a program that trains employees *and managers* around the world about how best to navigate the parental leave transition. They were the first company in the country to offer an employee-manager-aligned parental leave training and support program, a pilot so successful that it was rolled out globally.

Once I began working with companies on these issues, I realized how many challenges they face when it comes to parental leave. For example, beyond talent attraction, retention, and compliance issues, lack of a good leave policy also compounds risk management costs. If exhausted new parents come back to work too soon, they present an increased safety risk. AAA's Traffic Safety Advocacy and Research department reported that "a driver who has slept for less than five hours has a crash risk comparable to someone driving drunk."[5] Imagine how a sleep-deprived new parent plays that out in the workplace, especially if heavy equipment or important decisions are involved. Having someone come back to work too soon increases health care costs and jeopardizes health and wellness initiatives. If people don't get the time and support they need to heal and rest, their health suffers and insurance costs and absenteeism rates increase.

Ironically, the current trend of individual states passing paid leave can actually hurt companies, because those that operate in multiple states must keep track of and comply with many different (and complicated) laws. This adds a serious cost and administrative burden. I know many parents who couldn't care less about this administrative burden (like Rachael in the introduction) and are simply angry not to have paid leave through their employer, but that frustration is misplaced.

This is something our federal government should be solving, not individual companies. According to the Small Business Administration's Office of Advocacy, 99.7% of companies in the United States are small businesses.[6] When we think of companies, we cannot just think of the Amazons and Googles of the world, with a sense of what they "owe" us.

Small businesses are affected more than larger businesses because larger companies can afford to offer paid leave benefits that attract the best talent, and the administrative costs that come with them. Small businesses often cannot. Even though in most states our current system doesn't legally obligate them to provide paid leave, there are other detrimental financial effects—such as having to pay to replace workers who leave after becoming a parent.

Although I see many companies fighting against the idea that parents should be supported with paid leave to take time away from work to welcome children, I think this is largely due to a lack of information on this issue. It is not easy being in leadership at a company of any size, and leaders often push back on anything that could cut into the bottom line and threaten the solvency or the day-to-day functioning of the company. However, forward-thinking leaders realize that supporting new parents through generous policies and strong support practices can literally pay dividends. It costs far more to recruit and train a new employee than it does to retain an existing one (the Society of Human Resource Management reports the cost of directly replacing an employee can run as high as 50% to 60% of their annual salary; total associated costs of turnover can range from 90% to 200% of an employee's annual salary).[7] Last, studies show that parents who are healthy (and well rested!) are more productive, more innovative, and even more loyal to their company.[8]

Clearly, the best thing for families *and* companies would be a generous federal benefit that provides clarity and stability for everyone involved.

When We Get Parental Leave Right

There is a shortage of data about parental leave in the United States, but the data we do have from progressive organizations and other countries show that providing generous paid leave policies and supporting practices works. Let's look at some of the rewards of getting this right.

• Reward 1: Healthier Kids

It may seem obvious to say that when parents are supported through the parental leave transition, they are able to better care for their children, which means better health outcomes for babies. The data support this: a 2017 study found that providing 12 weeks of paid leave in the United States could lead to 600 fewer infant and post-neonatal deaths each year.[9] (In 2019, the infant mortality rate in the United States was 6 infants in 1,000 live births, twice that of the European Union, where health care and paid parental leave are widely available.)[10] Breastfeeding (if desired) can be smoothly established and last longer. Parents have time to take their child to get vaccinations and checkups as well as notice any developmental delays when an early intervention can mean a better outcome. Everyone sleeps better and has time for the crucial bonding that we know leads to healthier kids (and parents).

• Reward 2: Healthier Moms and Birthing Parents

Better supported parental leave also means better health outcomes for birthing parents. It's not just babies who suffer under the current state of things. The *maternal* death rate in the United States is actually on the rise, despite the global trend downward in the last few decades. In 2017, the United States saw 17 maternal deaths per 100,000 live births.[11] The European Union saw just 6 maternal deaths per 100,000 live births in the same year.[12] That's right, the maternal death rate in the United States is nearly *three times higher* than in the European Union and almost twice as high as in Canada.[13] It's clear that birthing parents are not getting the care and support they need to thrive. Black moms and moms of color are disproportionately affected[14] (more on this in Chapter 16). When moms are supported to take leave, they have the time and rest they need to recover more quickly and fully, and to get the treatment and screenings that prevent medical and mental health complications related to childbirth so they can return to the workforce more effectively.

• Reward 3: Healthier Dads and Non-Birthing Parents

Although dads often face different issues than moms, it is important to highlight their transition. Dads often feel extreme pressure to "provide" for their families, which can lead to overwork and a lack of self-care with serious health impacts. Dads and other non-birthing parents are not immune to perinatal mental health challenges, either. Research shows that 1 in 10 fathers experience depression and anxiety after their child is born.[15] Often, they do not seek help until they are in crisis. Partners of a birthing parent often internalize any emotional or physical difficulties that their partner or child may encounter as a reflection on them and something that they need (and want) to fix. They can be left feeling inadequate and unsure of how to step into their critical role.[16] When we look at outcomes in cases when dad gets paid leave and cultural support for time at home, we see how much it helps. For example, a study on a 2012 Swedish law that granted fathers more access to parental leave found that their partners' need for prescription anti-anxiety medications decreased by 26%.[17] When dads take paternity leave they are more confident as parents, have better relationships with their partners, and are less likely to be separated or divorced for as many as six years later.[18]

- ### *Reward 4: Healthier Relationships at Work and at Home*

When new parents have adequate time, space, and support during the transition to parenthood, it makes for healthier relationships in all spheres. At work, when communication is open and honest and leave planning is thoughtful and transparent, the relationship between the new parent and their manager (and often their team and HR) is strengthened. Team communication and trust as a whole improve when the handoff of duties is clear and well communicated and everyone understands their temporary role. Successful transitions can be used as a model for other teams in the organization and can become standard best practice. At home, parents can bond with their new child and—if there are two parents—with each other, to form equitable caregiving divisions that will prevent future strife and allow them to return to work with confidence that their home is a safe haven to refuel and restore.

- ### *Reward 5: Gender Equity*

Averaged across all races, women still make only 82 cents for every dollar men make.[19] Of S&P 500 companies, only 6% have women CEOs.[20]

One of the biggest reasons that women have not yet achieved equity in the workplace is our cultural assumptions about who should be responsible for caregiving at home. Women are de facto caregivers and face bias, whether conscious or unconscious, that they are not as dedicated to their careers because of their current or possible future caregiving responsibilities. When men are empowered to be equal caregivers, not just through policy but through cultural messages, women will finally achieve full equity in the workplace and men will at home. I encourage all employers to offer gender-neutral parental leave and find ways to encourage all employees to take their full leave benefit. It may take time, but the more examples we have of men taking extended leaves to care for their children or other family members, the less we will punish women in terms of pay and opportunity for doing the same thing.

- *Reward 6: Inclusion of All Types of Families*

Although we have made great (and long overdue) strides in this country to recognize and include all types of families, we have a long way to go. And though cisgender, heterosexual couples who have biological children represent the majority of family formations, it does no good to pretend that method of creating a family is somehow preferred or superior. Children, parents, and society as a whole will benefit when we recognize the value of all types of family compositions. No one benefits when certain parents or children feel marginalized. A future that welcomes all families is bright with the rich insights diversity brings.

You Are the Way Forward

If what you read in this chapter resonates with your own anxiety, I get it. I invite you to take a deep breath. You've got this. Reading this book means you are already ahead of the game. By learning the techniques in this playbook, you will have the tools and resilience you need to handle whatever comes your way. We cannot control the world or what life throws at us, but we can improve how we respond by deepening our emotional intelligence and practical skill set. Parenthood is the perfect opportunity to work on what you can control: your own knowledge, planning, communication, and attitude toward one of life's greatest adventures.

Chapter
Two

The 10A Transition
Touchpoints Framework

You MIGHT HAVE already asked yourself, "Why isn't there a manual for this becoming a working parent thing?" Everybody has this reality check at some point. For me it was when I left the hospital and looked down at my son all scrunched in his car seat and thought, "What the heck do I do now?" For Kisha, it was when she felt her baby's first kick and realized *this was really happening*. For Jay, it was when he saw his partner constantly breastfeeding and realized it was on him to care for their toddler while also working full time from home. Many people ask for a manual when they confront changing a first diaper or giving a first bath. Yet even with this nearly universal desire, there still isn't a universal manual. As mind-boggling as this may be, there is a good reason: *every child and every parent is different.*

What are we really asking for when we yearn for a manual? Do we really want someone to tell us what to do? Do we care, or even listen, if we don't think it applies to us? What makes that magic moment possible when something *clicks* and we can finally hear for the first time what we may have been told 10 times before?

I worked with Caitlin when she had her second child. After he was born, she reported, "Wow, it's so much easier this time around.

I'm much more relaxed because I know what to expect and I know that some of the things that were so scary before pass quickly. I really wish I had known this with my first." She hadn't believed her large family when everyone told her not to worry so much with her first—that she would find her way. They had even spent time giving her advice and showing her how to do certain things. She didn't listen to them because she didn't trust that they could understand the unique experience she was going through. Like most new parents, when Caitlin was offered an informal manual, she wasn't ready to receive it. With the birth of her second child, Caitlin was able to pay less attention to the critical internal voice that had accompanied her the first time around, telling her she was doing it wrong. She was more confident because she had learned that she could do this, and do it well. I could hear her contentment and see her whole body relaxing when she talked about it: "I'm not worrying that he hasn't eaten enough or that he's sleeping at the wrong time or about the hundred other things I used to think about. I'm just looking at him and thinking, how did I get so lucky?"

Caitlin was describing the comfort, confidence, and expertise we all get when we have lived through something difficult and discovered we not only made it through, but we got wiser along the way. Qualitative researchers talk about the value of learning from our unique and individual *lived experience*, through which we gain personal, even profound, firsthand knowledge about ourselves and the world around us, which enables us to grow and develop. We can be told or read about something, but it is in the doing that we learn.

In the consulting world, experiential learning (sometimes called action learning) is the gold standard when it comes to skill building and leadership development programs because it relies on lived experience to ensure what is being learned sticks and is carried forward. This is why I say (pun intended) *the parental leave transition is the mother of all experiential learning programs and companies would be wise to see it that way.*

As part of my research and theory-building for my doctorate over a decade ago, I wondered if we could capture the learning opportunities of this massive experience in a way that would support new parents to find their footing faster and bring what they were learning in warp speed at home into work, and, conversely, if there was a way for them to bring their expertise from work into what they were learning at home. Was there a way to allow for the uniqueness of the individual experience in a predictable and replicable process? I found there was.

The RETAIN Parental Leave Transition Coaching Model

When I had my first child, I realized there was a huge gap between new parent expectations of support and actual support within their companies—and in that gap lay an enormous missed opportunity.

I developed the RETAIN parental leave coaching pedagogy and method as a way to channel what I learned from my less-than-ideal experience of becoming a working parent into creating a new field of coaching to better support working parents, managers, and their companies. Today, RETAIN sits behind the manager training and new parent support work we do at my company, the Center for Parental Leave Leadership (CPLL), and gives our parental leave coaches a philosophy and method to use when working with expecting parents and their managers.

RETAIN is the first evidence-based, theoretical pedagogy for the growing field of parental leave coaching and is supported by over a decade of research and practical application as shown in the figure. I will say more about this foundation throughout the book where it is relevant. For now, all you need to know is that RETAIN is built on seven different academic evidence streams that play a role in how you experience your transition and how you can grow from it, including the research and theory of (1) executive coaching, (2) transition theory, (3) adult learning, (4) life stage theory, (5) career development, (6) role and identity theory, and (7) work-life conflict and enrichment.

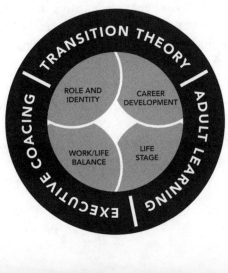

At its simplest, RETAIN is an acronym that stands for *Relate, Explore, Tailor, Assess, Instruct,* and *Next Steps*. This iterative process our parental leave coaches cycle through as they work provides a way for you to orient yourself along your journey.

Relate. Building trusting relationships in all areas of your life is one of the most important things you can do to ensure your successful transition. The *R* is first on purpose.

Explore. Deliberate exploration, with a curious mindset, of goals, desires, needs, and limitations—your own and those of the people around you—will help you uncover strengths and opportunities you may not have known you had and imagine solutions for any issues you find.

Tailor. You are an individual at a specific moment in time, with specific needs. Your next parental leave transition, if there is one, will be different because you will be different. The *T* reminds us that customization enables the transition to be effective and enjoyable and to meet the needs of *your* situation.

Assess. Taking stock of everything going on within you and around you by thoroughly assessing and reflecting on your transition will help ensure all your needs can be met by whatever plans you create (and you'll learn about yourself in the process).

Instruct. In a departure from traditional coaching, RETAIN coaches do a fair bit of overt teaching to clients. We recognize that sometimes when a person is learning an enormous amount of information in a very short time, it can really help to lay out the best practices and offer tips. This book and any further self-study you choose are that instruction.

Next Steps: Action Plan. All the previous elements fall flat if you do not pay attention to this last step and intentionally build what you have learned into a comprehensive plan to lead your leave. We call this plan your *Next Steps: Action Plan*, and there are three components of your plan: *preparing for leave, during leave,* and *returning from leave.*

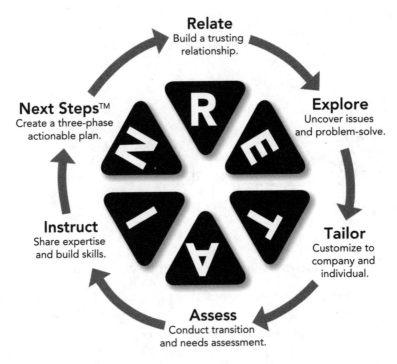

RETAIN Parental Leave Transition Coaching is a structured and holistic form of coaching developed to support working parents and their managers from a business and personal perspective throughout the three phases of leave with an overt goal of ensuring a successful, engaged, and sustainable return to work while thriving at home.

It's easy to read the word RETAIN and think it is only about employee retention. However, RETAIN is not simply about staying in your job, though one of my overt aims is to keep parents—especially women—in the workforce if that is where they want to be. This type of coaching puts you, the working parent, at the center while also considering the needs of your work organization. At its core, RETAIN is about staying in *all parts of your life*, about sticking to the career course you choose while also staying consciously aligned with your higher self and deeper knowing—which may mean some pivots and unexpected turns. Ultimately, tapping into that part of yourself is key to long-term retention in whatever you choose to pursue.

As you navigate your parental leave with the help of this book, remember that this deep RETAIN foundation is already built into the 10-touchpoint framework you are about to learn, so you don't have to think about it. It can be comforting, though, to know it is there.

RETAIN™ Parental Leave Coaching Model

Retain working parents in an engaged, supported, and sustainable way.

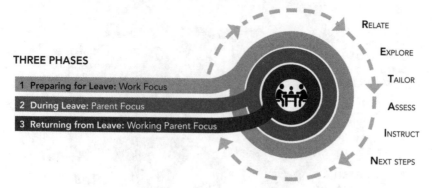

THREE PHASES

1 Preparing for Leave: Work Focus

2 During Leave: Parent Focus

3 Returning from Leave: Working Parent Focus

RELATE

EXPLORE

TAILOR

ASSESS

INSTRUCT

NEXT STEPS

The Three-Phase Parental Leave Transition

The 10-touchpoint framework of this playbook is built on the idea that the parental leave transition breaks down into three phases—each equal in importance. Don't think of this time as an *absence* as the word *leave* implies, but rather as a period of personal and professional *presence* in transition, defined by the three phases shown in the figure.

A supported transition, such as the one you imagined at the beginning of the last chapter, can help your family flourish. When your family thrives, you can bring your best self back to the workforce and help your work organization and your community thrive as well.

Each phase has its own focus, its own set of touchpoints, and its own set of role changes. When you understand how to handle these touchpoints and role shifts well, you significantly improve your chances of transition success—again, however *you* define success. First, let's look at the three phases of the 10-touchpoint framework. Then we'll discuss roles, identities, and routines.

• *Phase 1: Preparing for Leave: Work Focus*

In the first transition phase of the framework, you are still working and focused on career stability while you make preparations—both at work and at home—to welcome your new child. You are starting to feel the shift in your roles already, and you are working to figure out how this new parenting role will fit into the current picture of your life. Practically speaking, at home you are preparing for your child's arrival.

You may be rearranging your space or even moving to a larger home or to be closer to family. At work, you are trying to wrap up projects and create documentation for a clean handoff to whoever is covering your duties during your leave. You are also considering how to do everything in a way that makes your manager and team happy. If you have any extra headspace, you might be using it to think about setting yourself up for a smooth return.

The first mile marker or touchpoint we will go into for this phase is your *announcement* at work that you are expecting a child. This sounds simple enough, but in many workplace cultures an announcement can be tricky and expectant parents are often surprised by the way other people react. Even if you have already made your announcement by the time you are reading this book, we will explore ways you can look at the impact your announcement had and be creative about positive ways to talk about the arrival of your child going forward.

The second touchpoint of Phase 1 is about how to *assess* your transition. I'll show you how to look at your transition from some specific angles using a tool we call the *6-S System for Transition Success*. This process will help you identify everything working in your favor as well as anything working against you, in order to actively make the most of resources you have available to you and plan for mitigating challenging circumstances.

The third touchpoint has to do with leave planning and communication. I will walk you through how to create a comprehensive three-phase leave *action plan* that includes how best to get all of your stakeholders the information they need. You will use what you've discovered in your transition assessment from the second touchpoint to create a plan (and a backup plan or two!) for work and home purposes.

The fourth and final touchpoint of Phase 1 is to *acknowledge the transition to parenthood*. This section will help you understand why it is important to make time in your hectic schedule to soak in the enormity of the life transition you are embarking on so you can prepare emotionally and find ways to celebrate that feel right to you. Busy as you are, it's tempting to skip this part, but that never ends well. On a practical level, it pays to spend time thinking about the kind of parent you want to be and what your new life will look like so you can build it into your plans and goal setting. On an emotional level, giving yourself the room to truly acknowledge and embrace the magnitude of your new life path will help you develop and practice the self-awareness and emotional intelligence required of all working parents (and leaders).

I will give you tools and resources to handle the practical and emotional sides of the touchpoints in this phase, as well as each of the touchpoints in the next chapters.

• *Phase 2: During Leave:* Parenthood Focus

During Phase 2, you will be at home and able to naturally shift focus to your role as a parent while taking time to bond with your new child and whole family. This is a wondrous time—but it is not a vacation (and anyone who has been through it understands that; ignore childless people who think this is somehow the equivalent of three months in the Bahamas and read this spot-on comic: https://english.emmaclit.com/2017/06/04/holidays/). In transition theory, this phase is known as the *neutral zone*—the time in between where you have been (which is known) and where you are going (the unknown). However, *neutral* does not adequately describe how this phase feels. I think of it as the "messy middle" because it can feel disorienting and even overwhelming as you scramble to orient yourself, adjust, and learn the new tasks and skills that are required of you overnight.

Touchpoint 5, the first touchpoint of Phase 2, is to **appropriately keep in touch** with work. You will have developed a communication plan during the action planning touchpoint of the previous phase, and now is the time to put that plan into practice and make sure it's honored by your colleagues—or adjusted as you find yourself wanting something different than what you thought you would need.

Touchpoint 6 helps you **advocate** for yourself and your child(ren). During your transition any number of things may arise that require you to stick up for yourself or your family's needs. You may be healing or dealing with health issues for yourself, your partner (if you have one), or your child. You may be navigating tricky extended family dynamics. Enhancing your self-advocacy skills will serve you well now and for the rest of your career and life.

Touchpoint 7 happens toward the end of your leave as you make **arrangements to return**. This chapter walks you through the many things you will need to modify and arrange before you head back to work. This includes home basics like childcare, feeding plans for your child, dealing with separation anxiety, as well as work considerations such as how to best reconnect with your manager and team to ensure a smooth reentry to work. Again, having a plan—and a backup plan—is invaluable during this stage.

- ## *Phase 3: Returning from Leave:* **Working Parent Focus**

In this final transition phase, you will focus on integrating your dual roles of worker and parent into a new, singular working parent role (even if this is not your first child, this applies because you've never done it this way before). You will be heading back to work and slowly establishing your new normal through a series of experiments and adjustments. It's important to keep in mind that although you will appear, to your coworkers and boss, to be the same old you who went on leave, this may not match how you feel. You've undergone a significant internal transition (possibly accompanied by physical changes) that has brought you new insight and knowledge (again, even if this isn't your first child).

Touchpoint 8 is similar to Touchpoint 4, when you made the emotional space to reflect on the impact of your transition to parenthood. This touchpoint outlines how taking time to **acknowledge the transition to working parent** is equally important. Some can't wait for the day to come; others dread it. Either way, this is emotional and intellectual labor, the fruits of which you can bring back into your workplace as you continue building your career.

Touchpoint 9 is all about **adjustment**. Finding a new normal takes time and you will need to be creative and flexible in your thinking and actions to integrate your new dual identity as a working parent. Learning how to be gentle with yourself and others will be an important skill to practice in order to manage future transitions as your child grows and demands on your time and skills evolve.

Touchpoint 10—the final touchpoint of this framework—is about keeping **access** to ongoing career development front and center on your return. After an extended leave, especially one of this bedrock-shifting magnitude, a new parent can lose confidence in their abilities or question their commitment to their work. It is not uncommon to feel like hard-fought career aspirations are at risk. This section walks you through putting a plan in place to ensure your career is not derailed and that you can capitalize on all you have learned personally and professionally during this time. All of the work you have put into your development during your transition helps take you to the next right place in your career path.

Thoughtfully approaching each of these touchpoints, as shown in the figure, allows you to take charge of your leave experience and skillfully create your new normal in a supported way that helps you continue building your career.

10A Transition Touchpoints Framework™ by Phase

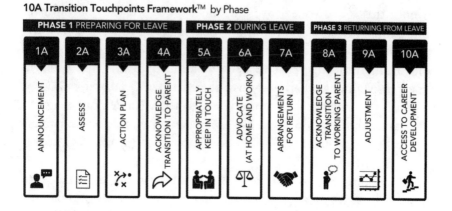

From Worker to Parent to Working Parent

The 10-touchpoint framework will help you integrate the massive role change of moving from simply being a grown-up with a career to becoming a parent, then a working parent. Roles and role identity are important; you have played countless roles in your life (good student, strong athlete, best friend, etc.) and you play a number of roles throughout each day. They are the various hats you don in different spheres of your life. Sometimes they feel like a part you play, but often they become a key piece of how you think about yourself. When this happens, that role has become an identity.

Throughout this book I will ask you to pay particular attention to how you transition between the various roles in your life and how an identity can begin to form out of these roles. I will also ask you to give some thought to the roles others have played in your life, what it means to be career-identified and/or family-identified, and how a parental leave transition can lead to role and identity confusion and, at times, even conflict between those two spheres of your life.

Roles and Identity

One client, Kenny, grew up in a traditional home in a rural part of the country. His dad worked a lot and was the family breadwinner. Even though his mom also worked full time, when I asked who raised him, he didn't hesitate to say it was her. He explained that she was the one who saw to his basic needs, made sure he had his favorite foods to eat, understood that some clothes just weren't cool enough to wear, and helped advocate for him at school when he was struggling. I watched his contagious smile spread when he described her as his go-to person if he was upset or heartbroken. He said he hoped his wife would have a chance to be that person to their new baby.

Yet Kenny found himself about to be a first-time dad in a city away from family support, with a wife whose job was more demanding (and lucrative) than his. Circumstances meant that it was more likely that he would need to be the go-to for his new child, but even though he was open to the idea, he believed he had no good role models for how to do that. His supervisor had some experience managing other dads through parental leave and had seen indications that Kenny might struggle to overcome some outdated notions of what a dad's role should be and rise to the challenge of what would be required of him at home. I was called in to work with Kenny because his manager was concerned that if Kenny was unable to find ways to be a successful caregiver at home, he would encounter difficulty, even strife, and that struggle would spill over into how he would be able to show up at work. With the authentic support from his manager and the focused time we had together, Kenny was able to recognize that he *did* have a strong working parent role model: his mother. He tapped into the skills she had taught him and was able to beautifully manage his dual roles.

Until recently, the prevailing presumptive (impossible) goal was for working mothers to achieve a harmonious balance between their work selves (career-identified role) and their home selves (homemaker and mother-identified role) and not feel torn between two conflicting identities. Today we also realize the way these stereotypes affect fathers.

Such presumptions have levied a heavy psychological toll on working parents, often resulting in personal feelings of inadequacy and being overwhelmed. We have not yet developed sufficient social and cultural structures to support new parents in this dual identity at home and work. As a result, new parents (still predominantly moms) are often forced out of traditional careers and into alternative work situations such as the part-time flexibility offered by freelancing or the schedule control possible when becoming an entrepreneur (which even has its own controversial name: *mompreneur*). I am seeing a silent wave of fathers facing these identity and role conflicts as well—Kenny is just one example. These solutions may work in the short term, but they can leave families vulnerable to financial strain, job insecurity, and a lack of health insurance. It also sets parents up for challenges down the road if they ever want to reenter traditional work, when they want to collect Social Security, or if they need to use the social service safety net.

Yourself

Whether you are a mom or a dad, the shock of this transition can be exacerbated by any role and identity confusion you might experience when you become a parent, and again when you go back to work. This can be particularly challenging if you are like many of our clients at the Center for Parental Leave Leadership and the work you do is a big part of your identity—after all, you have already spent a significant portion of your life building your career and the majority of your waking hours working. You may feel like you have your current work life pretty well figured out. You understand your role at work, and you have a home life that is, to some extent, chosen and predictable.

The shift to a working parent identity can bring intense inner turmoil as you try to balance and integrate changing priorities and increased responsibilities at home with those at work.

Societal ideals, personal values, and organizational pressures all contribute to shaping this new reality. Although mothers and fathers may share some similar experiences, they still face very different cultural expectations about their roles at work and at home. Women are particularly vulnerable to pressure to conform to the conflicting roles of ideal worker and good mother. For men, societal expectations about fatherhood tend to center on the ideals of the good provider and the involved father. Additionally, many working parents face the expectation that their return to work should be easy and seamless, which is based on the mistaken assumption that they are the same person they were before going on leave.

Although understanding your own role and identity changes through this transition is crucial, it can also help to think about the people around you and how the roles they play may affect your leave experience and employment (see sidebar *Stats: Moms versus Dads*).

Stats: Moms versus Dads

How Parenthood Affects Employment

- 56% of mothers and 50% of fathers say juggling work and family life is difficult.[1]
- Childcare and family obligations are the top reason keeping women "of prime age" (25–54) from working in formal employment. For men of the same age, the top reason for not working is health limitations, followed by inability to find work.[2]
- 46% of women and 23% of men list childcare or other family obligations as a reason they are not working.[3]

Full Time, Part Time, or No Time

- 76% of people think full-time work is ideal for fathers; only 33% say the same for mothers.[4]
- 96.2% of employed fathers work full time; 78.5% of employed mothers work full time.[5]
- 39% of people who believe one parent should not work full time say the mother should be the one to not work, or to work part time, as compared to 5% who say the stay-at-home (or part-time) parent should be the father.[6]

Mompreneurs

- 80% of mompreneurs started their business after having children, with 69% citing flexibility as the top advantage of having their own business and 71% indicating they are the primary childcare provider.[7]

(continued)

(continued)

Involved Parenting

- 80% of women and 74% of men believe that women face a lot of pressure to be an involved parent; 43% of women and 56% of men believe the same of men.[8]
- When both parents work, moms are more likely to take on more responsibility for sick children (47% moms versus 6% dads) and to be responsible for managing children's schedule and activities (54% moms versus 39% dads).[9]

The Value of Our Contributions

- Society puts greater value on men's contributions at work (53%) versus home (5%) and conversely greater value on women's contributions at home (28%) versus work (15%). There is a higher expectation that women contribute in both arenas (56%) as compared to men (41%).[10]

Parenthood Bias

- 27% of mothers and 20% of fathers have been treated as if they were not committed to their work.[11]
- 19% of mothers and 14% of fathers have been passed over for an important assignment.[12]
- 19% of mothers and 13% of fathers have been passed over for promotion.[13]

Driving the Point Home

- Having a baby changes the brain! Pregnancy and the post-partum period are associated with physiological and neuro-logical restructuring changes for moms[14] *and* dads.[15]

Your Manager

In an ideal world, your manager would act as a facilitator and lead communicator during your transition. Because most managers are not specifically trained or equipped to support parental leave, it is likely you will have to lead the conversations and "manage up" to ensure you get the support you'd like. Managers usually see their role as making sure your work gets done by someone in your absence. You can help your manager see that this is a time of opportunity for the whole team to improve communication and develop skill sets by taking on new roles and tasks. Being clear about the kind of support you want is mutually beneficial—everyone will know what to do and you will get what you need to come back strong, productive, and recommitted to your team.

Your Human Resources Representative

Ideally, your HR representative (or HR equivalent) would be helping you understand your organization's policies and practices on parental leave. A good HR representative can be a key partner in building your plan, providing a deeper understanding of how much time you may take off, how much pay you will receive while you are away (if any), and options for returning, such as a part-time or gradual return. Often, trying to make sense of convoluted federal, state, and local laws *and* company policies can be incredibly confusing. Even your HR department may be unclear. It is their job to aid your understanding, but I want you to be prepared to take the lead in case they don't provide adequate guidance.

Routines

Becoming a working parent will also have practical implications. Your morning routines must be reworked and the end of the day will be about bath, bed, and feeding. As wonderful as the arrival of the new child will feel, it will be disorienting to be out of your regular routines and learning new responsibilities. *When a new child arrives, a parent is born.* Your new child is just beginning to learn about their environment. You, too, are getting to know the world again from a different perspective.

Eventually, you will become less and less disoriented. You will return to work and reach a new normal where all things will start to fit into a more predictable pattern and routine. But finding a new normal takes time. Diving into the 10 touchpoints in these chapters will give you the tools (and help you recognize the ones you already have) to navigate this exciting time as it unfolds.

Lead Your Leave

Parental Leave Is Our Most Overlooked Leadership Development Opportunity

There is one more role I want you to consider taking on—a leader. As you continue reading, you will see that leadership is a key theme throughout this book. I invite you to imagine that your transition to working parenthood is a leadership development and personal growth workshop or retreat that makes even the most prestigious leadership program offered to C-Suite executives pale in comparison. You have already paid for it and put it on your calendar (even if the dates aren't exactly fixed!).

I mean this quite literally. What you will learn as you become a working parent is beyond what is taught in leadership development courses around the world. I know this because I have been creating such courses for more than two decades. In the mid-1990s, I was hired as the only employee for a new executive development and leadership coaching company being started by three trailblazers of the fledgling field, Drs. David Dotlich, Peter Cairo, and Stephen Rhinesmith. These master teachers took me under their wing and generously taught me everything they knew about leadership and the humanity at the core of it. We worked to create the most innovative off-site executive development programs of the time. My mentors held what is now a widely shared view but was a unique perspective then—that ideal leadership does not come from top-down commanders; instead, a true leader is someone with keen emotional intelligence who understands themselves and is attuned to their environment. These teachers invited program participants to pay attention to their head, heart, and intuition to become *whole-person leaders* (see their excellent book *Head, Heart, and Guts: How the World's Best Companies Develop Complete Leaders*[16] to learn more).

Decades later, everything we had created for tens of thousands of executives in those workshops and retreats was nothing compared to what I found myself learning as I became a mother and a working parent. I do not mean to minimize the profound impact a leadership development course can have, if it is done well. However, becoming a working parent was the most intense and rewarding experiential learning program I have gone through. It can be the same for you. Becoming a working parent is ultimately about the process of *becoming*—not just a parent, and not just a working parent, but a whole person more attuned to yourself, those around you, and the world. In other words, if you are open to it, this transition offers the possibility of becoming who you were born to be and what you were born to do. You started that process of evolving when you decided to become a parent; it is up to you how far you want to take it.

You can lead your leave by deepening your self-awareness as you navigate this major life transition. The exercises and processes you will find in the touchpoints throughout this book outline what to do in pragmatic terms. They go beyond practical matters, however, in digging into how to identify what matters to you and connect with your core values to guide you toward a more fully realized version of yourself.

You'll find a leadership box at the end of each touchpoint chapter to help you recognize and apply some of the whole-person leadership skills on offer during your transition to parenthood.

Your leave will be uniquely yours and shaped by your personality, situation, and beliefs. No matter what, you will learn and grow through this process. To the extent that you prepare yourself (practically and emotionally) and engage in the transition with a willingness to learn and lead, you will come out the other side stronger, wiser, and more connected to your life—at work and at home.

PHASE ONE
Preparing for Leave

✱ ✱ ✱

Work Focus

Chapter
Three

Phase 1: Preparing for Leave Overview

WHEN I WAS a kid, my family would travel a few times a year from Denver to a small town where my mom grew up in Wyoming. About 20 miles outside of Cheyenne, in the stretch everyone simply called "the badlands," you would begin to see billboards featuring penguins who counted down the miles until you arrived at Little America. In my child's mind, Little America was a high-class resort oasis in the middle of endless stretches of dirt, and the penguins enticed me to beg my parents to stop there. Each billboard was funny and novel, showing a penguin pumping gas, swimming, or wearing a hat. Each sign added another chapter to the story about what I could expect when I got there and reminded me of things I would need when I did: *World's Largest Stations with 65 Gas Pumps! 150 Motel Rooms! Ice Cream! Swimming Pool!* Then when I thought I could barely wait another minute, the magnificent final sign: *Almost Home.* These penguins made that long stretch of drive more bearable, cutting the interminable journey into manageable chunks and giving me something to look forward to, not just at the end of the journey, but with each sign. Instead of dreading an unbearably long journey to Wyoming, I left the house excited to see the penguins and quietly watched the roadside until the first one appeared, at which point I read it out loud and started my campaign to get my parents to stop. The signs told me exactly where I was and how far I had to go, and when I should start asking for ice cream.

As you navigate your leave, these touchpoints give you a heads-up about things you need to pay particular attention to in order to bend things to your advantage (and, yes, you should ask for ice cream—I'll talk about self-advocacy skills in Chapter 10). The figure highlights the first four touchpoints that make up Phase 1 of your transition.

The 10A Touchpoint Framework™ Phase 1

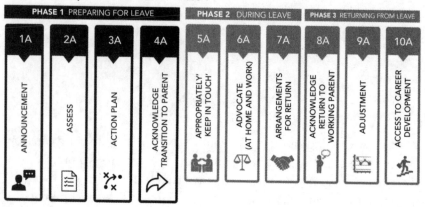

The Emotional Passage to Working Parenthood

If you've ever been on a long trip like those drives we used to take to Wyoming, you know that at some point in the journey, everyone involved will get excited, cranky, scared, and awestruck by turns. This is true of your passage into working parenthood as well. The figure depicts the emotional hills and valleys of becoming a working parent. Over the course of your transition, you can expect to revolve through emotions like anxiety, happiness, guilt, even disillusionment. The key takeaway here is this: having emotional ups and downs does not mean you're doing it wrong. It is to be expected on your way to empowerment.

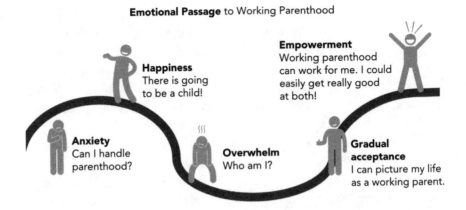

Emotional Passage to Working Parenthood

Empowerment
Working parenthood can work for me. I could easily get really good at both!

Happiness
There is going to be a child!

Anxiety
Can I handle parenthood?

Overwhelm
Who am I?

Gradual acceptance
I can picture my life as a working parent.

As we go along through Phase 1 and beyond, I will point out the places where action and attention are recommended. I will offer reflection questions, exercises, and models that others have found useful in handling the practical and emotional aspects of their parental leave. It is up to you how you engage with the material and how deep you go. I encourage you to spend extra time in the areas that make sense for you and quickly skim over things that don't feel relevant, or at least not relevant yet. You've got a lot going on, and skimming is an efficient way to notice information that you may want to go back to at a later date.

Don't Expect Others to Have a Plan

As I emphasized about leadership at the end of the last chapter, one of the overarching principles I want you to walk away from this book with is that *there is power in listening to your head, heart, and intuition to lead your leave, and you alone hold the keys to that power.* I know how much you have stacked against you as a working parent. There are countless people and systems in place that could block you from your power—whether by design or lack of it. It is with this awareness that I encourage you to accept two fundamental truths: (1) for the most part, for better or for worse, it *will be up to you* to lead your leave experience for yourself and those around you and (2) embracing this opportunity will serve you better than almost anything else.

When my coauthor Sue was pregnant with her first child and working for the HR department of her city government, she excitedly told her boss she was expecting and then waited for everyone to tell her what to do. Like many new parents, she was surprised that her organization largely took a play-it-by-ear approach. To her, it felt like the most important event of her life was being treated like planning for a week of vacation.

There was nowhere her manager could direct her to learn about the leave process or even a central location for compliance forms and deadlines. There certainly wasn't anywhere for her manager to find out how to best support an employee during a parental leave transition. With each new leave taken by someone in her organization, as is usually the case in the United States, managers and expecting parents had to reinvent the wheel. Luckily, Sue's boss was a parent herself and deeply empathetic. (Sue had won the boss lottery!) To the best of her ability, she tried to think ahead and support Sue in all the ways the system allowed. I see many expecting parents who are not so lucky. If you are with an organization that has no system in place to support new parents, it will be up to you to create one. The alternative is to experience the tumult that is bound to occur when you and everyone around you are in reaction mode without a plan or a leader.

Sue learned from her initial experience and from her side work with me at the Center for Parental Leave Leadership. With the arrival of her second child, she took charge of her second parental leave transition from the moment she announced her pregnancy. It made all the difference in the ultimate outcome *and* her day-to-day experience.

Frontload the Work

The work necessary to manage your transition in this first phase, as you prepare for your leave, is more intense and takes longer than the work in Phases 2 and 3. In order to set yourself up well, you will want to do a lot of what we call *frontloading*: doing the heavy lifting of planning for each phase toward the front end—here in Phase 1, while you are preparing for leave. **I recommend reading the entire book before finalizing your parental leave transition plan and then revisiting the touchpoints of Phase 2 once your child arrives, and of Phase 3 when you return to work.** What you get out of those sections will change as you move through this transition.

Phase 1 is also where you will be doing the inner work of orienting yourself to the type of parent (and then working parent) you want to become, with the *assess* and *acknowledge* touchpoints, and making sure your plans are designed to get you there with the *action plan* touchpoint. This frontloading is purposeful and, thankfully, it also coincides with when you have the most attention and time (though it may not feel like it) to set yourself up well. Things like thinking through and creating your off-boarding plans, setting up your return, and making sure you give yourself multiple backup plans in case anything unexpected happens are worth carving out time for now. I've never heard a new parent say, "I wish I hadn't done so much practical and emotional preparation before my child arrived."

So, let's dive into the first touchpoint of Phase 1, your *announcement* at work that you will soon welcome a new child into your family.

Chapter
Four

Touchpoint 1
Announcement

JANELLE FOUND HERSELF revealing to her boss that she was expecting while at a company party. They were chatting in line for dessert when her boss left for a second to get in the champagne line. She came back with two glasses and offered Janelle one. Caught off guard, Janelle blurted out, "No, thanks, I'm pregnant. Surprise!" To her relief, her boss laughed and hugged her, and they offered the extra glass of champagne to the guy behind them, who laughed, too.

Javier, equally caught off guard, didn't have such a positive start. His manager called him into his office to ask if the rumor that Javier and his husband were adopting was true. When Javier responded that, yes, the news was true, his manager did not smile or congratulate him. Instead he took a passive-aggressive approach and indicated his expectations by reminding Javier that the company policy offered men only two weeks paid leave; the three-month paid leave policy was reserved for birthing mothers. Javier, who had thought he had more time before he had to make his announcement, was unprepared for how to best respond.

As Janelle and Javier's stories show us, you can't always predict when your announcement will happen. However, as much as possible, it is a good idea to try. Your announcement is your first opportunity to kick-start a successful leave and return and can set the tone for your entire three-phase parental leave transition. Although you may have legitimate fears of pregnancy discrimination, being passed over for an opportunity because of impending leave, or worries about how others will perceive your commitment to work, your power lies in setting the scene and striking the tone for your announcement, as well as how you interpret and respond to the reactions you get.

If you have already announced and you don't feel like it went as well as you would have liked, don't worry: there are plenty of ways to reposition yourself and reclaim the tone and direction your transition takes.

When It Goes Badly . . .

There are many cautionary tales of announcements that have gone off the rails. They mostly involve managers or coworkers having knee-jerk reactions and/or saying something inappropriate or hurtful. Of course, how other people respond to your news is beyond your control (and almost always about them, not you). However, announcements that are poorly timed or communicated can contribute to a rough transition— and that *is* within your control. Javier made the mistake of telling his coworkers before he told his boss and ended up feeling cornered and unprepared. His boss likely felt caught off guard, too, when he heard from someone else about Javier's plans and was left wondering if they were true and why Javier wasn't telling him. (Whether his boss realized it or not, he may have called Javier into his office and responded from a negative place because his feelings were hurt by not being included earlier—a very human reaction.) By telling his coworkers first, Javier put his boss in an uncomfortable position where he was left with few choices other than asking Javier directly if the rumors were true, which was bound to feel confrontational. If Javier had chosen to tell his boss before his colleagues, his announcement would have happened on his own terms. Plus, it never feels good to a manager (or anyone!) to be left out of news that affects them. I have yet to see this approach go over well with leadership.

When It Goes Well . . .

When you make a well-timed, thoughtful and confident announcement, you, your manager, and your team are given the time and clarity needed to communicate and prepare for your absence. Identify and propose ways your leave can be used as an opportunity to improve team communication and cross-train or skill-up junior staff. Using this approach, you'll feel confident and supported as you prepare for your vital time away and your manager and team won't feel like they have been left holding the bag, which can create a breeding ground for resentment and make your reentry more difficult.

Preparing to Announce

Before you announce, it will be helpful to spend some time reflecting on how you want the conversation to go. Picture the outcome you want and think of ways you can frame the announcement and what language you can use to steer things to a positive interpretation of your news. Even with scary managers and in companies with dreadful cultures concerning leave, I have seen time and again that when clients assume it will go well, it does, and when they assume it will go poorly, it also does. I'm not saying you can control what others feel, do, or say, but they are influenced by your mindset, tone, and approach.

Reflection Questions Before You Announce

Ideally, do this reflection exercise before you announce, but if you have already made your announcement, it's still helpful to think back on how it went—not to beat yourself up, but to use some of the lessons learned as you move forward.

Your announcement is your opportunity to set the tone for your entire three-phase transition. Consider what tone you would like to set and how you would like to go about setting it.

* Consider when and how you will announce your upcoming transition to your manager and team. What is important to remember as you plan your announcement? Are there announcements from others you admired and can use as a model?
* What concerns do you have in announcing that you are expecting, adopting, or fostering a child?
* What reaction are you expecting from your manager? Is your expectation based on experience, and do you think it is realistic? Could it be fear-based and actually unlikely?
* What reaction are you expecting from your team? Again, do you think that it is a fear-based expectation or a realistic, experience-based one?
* If you could wave a magic wand and get any reaction you wanted, what would that be? Think through your ideal reaction in detail (write it down if you can). Really pay attention and notice what is going on. Where are you? Are there any noticeable feelings, locations, or other contributing factors?
* Think of what you can do to inspire this ideal reaction. Is there an energy or tone you want to bring to the conversation? Is there a certain time of the day or location that you know will be helpful?

It's important to recognize any expectations you have about what will happen when you announce. Expectations often set us up for disappointment, and humans are often bad at predicting the future, particularly the behavior of others. Recognizing ahead of time that you are telling yourself a story can help you detach from it and instead be curious about what will really happen. Noticing your expectations will help you make a plan while also helping you figure out which fears are realistic and which are fantasy.

Key Elements of a Good Announcement

Here are elements to consider before making your announcement.

Source: Cartoonresource.com

• *Timing*

When planning your announcement, choose your timing thoughtfully. Who you tell and in what order can be important, depending on the unique politics of your workplace. The more time for planning and preparation you and your manager have before your leave starts, the less stressful and more successful your transition will be for both of you.

Of course, you want to balance your personal timing comfort with the importance of telling your manager before they hear it at the water cooler (like Javier's boss). In practical terms, if you are welcoming a child via birth, consider if you would like to wait until the end of the first trimester to announce or if you would like to announce as soon as you find out. Some people find it easier to deal with morning sickness and fatigue if they are not trying to hide it or pretend something else is wrong.

One important consideration is that pregnancy loss most frequently occurs before 12 weeks. Some people prefer to keep loss private and others appreciate the support colleagues can provide when they know. If you have a close relationship with your manager, you may wish to share the news earlier in hopes that your manager will be understanding and accommodating in the event of a loss. Too many grieving expectant parents suffer in silence unnecessarily.

The same considerations apply if you're welcoming a child via adoption, fostering, surrogacy, or any other means. These ways of becoming a parent can also result in unexpected loss, such as a birth mother changing her mind or a surrogate miscarrying. Consider if you want to wait to announce until all approvals are in place and you know it's a done deal with a fairly solid date to welcome your child or if you would like to bring your colleagues along through the full process so they can provide you support when you need it and celebrate with you when all goes well.

For many it can feel difficult to go against the cultural norm of keeping home and work separate, but I have seen many expectant parents form deeper bonds at work by allowing teammates or managers into their emotional journey to parenthood early on. For one thing, it will be much easier for your boss to accept a future request on your part to miss a day or adjust a deadline if they have more context to understand why you are asking. Conversely, you may work in a climate where your direct manager or teammates are not understanding or supportive—perhaps even the opposite. Consider your situation and whether announcing earlier will only result in your being penalized earlier, and plan accordingly.

There are no firm rules that apply to everyone in terms of timing. Much of the decision depends on your personal situation and comfort level. Announcing earlier may mean having to share painful news. Announcing later may mean that people have already figured out something is up and gives you less time for communication and planning and fewer people supporting you from the beginning of your transition.

In any case, it is important to think through the basics of your transition plan before you make your announcement to your whole team, so you can go into the conversation with ideas on how to make it successful for everyone involved.

• *Tone*

Choosing your tone consciously can show your excitement and willingness to do the hard work it takes to plan a smooth transition. Though you may be tempted to say sorry in advance for a lengthy absence, there is no need whatsoever to apologize. *Apologizing sends a signal that something has gone wrong, and nothing is wrong here.* Remember that you are a human on a team full of other humans and the reality is that, at any moment, any one of you may experience something in your personal life that requires an extended absence. Even though our culture is still shrugging off outdated norms, you have nothing to be sorry about, especially when you plan and communicate well.

Your tone can also convey that you are excited to see what your team can do while you are away and excited to take things on again when you return. You can even be forthright about your belief that becoming a parent is bound to offer you many lessons that you can bring back to work. An air of prepared confidence will go a long way to reassuring your manager and team that taking parental leave does not automatically mean a negative impact on the business or that you won't come back. You are about to show them how it is done.

Sample Script for Announcing to Your Boss

Although every announcement will be different, it is often most effective to schedule a short meeting when you can have a discussion in private and schedule multiple follow-up meetings to plan logistics.

You know you and your relationship with your boss best. Put yourself in their shoes. Would they like to hear the news over lunch or in a more formal setting? In person or over email? At the end of the day or the beginning? Your goal is to pinpoint as best you can what will bolster your news and put it in an empowering light, given your particular manager and circumstances.

> "I have some exciting personal news to share that will affect work, and I want to allow plenty of time for planning. I'm/we're expecting a child/baby in x months! I know from some research I've done that the better my planning is, the smoother the transition will be for me and for our team as a whole, which is very important to me.
>
> "I'm looking forward to learning anything you have to teach me about this process, but in the meantime, I've started putting together an action plan for my leave and I'd love to schedule another meeting soon to go over that with you and get your feedback so I can fine-tune it.
>
> "Can you think of anything you want me to know about or consider as I put this plan together?"

Sample Script for Announcing to Your Team

Talk to your manager about whether they would like to make the announcement to the larger team and then have you share a few words or if they would prefer you take the lead. Either way, use this announcement to send the message that you and your manager are working closely together to plan for how to minimize the impact of your leave on the team. Here is an example of how to approach this:

> "Thank you all! I'm/we're very excited. I know from some research I've done that the better my planning is, the smoother the transition will be for me and for our team as a whole, which is very important to me. I'll share details in the coming weeks/months about my transition plan, as I work closely with [boss's name]. I'm excited to see how we can make this process work for the whole team and will be reaching out to some of you to get input about what would be helpful. I will be doing everything I can to make this as easy on you as possible! If there are any parts of my role that you are particularly interested in learning about and possibly covering for me while I'm away, please let me know. Thanks again. Your excitement and well-wishes mean a lot to me."

If You've Already Announced

If you have already made your announcement before reading this book and you are feeling a negative impact from it, do not lose sleep over it. There is no time like the present to pivot and adopt a tone and planning strategy that can turn things around. Again, even though you can't control the reactions of others, attitude is contagious. An apologetic tone sends the signal that there is a problem. A self-assured tone will help put people at ease. If, however, there *is* something to apologize for, by all means do, and then move on.

If you are experiencing major fallout from the way you announced, you may need to schedule a few one-on-one discussions to set things right. Alfonzo, a project manager and father expecting twins for his second time around, wanted to take an extended leave to support his wife on bedrest and then be there to share in caregiving after the birth. His announcement had not gone over well, and his manager had made it clear that he didn't want Alfonzo to be gone long for paternity leave because they were all working under a tight deadline. Alfonzo knew a reset was needed. Given the animosity he was feeling from his manager, we decided the best place for him to start would be with his HR representative. This enabled Alfonzo to informally document the issue and get advice from someone who could influence outcomes. He was able to get more information about his company's policies and create an ally whom he could call on if needed. But rather than go back in frustration or anger, Alfonzo decided to reapproach his manager with a plan that addressed his biggest concerns. It was as simple as him saying that he had been thinking about how he wanted to handle his leave given the tight deadline his manager was working to meet. He consciously reset the tone to one of open communication, showing confidence in his plan as he shared his ideas about what he could get done ahead of time and which pieces he would transfer to whom. Doing this demonstrated empathy toward his manager's predicament, and, though admittedly not thrilled, his manager felt like his concerns were addressed. He agreed to Alfonzo's proposed plan and backed him in making it happen.

Ongoing Communication

After your announcement, make open communication an ongoing priority by scheduling regular meetings with your manager. Together, you can plan what needs to be communicated to the larger team and when.

Depending on your organization's size and your situation, you may also want to contact your HR representative so you can learn your organization's parental leave and flexible work policies. (Keep in mind that, depending on the size of your organization and how much thought this topic has been given by HR, you might be disappointed with what you find. It is not uncommon for companies to have no policies or direction.) Often, if there is good information to be had, you can find it on your company intranet or employee assistance program (EAP) web-site. Do not be afraid to ask questions and get clarification on anything that is unclear. The patchwork of laws and policies that govern leaves is often confusing—even to people who deal with it all the time.

In companies with policies and those without, it can be helpful to reach out to a trusted colleague who has recently been in your shoes and ask them to tell you about their experience, including anything that went well, things that were unexpected, and things they wish they had done differently. More and more workplaces offer parent support groups or employee resource groups (ERGs) devoted to working parenthood. These are useful places to learn from the experiences of others and gain a sense of community. Many parents have told me how the people they met in these groups became their dear friends as they navigated working parenthood together, sharing tips, experiences, and mutual support as their children grew.

When Someone Says the Wrong Thing

It is a good idea to assume that someone will make a thoughtless or insensitive comment at some point once you announce. This can be destabilizing in the moment, but expecting it will happen helps reduce the sting. When humans encounter a new situation, see someone doing something differently than they think it "should" be done, or see someone doing it how they wish they had, they can often respond defensively or in an off-putting manner. This usually has nothing to do with you and everything to do with them. As a working parent you are going to encounter comments that feel judgmental or intru-sive. They may be minor, like when a client's neighbor told her, "My babies always wore hats from September through April," while point-edly staring at her baby's hatless head, or they may be more harmful, such as when a different client's teammate told their boss that he should be given an important work trip instead of my client because "he's got a new baby at home; do you think his wife is going to let him go anywhere?"

Use any jarring responses to your announcement as welcome prompts to get yourself to think about and practice how you want to respond to these types of comments now and far into the future. You can choose to be annoyed and add another check mark in the mental column of reasons to avoid that person, or you can use it as an opportunity to develop your mental strength and agility—a key skill of working parenthood now and, well, forever.

Amy Morin, author of *13 Things Mentally Strong People Don't Do*,[1] puts it this way: "Allowing others to control the way you think, feel, or behave gives them power over you. And you certainly don't want to let negative, snarky comments influence how you feel about yourself. . . . Reframe your upsetting thoughts, take deep breaths to stay calm, and walk away from the situation. . ."[2]

The Broader Impact of Your Leave

Bear in mind that parental leave will bring about a transition for your broader team and clients, too. Some team members will be excited about your news, and others may be concerned about what it means for them. In the same vein as your response to judgmental comments, use this as an opportunity to focus on not getting defensive if you are met with some attitude. Defensiveness only escalates conflict and makes it harder for you to reach your goals. Instead, adopt a curious mindset to better understand where their concerns lie and work to reassure them that your plans aim to create a smooth transition for them, too. As much as possible, refocus attention on whatever task is at hand. As concrete plans come visibly into focus, other people's concerns are likely to decrease.

Take the Lead

As you navigate these early days of your transition, don't wait for others to make the first move. Managers and colleagues can feel uneasy about overstepping boundaries when it comes to your personal family life, and even if they are not conscious of it, they may be looking for you to take the lead—and are relieved when you do. Remember, this is an opportunity for you to set the tone with confidence and clarity.

Leadership Lessons of Parenthood

Touchpoint 1: Your Announcement

By thoughtfully considering and leading your announcement and by being open to reactions and feedback in ways that don't knock you off your center, you are stepping (further) into your power.

Here are a few of the *whole-person leadership* skills you'll be practicing during this touchpoint:

- Holding steady in the face of unpredictable reactions
- Stepping into your power
- Taking the proactive lead in your leave transition for the good of everyone, rather than waiting for things to happen to you and your team
- Communicating authentically and with empathy
- Engaging in courageous conversations

Chapter
Five

Touchpoint 2
Assess

A THOROUGH ASSESSMENT of your transition is one of your most important tools in preparing for leave. It reminds you to stop and reflect on how this change will affect you and those around you at work and at home. Taking your time in the assessment phase will pay huge dividends throughout your leave and beyond.

Although it can be tempting to focus your efforts on the things that seem urgent, this touchpoint is situated in second place to prompt you to resist the instinct to jump straight into planning (which is the third touchpoint and comes *after* this one). You are going to create a stronger plan and better harness the opportunities of this transition if you take the time you need to consider the big picture. Understanding yourself, your guiding values, and your goals, as well as what you have working for you and against you during this transition, are key to any successful leave plan.

When you become a parent, you are not just experiencing a change, you are undergoing a fundamental life transition. William Bridges, a prominent transition theorist, researcher, and organizational consultant, explained the difference between change and transition this way: *"Transition is not just a nice way to say change. It is the inner process through which people come to terms with a change, as they let go of how things used to be and reorient themselves to the way that things are now."*[1]

Change happens rapidly and can be entirely passive; transition happens over time and is often intentional. Examples of common life transitions include graduating from school, getting married, moving from one job to another, and, of course, welcoming a child. Understanding parental leave as a transition enables us to define the steps and stages. This can help us appreciate that there are predictable, sequential elements to any transition process and that because this is a time-bound transition, at some point we will be on the other side of it. This perspective shift can bring you a sense of clarity and self-efficacy and can go far in easing any associated pain or confusion that may have you questioning if you will ever make it through or get a handle on all that has changed.

Transitions are not by nature positive or negative. You get to decide what your transition is for you. That means you can take some pressure off of yourself. When you become a parent you are *changed* overnight, but you will be *transitioning* in various ways for the rest of your life. You don't need to figure it all out today.

Transition Shock in Parental Leave

Transitions by definition involve change, and if you are like most humans, you probably have a knee-jerk reaction against change. Although there are an infinite number of normal responses to change, transition theory shows us some patterns. Frequent responses include (1) a sense of confusion due to the absence of previously known life markers and/or the introduction of new ones, (2) feelings of loss (even when the change is eagerly anticipated and planned for), and (3) the experience of feeling threatened, which can make you want to defend yourself. These types of responses to transition have been given a name—*transition shock*—which is defined as the state of loss and disorientation we experience during any change in our familiar environment that requires adjustment.

Though many new parents can relate to this feeling, not everyone who undergoes a transition will experience transition shock. I mention it here simply to acknowledge and normalize any disorienting feelings and defensive reactions you encounter in yourself, whatever their magnitude.

Introducing the 6-S System for Parental Leave Transition Success

When I started this work there was no easy way for expectant parents to assess their transition in a way that gave them a holistic picture of their strengths and challenges in all the areas that affected their experience. I needed a way to measure the external pressures of such a big, life-changing transition, as well as the physical, psychological, and emotional states of my clients. In response, I developed a self-assessment tool based on a process I called the 6-S System for Parental Leave Transition Success. This tool was inspired by the work of transition expert Dr. Nancy Schlossberg and her colleagues. I use this process to help expectant and new parents identify what elements they have working for them (their *assets*) and what they may have working against them (their *liabilities*) as they navigate through their parental leave and return. Research shows that every little bit that you increase your assets and decrease your liabilities creates a quantifiably greater chance of transition success. Schlossberg's theory and related 4-S System have demonstrated usefulness over roughly 40 years to help make individual experiences of all types of transitions easier. My adaptations focus specifically on the parental leave transition to make it even more relevant for today's working parents.

At the Center for Parental Leave Leadership, we've automated this process by developing an online self-assessment tool called the *Parental Leave Transition Assessment (PLTA)*, which is the first evidence-based survey and report for setting up parental leave, asking a comprehensive series of questions that lead you through the various areas of the 6-S System. The resulting customized report outlines your assets and liabilities and includes your risk score, which is a calculation that identifies the level at which your transition success is at risk. It's illuminating to work through this process, and in the rest of this chapter I will show you how to do so on your own (or you can find this tool on our website: www.cplleadership.com).

This is not a self-assessment of *skill*, but rather a picture of *resources* available to you and *conditions* working against you at this moment in time. In this process I'll ask you to look at your strengths and challenges in six areas that have been shown to have a direct link to your transition success. Although transition success looks different for each person, parental leave transition success can be broadly defined as *the engaged, supported, and sustainable retention of working parents within their work organization while they are also thriving at home.*

Transition Success Requires:

INCREASED ASSETS

DECREASED LIABILITIES

Walking Yourself Through the 6-S System for Parental Leave Transition Success

Each of the six topic areas that this process covers is conveniently named for a word beginning with an S, hence the 6-S System. The first four—**situation, self, supports,** and **strategies**—ask you to consider questions related to these four dimensions. Your answers will help you identify your current assets and liabilities related to your parental leave transition. This knowledge wil l help you understand where to focus your energy to leverage the assets you identify and decrease any liabilities.

Sometimes, when it is not yet clear whether something is an asset or a liability, it can fall somewhere in the middle. We call those things *pivot points.* Actively working to turn these more neutral pivot points into assets, rather than letting them slip into becoming liabilities, can increase your overall number of transition assets.

The fifth S area—**sabotages**—asks you to identify any external or internal derailers that may affect your transition experience. These are tendencies or circumstances that, if not brought to light, can upset even the best-planned transition. Often sabotages may be opportunities for quick wins if you can easily head them off or defuse them. Sometimes, sabotages present a greater threat to your transition experience and need more focused energy and planning for improvement.

The final S dimension is **suggestions**, and I include it to create a feedback loop for you to share suggestions about how your peers and work organization can help support you—and others facing their own parental leave transition in the future. See the figure for an overview of the areas to consider during your 6-S System self-assessment.

6-S System for Parental Leave Transition Success

1 SITUATION   **2 S**ELF   **3 S**UPPORTS

4 STRATEGIES   **5 S**ABOTAGES   **6 S**UGGESTIONS

Take Stock

As Dr. Schlossberg explains in her work, in order to take charge of a transition, one must first take stock. In this next section, I will walk you through how to do this yourself. First, let's look at each S dimension one by one through the lens of *your* transition. You can follow along with this process in your head, or if you prefer something more concrete, grab a notebook or go to www.cplleadership.com/playbook to download a worksheet and take notes as you read through this section.

1 SITUATION

This is the *what* of your personal equation. Think specifically about what is happening to you. What is going on in your environment? What is your job like? How much time do you have for leave? Are finances tight? Do you have multiple responsibilities? Are you in the middle of a move or other simultaneous transition? Did you plan for this child or plan for them to be joining your family right now? Do you have other children to consider?

Write down a list of your situation assets. For example, do you have an understanding manager? Put it in the asset column. Is this happening at a good time in your career? Asset! Do you feel like you have some control over the details of your transition? Asset! Are you excited to welcome this child right now? Asset! (Maybe you are excited, but a part of you wishes it was happening a year from now. If so, that could be a pivot point.)

Common assets I see with clients include high job satisfaction, having a supportive manager, being satisfied with the length of leave they have available, having a partner who can take leave, and having previous transition experience. Remember, these are *your* assets, so write down whatever feels supportive related to your situation (not the things that someone tells you are supportive, but don't feel that way to you).

Next consider or write down your situational liabilities. For example, is your childcare unreliable? That is a liability. Is your job changing when you return? Potential liability! Are you taking care of an elderly relative as well? Likely liability! Are you struggling with a perinatal mood disorder such as anxiety or depression or another health concern? Liability.

Common liabilities include poor timing of your leave, concurrent stressors, and uncertainty about your role when you return to work.

The more liabilities you can identify, the better. This is not a time to pass judgment or make plans. *Don't get discouraged as they begin to add up; you are just taking stock.* Getting liabilities out in the open with a discerning eye toward strategic planning will enable you to better understand how to transform your liabilities into elements working in your favor.

2 SELF

This is the *who*. You bring your own unique history, issues, personality, and habits to your transition. Who are you? Do you thrive in the face of change? Do you set realistic expectations? Do you have positive examples of working parents from your childhood? During a parental leave transition, these are all assets!

Common assets I see in my clients also include having a strong sense of self, having a curious, open mind—especially about themselves—being resilient, and having strong self-care habits.

As you make your list, consider this—when things go wrong, do you blame yourself? That's a liability. When you think about this transition, do you feel overwhelmed? Liability. Do you find it difficult to take care of yourself or tend to put others' needs ahead of your own? Liability. Are the parenthood examples in your life a far cry from what you hope to model for your own child? Liability. Common liabilities I see include being easily stressed or anxious, difficulty adjusting to change, fear of conflict, and blind spots in self-awareness.

Write down your unique assets as well as any potential liabilities you discover. Some people find it helpful to ask a friend for perspective; often those who love us can see us with kinder and/or more objective eyes than our own. This is about *your* perception, so only accept what feels authentic to you. The goal here is to get an accurate accounting so you can start turning the things that are working against you into things working for you.

3 SUPPORTS

Support means the type of help you perceive as available to you and from whom. First, identify and write down the types of actions from others that feel supportive to you as assets and the ones that are likely to be offered but don't feel supportive as liabilities.

For example, you may love the idea of having your mother come stay as you welcome your child (asset!), or that might make your stress level go through the roof (liability!). Reflect on what you need to feel fully supported during your transition. Do you need a meal train? A regular meeting with a lactation consultant? A therapist, nutritionist, or house cleaner? Time with your buddies outside the home? Will you implode without daily exercise? Setting these things up for yourself means assets! Where you identify gaps or unwelcome "support" means liabilities!

Next, consider *who your available supports are.* Is it your partner or spouse, if you have one? Your family or friends? Your religious community or work colleagues? Who is available and to what degree? Is there anyone you would like to be more available or available in a different way? Again, your desired supports are your assets. Your identified gaps are your liabilities.

Common support assets that I see include having a key support person (this could be a close friend, spouse, or partner), having helpful extended family nearby or friends who wish to help, or having a supportive community—religious or otherwise.

On the flip side, the liabilities I often see in this area can include not having any supportive people in your life, resentful coworkers, or inequitable gender roles in your household.

Adequate support *at all stages of your transition* is critical to transition success. Many people feel more comfortable requesting support at certain culturally approved moments, such as asking a relative to take care of other children while you are giving birth or traveling to pick up your new child. It is much more difficult to set up support that pushes that norm. Take a page out of another less individualistic country's book if it helps (see the sidebar). It is better to have support in place and not need it than to find out you need it and not have it there. Do not buy into the false idea of wanting to do it all by yourself. People love to be helpful; it gives them a role and makes them feel useful. Let them! Set up support all around you so you can thrive during your transition.

If this is an area you struggle with, as many do, try this thought exercise: imagine someone you care about needing help and asking you for support. Would you willingly say yes? What about if they didn't ask for support and you found out later they struggled without telling you? Most people find they would eagerly offer support and be disappointed if their friends and loved ones didn't reach out. *Remember that is how your loved ones feel when you do not let them know what you need.*

How Countries Around the World Have Traditionally Marked the Transition to Parenthood

Bali. People take turns holding the baby so its feet do not touch the ground for 210 days.

Finland. All mothers can choose between a care package of diapers, clothes, bedding, and the like—or a cash grant from the government.

Guyana. The celebration to welcome the baby is not held until nine days after birth, when mothers take their first post-baby bath. Some burn the placenta to represent the separation of mother and child.

Japan. Traditionally, the new mother will stay at her parent's house for a month after giving birth, resting in bed for 21 days while friends and family do housework.

Mexico. Mothers observe a 40-day quarantine, with no physical activity. Female relatives and friends do all housework to allow the mother to rest and focus on the baby. Mothers practice belly wrapping using a type of wrap called a *faja*.

Nigeria. *Omugwo* is the word for Nigerian postpartum care. An integral part of this is the baby's first bath, usually given by the grandmother or other female relative to represent that the mother will have community support in raising the baby.

Turkey. To help kick-start lactation and celebrate birth, mothers are given *lohusa serbeti*, a postpartum sherbet drink made of water, sugar, cloves, red food coloring, and cinnamon. There are no baby showers in Turkish culture; all baby-related celebrations take place after the baby is born. Mom and baby stay at home for 20 days after birth and receive visitors, who are also offered *lohusa serbeti*.

Vietnam. Celebrations are held 30 days after the birth; any earlier would draw the attention of the baby's previous mother (the baby's guardian angel) who might snatch the baby back.

4 STRATEGIES

This is the *how*. Each person will navigate their transition differently and use unique techniques to cope. What are your effective strategies when you are facing something unfamiliar or a tight deadline? Those are assets. Are you an expert at communicating your plans at work? Asset! Do you recognize when it is time to step away and take a moment alone to recenter? Asset! Are you known for your special skill in making your colleagues feel appreciated? Asset!

Common strategy assets during this transition include good negotiation and goal-setting skills, being comfortable taking action, mindfulness habits, strong time management skills, being assertive in ways that are not off-putting, and a sense of humor.

Do you have tendencies or have you tried strategies that blow up in your face or just don't work? Those are liabilities. When the going gets tough do you tune out, but your partner needs you to tune in? Liability! Do you deflect when your manager needs you to take responsibility? Liability! Do you become inflexible when the situation calls for flexibility? Liability.

Common strategy liabilities I see include poor relaxation skills ("workaholics" who don't know how to relax or be present with themselves or others outside of work), negative self-talk, and a lack of daily transition rituals between work and home (such as listening to your favorite song or podcast during the commute home or taking five deep breaths before you walk in the door).

5 SABOTAGES

This fifth S is a little different than the previous four. To start, *all sabotages are liabilities*, often ones you've uncovered in one of the first four S areas, but they present an added risk to your transition success. Sabotages can take many forms. They can be internal, such as derailing attitudes or behaviors often rooted in ambivalence or self-doubt. Sabotages can also be external, such as someone vying for your job while you are on leave or an unsupportive partner at home.

Sabotages can be subtle—even unconscious—or obvious. Your job is to identify them and then neutralize them or at least diminish their impact.

Ask yourself which of the liabilities you identified have the potential to knock you off course and derail you from reaching your goals. Write down a list of any sabotages you are aware of, internal and external, and then ask a trusted friend (ideally one at work and one outside of work) if they are aware of any others. Soliciting a friend's perspective can help get at those pesky, unconscious sabotages or even ones you just don't want to face.

Common *external* sabotages I see derail clients' success include having an unsupportive or untrained manager, childcare complications, health and safety concerns at work, conflict with a spouse or partner, and receiving negative or inappropriate comments about parental leave or pregnancy at work that make you fear for your job. Common *internal* sabotages include having poor working parent role models, having had a previous negative experience of leave, mixed feelings about returning to work, and health and wellness struggles. Although sabotages seem scary, recognizing they exist is the first step to figure out how to remove them from your path.

6 SUGGESTIONS

You are not transitioning in a bubble. There are people all around you who are involved in your transition and who are themselves affected by it. This last S is designed to give you a structured way to determine what you need from people in your life and to encourage you to ask them for what you need to make your transition successful. Too often new parents are hesitant to ask for the things they want or need because they are worried they will be categorized as difficult. They think they should be able to handle everything on their own. Don't set yourself up for an impossible load to carry. Give yourself permission to make suggestions to those around you about how they could help or propose a small adjustment that would serve everyone well.

Would it be helpful for your manager to send you a regular update email while you are on leave? Suggest! Does your partner need to share more home responsibilities? Suggest! Does your mom need to stop popping by unannounced? Suggest!

This S is also a reminder for you to stay open to suggestions from others during your transition. It is easy to get overwhelmed when everyone has something to add (often contradictory or annoying), but this is an opportunity to practice sifting through information and distilling it down to the gems that work for you. You will be enhancing this skill throughout parenthood. Think of it as a gift from others to help you begin to work on this life skill now.

Script for Suggesting

"I've been thinking about how to handle [x] (task or issue), when [y] (the child comes, I go back to work). It will be tricky because [reason]. One idea I had was that you could [z]. Would you be willing to do that so that [desirable result]?"

Your Score

Some people like a more quantitative accounting of their assets and liabilities. If that describes you, I'm going to walk you through a rough way to score yourself. (The online Parental Leave Transition Assessment uses a much more precise algorithm to do this for you and has an added risk score calculation. See www.cplleadership.com/playbook.)

To calculate your rough scores, take a moment to look at your responses in each of your first **four** S areas (situations, self, support, and strategies) and give yourself one point for each *asset* you have noted or written down. Add them up to get your *total asset score*.

Next count up all of your *liabilities* in the first **five** S areas (situation, self, support, strategies, and sabotages). That number is your *total liabilities score*.

Does one heavily outweigh the other? Are they nearly the same? If your overall assets outweigh your liabilities, congratulations! You are in a good position for starting your transition. If your liabilities are greater than your assets, focus on improving that ratio. Make sure to notice your pivot points and where you can easily move ones toward becoming an asset. *Remember, the more your assets outweigh your liabilities, the greater your chance of long-term sustainable transition success with fewer bumps in the road.* You now have a clearer idea about what you have working for and against you as you lead your leave so you can focus your attention accordingly.

Take Charge

Once you have taken stock and identified your assets and liabilities, your next step is to take charge by looking for ways to increase your assets while also working to decrease your liabilities. It can be encouraging to start by going down your list and highlighting some easy wins. Are there obvious areas where you can increase your assets? This may mean doing what it takes to transform a pivot point into an asset. For example, if you're unclear on what role you'll assume when you come back to work, you can schedule a meeting with your manager to get clarity and maybe even a firm commitment. You can also try to increase the effectiveness of an asset you have identified; for example, if you already see a great therapist, you could increase the frequency of your sessions for a while. Make what you already have working for you work even harder.

Conversely, are there liabilities that you can easily mitigate, turn into assets, or in other ways decrease their potential for negative impact on your transition? For example, one client noticed a pattern of liabilities that had her putting her health and wellness last, so she called a neighbor and made a plan to walk together three times a week. Another could not make concrete plans because his company had no written policy and he was not totally sure how much leave he was allowed to safely take—even though his manager said he could take what he needed. He reached out to HR and asked that they send him in writing what he was approved for that would not put his job in danger. Don't let any internal resistance to accepting support stop you from taking charge and moving your transition forward in a positive way. Again, ask for what you need.

Once you have taken care of your easy wins and are feeling confident, tackle the harder stuff. To do this deeper work, you may need to schedule a conversation with your manager or HR department, or enlist a mentor or coach to advise you. On the home front, this could look like doing an overhaul of your financial plan to find ways to afford more help, or it could mean you start working with a therapist to overcome mental roadblocks or other personal challenges. Don't shy away from tackling a big issue, it may mean the difference between suffering through parts of your new parenthood and truly enjoying it.

Reflection Questions for your Assessment

* What surprised you most during your 6-S self-assessment?
* What's the one thing (or two) that came up that you least want to address? (Pro tip: This is probably the most important one to get working on.)
* Did you notice any common themes influencing your answers? Pay attention to these as they may be able to point you to your core values. Knowing what your guiding values are and basing your plans on them will help you build the life you want. (I will walk you through an exercise about this in Chapter 13.)
* Are there any other assessments, reviews, or reports that you have done in the past that could help you now (360, MBTI, performance review, etc.)? You are in a process of self-discovery. Previous feedback may open up new insights or highlight things you can include in your efforts now.
* How does what you identified and uncovered fit with the future you want to build (at work and home)? Notice what pieces are in alignment with that future and which ones are not.

Using Your Assessment Results

Your thoughtful use of the 6-S System adds an important tool to your transition toolkit because it deepens your understanding of what you face during this complex time and builds your own self-knowledge. The information you uncover is key to making your own customized action plan for reaching the goals you set at home and work in ways that feel authentic to you.

The usefulness of this assessment goes well beyond your leave planning. It is a self-assessment process that you can quickly walk yourself through anytime you need a little pros-and-cons clarity. Remembering to pull it out and use it when times get tough can go a long way toward making your transition an empowered and meaningful one.

In the next chapter I will show you how you (in collaboration with your manager) can use this information to create a road map—your leave action plan—that plays to your strengths and minimizes potential liabilities.

Revisiting Your 6-S Assessment

You will use your 6-S assessment to help plan your leave, but as circumstances change and as you change, you may find it helpful to complete another 6-S assessment further along in your transition—for example, as you prepare to return to work. It can be a great tool to provide the kind of clarity that will help you revise your plans when needed.

Leadership Lessons of Parenthood

Assessment

Deepening your emotional intelligence (EQ) by better understanding yourself and others is the bedrock of effective *whole-person leadership* and foundational to living a thoughtful, considerate, and happy life. The better you understand your own skills, motivations,

(continued)

and drivers, as well as what you have working for you and against you, the better you can recognize areas that need your attention and use your new insights to find creative solutions.

Here are a few of the *whole-person leadership* skills you will be practicing during this touchpoint:

- Deepening EQ by cultivating self-awareness
- Developing a strategic point of view
- Determining what is important to you
- Understanding your impact on your environment and its impact on you
- Engaging in reflective thinking
- Recognizing what you can draw on (internally and externally)
- Identifying and overcoming potential sabotages or derailers
- Acknowledging paradox exists and navigating complexity

Chapter
Six

Touchpoint 3
Action Plan

THE PATH TO parenthood is inherently unpredictable. Still, a comprehensive and clear—yet flexible—plan is your best asset as you prepare for parental leave. Taking the time to think through your vision for this exciting life transition and then putting it in a format that can be shared with stakeholders will pay off (I promise!), even if you have to abandon your plan A in favor of plan B.

For some lucky folks the structure and process of action planning is exciting and lights them up—they can't get enough. Although I admire them, the very words *action planning* make my eyes glaze over a bit. In my imagination I see spreadsheets and hear a voice droning on about things I'm not interested in paying attention to. When I'm already feeling too busy, you would have to pay me handsomely to add something like this to my overflowing plate—even if an expert promises it will help me.

If you share my ingrained distaste for this sort of thing, here is a secret: action planning does not have to be tedious. It can be empowering and help you develop as a leader and human. This is one of the biggest events of your life and it deserves the time and headspace to reflect and plan it well. This gift of time and presence with your own thoughts is something many of my clients feel is difficult, even impossible, to give themselves. They rationalize that they have so many other more important things going on that they will try to fit it in after dinner or on a subway ride home. Try to see it, instead, as an essential act of integrity and self-care to ensure your wants and needs stay centered in this transition. Everyone will be looking to you for guidance and clarity. If you are able to make the time you need to get grounded, clear, and calm, others will follow your lead. By practicing this thoughtfulness now, you are exercising the muscle that will make it easier to do so in the future. The ability to find time to go inward and connect with yourself, and then move outward to live and share what you have learned with those around you, is one of the many leadership skills that you will develop during this time.

You can also make it fun. You decide the structure and format and you decide the content. Get creative, get comfortable, get your favorite drink and snack, have a friend help out—do whatever it takes to make it something you look forward to (and needless to say, all of the above is encouraged if you *love* planning, too).

Plan Overview

When deciding which action plan format works for you (spreadsheet, word or google doc, Asana project, Trello board, etc.), consider what will be useful to your stakeholders as well. Whatever your chosen format, you'll want a section that covers each of the three phases of your leave transition. If you'd like a free template to use in this chapter, you can download a spreadsheet of the *Next Steps: Action Plan* I use with my clients at www .cplleadership.com/playbook. The template has tabs for each section of the plan covered in the following sections. Be sure to keep your 6-S assessment from Chapter 5 at hand, too. Your awareness of the assets and liabilities you identified there will inform the tangible strategies you will build into your plan.

In this chapter I will guide you through planning the three phases of your leave (Phase 1: preparing for leave, Phase 2: during leave, Phase 3: returning from leave) and cover all of the elements you will want to include in each phase to ensure you create a comprehensive plan—and backup plans—to tackle your parental leave transition with confidence and clarity.

It *almost* goes without saying that having a plan does not mean that everything (or anything) is guaranteed. Indeed, assuming that everything will *not* go according to your original prototype plan, and expecting that iterations will follow, is a built-in part of the creative growth process of design thinking and experiential learning. Each school of thought recognizes that the act of creating a detailed plan will help you think through how to manage contingencies *and* handle them more quickly when they inevitably arise. Having a plan helps relieve stress by getting it all out of your head and into a format you can share and improve with feedback. At work, a plan also helps assure your manager and team that everything will be covered in your absence. Set up regular check-ins with your manager to discuss your plan and solicit input, support, and approval. At home, a plan ensures that you and your supports, friends, family, partner, or spouse are clear about division of roles and responsibilities and that they have the information necessary to jump in and take over if you need them to do so.

Regardless of how much leave you are planning to take, the arrival of your new child will mean unexpected events. Expecting that your plans are likely to change will help you adjust and be flexible if they do. This appreciation for unpredictability is beautifully illustrated in the Japanese practice of *wabi-sabi*, where accepting asymmetry and deliberately incorporating imperfections is a nod to the ingenious integrity of the natural world. We also see it in Navajo culture, when rug weavers incorporate small imperfections around the border called *ch'ihónít'i* or a "spirit pathway." They believe that the weaver's spirit and the rug come together during creation and this pathway gives their spirit a way to exit the rug to move forward. In much the same way, you will put yourself into the weaving of your leave plan (and your birth plan, if that applies to you). Thinking of it as only one part of your larger work—and giving yourself an exit pathway (even if only in your mind) to move on to a new plan when it's time—is empowering.

It is worth saying again: I recommend you read this entire book *before* making your three-phase plan. Later parts of the book will help

PHASE 1
PREPARING
FOR LEAVE

- Off-boarding plan
- Contingency plans
- Keep in Touch (KIT) strategy
- Leave logistics

PHASE 2
DURING
LEAVE

- Parenthood plan
- Contingency plans
- Birth plan (if applicable)

PHASE 3
RETURNING
FROM LEAVE

- Onboarding plan
- Contingency plans
- Return logistics

guide your thinking and planning. Then, as you move through your actual leave and return, certain aspects of your plan will need to be revised and certain sections of the book reread when life throws you the inevitable curveball or two.

Ideally, you will create your entire plan before going on leave. If it is too late for that, you will find this process and format useful at any point in your transition.

The Benefits of a Thoughtful Three-Phase Parental Leave Action Plan

- **Relief.** I've heard many expectant parents describe a weight lifting off their shoulders when they got their thoughts out of their head onto (often virtual) paper.
- **Alignment.** By being explicit about needs and wants, you and your team (at home and work) are able to get on the same page to ensure that the processes are uninterrupted and clear.
- **Communication.** By planning together, you will improve communication and avoid assumptions and expectations, which are the source of most problems I have seen arise for new parents. With a clear strategy for communication, which

has built-in opportunities to be adjusted along the way, your supports can be clear on how to pick up where you leave off.

- **Empowerment.** By making your needs clear, you will be more empowered to set healthy boundaries going forward.
- **Agility in the face of work life challenges.** Do not underestimate the number of unexpected scheduling changes that may come up for you as a new parent. A plan that includes contingencies you have thought through will help you easily and efficiently put those into place as needed.
- **Work-life integration.** Planning helps you find opportunities for work and life to complement and enrich each other as opposed to feeling in conflict. It will provide a neutral document you can systematically go over with all stakeholders to confirm you are on the same page.

Plan Elements

Phase 1: Preparing for Leave

In this work-focused section, capture the specifics of how you will hand over your duties as you leave work to welcome your new child. You will also create a section that details any leave logistics you need to specify as well as how you want to stay connected with work while on leave (if at all)—we call this your Keep in Touch (or KIT) strategy. This section is meant to be shared with your manager and any stakeholders such as teammates, HR, or key clients. *Use Phases 1 and 3 of your plan as an explicit intention agreement among you, your manager, your team, and HR. This will give you all a clear document to refer to and revisit as needed throughout the three phases of your leave.*

Phase 2: During Leave

This new-parenthood-focused section is designed to be confidential from work. Here you can turn your attention toward the more personal elements of your transition to ensure you have everything in place at home to welcome your new child. For birthing parents, this is also where you will consider any birth plans you want to make, baby showers or other celebrations, what you would like your immediate and longer-term "fourth trimester" bonding with your new child to look like, and in general how you will get the support you want and need from friends, family, and your health and wellness providers (obstetrician, midwife, doula, lactation specialist, etc.). If you choose, it can be helpful to share this part of your plan with your personal support team (friends, partner or spouse, family, etc.) to ensure everyone is on the same page.

Phase 3: Returning from Leave

This working parent–focused section of your plan is a chance to consider *months ahead of time* when and how you would like to return from leave, including how your work will be handed back to you. In this section you will also outline your career goals as they are now, before becoming a parent to this child, and think through steps you can take to ensure those goals are met. Like your plan for Phase 1, this part of your plan is meant to be shared with your manager and work team.

*****

Your action plan is a key aspect of leading your leave. In most organizations it will be up to you to drive the development of your plan while communicating and collaborating with those involved. You might work with your manager on this plan from the beginning, or they may expect you to first come to them with a completed draft plan that they can respond to—every situation is different. Take as much initiative as you can and use this as a chance to strengthen communication and trust with your team.

Don't hesitate to ask for what you need and to ask others what they may need from you. By asking, you avoid assumptions and unpleasant surprises. To the working parent, delegation and communication skills become more critical than ever, and expecting the unexpected is empowering and a form of kindness to your future self. Use this planning time to anticipate how you would like to communicate about changes as they come up.

Keep in mind that although this chapter is intended to cover the elements you need to think about, *there is no formula, and your plan will be unique*. You may find there are pieces here that don't apply to you, or you might feel like something is missing. Strive to craft an action plan that suits your circumstances, not just how you *hope* it will go (be mindful, though, to build elements into your plan that help you reach your hopes and dreams).

The planning you do today will enable you and your manager to outline how work will be handed off, whether in advance of an anticipated long absence or for a shorter time. If you are like every person I have worked with, you will likely also have some unexpected child-related obligations that take you out of the office at some point after your return. Your best move is to set up how you would like to hand off your work and to whom. Work with your manager to decide who your stakeholders are and how to share your plans with them well in advance of when you think you will need to, and then keep that information updated. Your plan will also help you think through what you need at home and how to communicate with your "stakeholders" there.

In this chapter I will walk you through the plan one phase at a time. Later in the book, when we get to the touchpoints that help with your return planning, I will ask you to revisit this original return section of your plan to update it with your new parent circumstances, needs, and wants. Just prior to your return, share that updated version with your manager and schedule a conversation about any changes you are requesting.

Importance of Contingency Planning

Remember what I said about expecting the unexpected? Becoming a parent is inherently unpredictable and even the best planning often has to rely on contingencies. Using a backup plan does not mean you have failed *in any way*. I doubt I have worked with any new parent whose plan went exactly as they thought it would. Often it is in those unpredictable moments that some of the greatest joy and self-development come. Make space to welcome them, even as you try to anticipate them.

Dozens of factors may affect your transition at any moment: the timing of your child's arrival, the mental and physical health of your child or partner if you have one, role changes of others at work, a company acquisition or restructuring, and later on, childcare—to name just a few. Creating contingency plans will let you be more involved as a parent without sacrificing work. Even if you are not taking an extended leave, creating contingency plans will show your manager and team that you are proactive, which is a benefit in itself.

It will be helpful to think of this in two directions:

1. What will you do if something does not go according to your ideal plan *at home*?
2. What will you do if something does not go according to your ideal plan *at work*?

How would you manage the other domain if this were to happen? In each section of the plan, I will give you some *what ifs* to consider. Let's get started.

Phase 1 Planning: Preparing for Leave

This first phase of your leave plan helps you turn your thoughts about how to hand off work and communicate with colleagues into something tangible that you will share with your manager and team as appropriate.

The first phase of your plan should include these components:

- *Off-boarding plans:* a detailed list of your responsibilities and necessary details to hand off to your cover team (I'll teach you a process I use called the TASCARS method)
- *Contingency plans*
- A *Keep in Touch or KIT strategy*
- *Leave logistics:* the little things such as security cards, passwords, remote access, time sheets, paid leave paperwork, and so on that must be dealt with

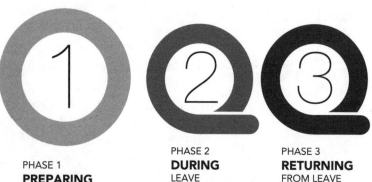

PHASE 1
PREPARING
FOR LEAVE
- Off-boarding plan
- Contingency plans
- Keep in Touch (KIT) strategy
- Leave logistics

PHASE 2
DURING
LEAVE
- Parenthood plan
- Contingency plans
- Birth plan (if applicable)

PHASE 3
RETURNING
FROM LEAVE
- Onboarding plan
- Contingency plans
- Return logistics

Don't Forget to Incorporate Your 6-S Self-Assessment

Before you begin your plan, consider what you learned from the 6-S self-assessment you completed in Chapter 5. Remind yourself of the assets you want to grow and any liabilities you want to minimize, then build that into your plan.

For example, if one of your liabilities is a lack of strong support at work, you may want to choose some people to casually connect with before you go on leave (over coffee or lunch) or include them among the people you would like to share pictures and updates with while you are on leave. It is much easier for someone to have your back when they are emotionally invested in you. You may also realize that you need to expand your support network to include support from new people. Is there anyone in your organization who has recently been through their own parental leave experience and could be a mentor? Noticing where you have a support deficit and actively building in ways to turn that around is an example of mitigating a 6-S liability.

Work Handoff: Using the TASCARS Method

Your cover team will thank you if you're able to hand off your work in a detailed and organized manner. In my coaching method I use TAS-CARS, a process developed while piloting RETAIN in Australia, to create a list of duties suitable for sharing with a temporary replacement. Following this TASCARS process helps you ensure that the handoff of your work happens efficiently and on your terms before you go on leave. (This method is included in the free action planning template resource at www.cplleadership.com/playbook.)

TASCARS is an acronym (Tasks, Accountability, Stakeholders, Conversations and Actions, Resources, Status) that helps you walk through the steps necessary to ensure a thorough handoff of your work as shown in the figure.

For example, let's say one part of your job is to put together your team's update for your company's quarterly report. TASCARS prompts you to break down that job into each of its sub-elements and put them into the **task** column. Now let's say you and your manager have agreed that your teammate Alex is the person who will learn the most about and be most responsible for taking over this task. You will put Alex's name

TASCARS: Preparing for Leave

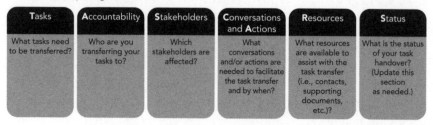

Tasks	Accountability	Stakeholders	Conversations and Actions	Resources	Status
What tasks need to be transferred?	Who are you transferring your tasks to?	Which stakeholders are affected?	What conversations and/or actions are needed to facilitate the task transfer and by when?	What resources are available to assist with the task transfer (i.e., contacts, supporting documents, etc.)?	What is the status of your task handover? (Update this section as needed.)

and contact info in the **accountability** column. Alert stakeholders that Alex will be taking over while you are away (and Alex will need to know whom to get updates from and who should get the final write-up). List all of these names in the **stakeholders** column and next to each name use the **conversations and actions** column to describe what needs to happen to ensure all goes smoothly. Alex will want to see write-ups from previous years to know what is expected. You can put a link to those in the **resources** column. The final column, **status**, is where you can make notes about where you are in the process as you get closer to your leave handoff and track what you have left to do. This ensures that if you need to leave unexpectedly, Alex will know what needs to be done.

Keep the following questions in mind and build them into your plan: how would you like to take back your work when you return? How can this be an opportunity for others to grow, too? What does your team need? Be as clear as you can about your return plans before you go on leave so colleagues can know what is expected of them and when that expectation ends. Be sure to build in extra time to account for a common problem researchers call the *planning fallacy*—a phenomenon in which people underestimate the time it takes to accomplish their own tasks (but not those of others).[1]

General Considerations for Work Handoff

Take a moment to reflect on the following questions, which will guide this section of your plan.

- How can you set up your off-boarding in ways that best support reentry after your leave? (For example, if you know that your colleague Tim would benefit from a few months of doing a certain part of your job, and you hope he can support you with that piece on your return, make sure that task goes to him.)

- As some of your long-term duties are temporarily transferred, can you take part in projects that have short-term deliverables before you leave or on your return as you ease back in?
- In considering the resources required, is access to any archival data or secure information required? Are there any passwords or confidential data that should be delivered with extra care to your cover team?
- Is lead time required for any training that is necessary to ensure a task is adequately covered (in line with its level of complexity and reporting requirements)? Have you built that in?
- Do you have any additional work roles beyond your key tasks that need to be considered (such as social clubs, committees, first aid or safety warden, etc.)? If so, who would you like to cover you there? Is there anything you would like them to keep you updated on?
- If applicable, what are the best ways to inform clients/customers of your leave and leave coverage arrangements? (Different approaches may be needed for different clients.)
- Are there any other stakeholders to be notified of your leave in addition to those already included? Think broadly. If so, who are they and how will this be done? It can be helpful to look back over the last year in your calendar to see if any cyclical events need to be considered.
- How will you build in appreciation with your task transfers? Whoever you are asking to support you is going out of their way to do so. Find ways to show your gratitude and deepen your relationship with them.
- If applicable, have you filed the appropriate paperwork requesting to get paid leave and double-checked it is logged in the system? If you are unsure, how and when can you confirm that this has been done? If you live in a state with a paid leave insurance program, you may have to do different paperwork for your company and your state.
- Can your leave be a development opportunity for members of your team? If so, who and in what ways? How can you foster that development mentality and support your team as they grow through your leave?

- How can you use your leave plans to deepen your relationships at work and at home?
- Have you explored if your workplace has any internal resources that may be available to support your full leave and return transitions? If so, how can you harness these supports? If not, how can you find out more?
- What will it take for you to fully switch off from work to be truly present for one of life's most meaningful experiences? Is there anything that's usually one of your responsibilities and isn't already addressed? What do you need to do to ensure it is taken care of and crossed off your mental list?

Contingency Considerations for Work Handoff

What will you do if the following situations occur?

- Decisions are delayed regarding how and who will take over your current roles and/or responsibilities. Often this decision is made by someone higher up in the organization. If this is the case for you, you may need to be a squeaky wheel to ensure decisions happen in a timely way.
- Challenges arise due to insufficient time and/or high demands. Be proactive so you don't find yourself in a situation without enough time to transfer over your tasks and knowledge before you go on leave.
- An organizational change, such as a new manager or restructure, occurs while you are away. Do you want to hear about it, or will that cause unnecessary worrying at a time when there is nothing you can do about it? Maybe you would like to know one week before your return so it is not a shock. Put all that in the Keep in Touch section of your plan.
- You have difficulty engaging your manager and/or team in your transition plan, or they only become motivated at the last minute. (One client, due with her second child, was particularly stressed when this was happening to her because her first child had come three weeks early. When she mentioned this fact to her manager it worked wonders to speed things up!)
- You have to begin parental leave earlier than planned (due to pregnancy sickness, complications, or the early arrival of your child).

- You realize that some parties may have unrealistic expectations of what is possible or required before leave, and may not be as supportive as would be ideal.
- There isn't anyone to hand your work off to. If it is going to be put on hold until you return, what must be taken care of in case you are out longer than planned?

One of the skills you will get to practice during this time is the ability to let things go. As this list highlights, much of this is beyond your control. Your goal here is to think through how you want to respond if you come up against any of these common challenges to your ideal plan. After you have put your best contingency planning in place there will come a point where you will have to let go and let your answer be, "I will let my manager or team handle that one for me."

Your Keep in Touch (KIT) Strategy

The next key element of this phase of your plan is your KIT strategy. This is another concept I learned while piloting RETAIN Coaching in Australia, where the country's parental leave policy has up to 10 paid "keeping in touch" days to use while you are on leave. Australia offers up to 18 weeks of paid leave for the primary caregiver, which is a longer leave time than all state programs and most company benefits in the United States. They also have up to a year of job protection, which means leave can be longer than 18 weeks for many. Australia has built these paid check-in days into the extended leave so that employees don't drift so far from work that they feel unprepared or unconfident to return. As part of their leave planning, expectant parents consider how they would like to use their KIT days. In the United States, the law states that FMLA-protected employees cannot work while on leave and that employers are breaking the law if they ask them to. Because of this, US systems for leave are missing this valuable connection tool. For our purposes here, use this section of your plan to consider and detail how you would like to stay in touch (if at all) with work while you are away.

As you are planning, remember, during your leave you will be doing the important work of becoming a parent to this child or, if you are welcoming multiples, children! *This is a really big job.* You will have your hands full and may not want or need to be disturbed—or you may want or need more contact. Your KIT strategy is where you outline your work and home boundaries, as well as any expectations you have about staying in contact during your transition. This is an individual decision and could range from no contact to regular contact; the choice is yours. Your KIT strategy will be unique to you and should include all necessary details for your colleagues to understand your contact parameters.

- **Who.** Who may reach out from work? (You may want to assign one contact person.)
- **What.** If you are out on extended leave, do you want to receive any regular team updates? Or do you only want to be contacted if there is a real emergency (death, reorganization, etc.)? Maybe not even then? It's up to you. Put yourself in your colleagues' shoes. If you know they would enjoy pictures and updates as you learn your new parent role—send them. Consider including them in your social media circle. This is an opportunity for you to rewrite relationships and start them from a new place when you go back.
- **When.** How often you do plan to check your chosen communication channels, so they know when to expect to hear back from you (and what to do if they don't in that amount of time)?
- **How.** What email address and phone number should they use to reach you while you're away and for what purposes? Will you be on social media, communications apps, email, company intranet, or other?

Your KIT strategy is so important, it has its own touchpoint. For more details on how to customize the KIT strategy elements that are right for you and how best to implement them, read Chapter 9.

Leave Logistics Considerations

Take time to think through the logistical considerations that need to be included in the first phase of your leave plan and outline them. Following are some examples.

- **Ramping down.** Have you considered a ramping down strategy that includes a build-down of days, hours, or task responsibility?
- **Out-of-office notifications.** Have you set up your out-of-office email reply and extended leave voice message? Do your messages reflect how you want to position your parental leave experience? Do they set you up well? (See www.cplleadership.com/playbook for a collection of auto response examples or to add yours to the collection!)
- **Organizational documentation requirements.** Is there any organizational documentation that you need to have completed and/or signed off before leave (payroll forms, HR paperwork, insurance forms, etc.)?
- **Property, equipment, vehicle, and so on.** Do you need to coordinate holding onto any property or equipment while you are away, such as your laptop, cell phone, or work vehicle? Is there anything you need to be sure to hand over before you leave?
- **IT system/building access.** Have you spoken to the necessary departments regarding your access needs while on leave (IT, security, etc.)?
- **Performance review finalization.** Have you completed a performance review prior to leave? Do you need to?
- **Professional development, certifications, and registration plans.** Do you have any continuing professional development activities or certification renewals that should happen or be officially deferred while you are on leave? If applicable, do you wish to maintain your registration(s) and/or can you take a leave of absence?
- **Baby shower** or other acknowledgment of your transition to leave. Have you considered what you would like for your leave launch celebration? Has this been communicated to your manager/team?
- **Birth/arrival announcement arrangements.** Have you finalized your announcement list? Have you given your list to the person who will be sending out the announcement of your child's arrival

on your behalf? Have you considered how you would like to notify your work team that your new child has arrived? Have you included this key contact person on your announcement list?

- **Other.** Are there any other leave logistics that you need to consider in order to comfortably disengage from your paid work while on leave?

Phase 2 Planning: During Leave

In the second phase of your leave plan, you will shift your attention from work to the planning needed at home. Whether you want to share this part of your planning with anyone else is up to you. We will focus on what you need personally, what supports you need at home, and about what kind of parent you want to be. Once you've identified your parenting values (see the exercise in Chapter 13), you can integrate them into your plan. If you are a birthing parent, I recommend you include a birth plan in your Phase 2 plans. Birth planning is not my area of expertise; however, in this section you will see a sidebar about birth planning to get you started. (To learn more about using your birth plan as a tool for self-advocacy, see Chapter 10.)

PHASE 1
PREPARING
FOR LEAVE

- Off-boarding plan
- Contingency plans
- Keep in Touch (KIT) strategy
- Leave logistics

PHASE 2
DURING
LEAVE

- Parenthood plan
- Contingency plans
- Birth plan (if applicable)

PHASE 3
RETURNING
FROM LEAVE

- Onboarding plan
- Contingency plans
- Return logistics

Being on leave offers you a window of time to really get to know what parenting your new child means and to practice those skills before integrating them with your work role. In this section you will write down what you'd like that to look like, keeping in mind that it is likely to change when you meet your child and adjust to what *they* need!

This second phase of your plan will include these aspects:

- *Parenthood plan:* the type of help you'd like and how you will get it while you prepare for, welcome, and bond with your new child
- *Contingency plans*
- *Birth plan* (if applicable)

Help and Support

As you prepare for parenthood, it is natural to have countless thoughts running through your head. Remember, this is the disorienting middle zone of your transition—before you hit your stride in your new normal. Planning will help you feel calmer and better prepared.

One of the key pieces of advice I offer on behalf of all the parents who came before you is to *ask for help!* For most people, asking for what they need is an underdeveloped muscle. This common deficit affects moms *and* dads and has significant repercussions, especially concerning parental leave. This is such an important skill to develop and build into your parental leave transition plans that it, too, has a whole touchpoint devoted to it: Chapter 10 is all about advocating for yourself and your child.

To repeat, our culture doesn't do this very well. Other cultures have customs that support new parents during and after the arrival of a child (see sidebar examples in Chapter 5), promoting better experiences of parental leave and early parenthood.

If you live in the United States, it is largely going to be up to you to ask for help. Even though it may be uncomfortable, *asking for the support you need during this crucial period can make or break your experience.* Research shows that perinatal social support is related to lower rates of postpartum depression,[2] greater mother-infant bonding,[3] higher parenting self-efficacy[4] and parenting satisfaction,[5] and an increased sense of self-worth.[6]

Mapping where you can get support ahead of time can make the act of asking for help much easier, should you actually need it. In this section of your plan, you will consider and document all of the various types of support you might want or need—the *who, what, when, where,* and *how* of support.

The structure shown in the figure will help you build out your list of the supports you can reach out to while on leave. List each person in your support network, including the type of support they best offer, when that support might be available, and how to reach them. Keep this list handy; share it with your partner, spouse, or friend in case they need to reach out on your behalf; and refer to it often. It is easy to forget how much support is on hand amid so much change. This is the type of self-care that matters, and it should be built into your plan.

SUPPORT

WHO?	WHAT?	WHEN?	WHERE?	HOW?
Support source	Description of support and need	Times when support is available to help	Contact information for support	Specific ways support will help

General Considerations for During Leave

As you fill out your list of supports, consider the following:

- Whose support do you value? Is there someone who has offered support, but you've never taken them up on it? Brainstorm everyone you can think of, making specific notes on how each person or organization can help.
- Are you aware of all the supports available to you through your work organization and external sources such as a religious, school, or neighborhood community? If not, do the research now to find those resources and sign up for any newsletters that will remind you they are there.
- Given all the demands of parenthood, how can you ensure you create time for yourself, time with your new child and any additional children, and/or time with your partner or spouse, if applicable? In

your Chapter 5 assessments you thought about the family culture you want to cultivate moving forward. Be sure to incorporate those reflections into your plan here. Cut yourself slack at every turn and prioritize in ways that will meet urgent needs and get you to your long-term goals.

- Your friendships matter, too, and not just for the logistical support they might offer. To be sure you don't lose touch with friends, build time in for them, too. Parenthood can be isolating. Your support network is an important form of community, and the more community you can build for yourself in these early years the more rewarding and enjoyable they will be.
- Many people start leave before their child arrives. Have you thought about your first days home, when the phone stops ringing, the calendar is clear, and your child has not yet arrived? Keeping plans flexible, what might you like to do during this period?

Contingency Considerations for During Leave

What will you do if you are in one of the following situations?

- You have another major transition happening at the same time, such as a plan to move. Do you need to consider setting up networks and supports in a new location (for example, which parent groups will you join, what childcare center or pediatrician will you choose)?
- Your child arrives early, and you were relying on the support of your parents or someone else coming to visit at a set date. Who can fill in until they are able to arrive?
- You have an older child who needs care while you are welcoming your new child. Who is your backup for that person in case something prevents them from being able to help at the last moment?
- Your spouse or partner (if applicable) returns to work and/or your extended family returns home earlier than what you are ready for.
- You need additional support but are unable to ask for it. Choose whom you would like as your first-line support team, then as your second string. Do they know about each other and how to contact each other, should they need to?

When it comes to asking for support, start with the small things. It's OK to feel conflicted about doing anything more than that at first. Keep it simple. To practice self-care I recommend my clients put SMART goals in place: *specific, measurable, achievable, realistic,* and *time sensitive.*[7] For example: *I'm going on a hike on Sunday at 10 in the morning with James. I'm going to get a babysitter on Tuesday from 2:00 to 4:00 p.m. so I can go to the gym.*

Remember, *there are no right answers.* Make the best choice you can in your circumstances. You can change your mind and your plan later if you need to. Parenthood is a constant process of managing change. If you were looking for places to practice and improve your change management skills, you are in luck!

Plan to Sleep

Sleep deprivation is literally a torture tool. Initially, many of my clients with new babies think they'll be fine and don't bother to nap or go to bed early. When the baby sleeps, they are often desperate to have some time alone to finally catch up on chores, social media, or zone out watching a mindless show. Unfortunately, this is a seduction that will only cause you pain and make this time more difficult. *Sleep will restore you.* Don't ignore it. In fact, find ways to create more opportunities for sleep.

This could look like setting a SMART goal for yourself such as this: *on Saturday from 11:00 to 2:00 p.m., I will have my mother-in-law come take the baby for a walk and feed her lunch while I take a shower, eat in peace, and take a nap.* It might mean getting a white noise machine or app and ear plugs to prevent environmental noise from waking you up. You will want to decide where the baby can sleep that allows you to sleep, too, confident the baby is safe. This can be a difficult element to sort out, and you should do whatever works for your family. I have seen *every* possible scenario, from everyone in different rooms, or even different floors of the house, to everyone in the same bed. There is no wrong way as long as it allows you to sleep as much as you possibly can. Period.

Take a pragmatic and creative approach to making sure your own needs are met during your leave. Even if solutions end up looking nothing like what you carefully organized before your child's arrival, it is good training for the kind of adaptive self-care you will need to prioritize in Phase 3 of your plan when you return to work.

Birth Plan Tips

A birth plan outlines the choices you make, in advance, for the arrival of your child. It serves as a playbook for your birth attendants to support you on your terms during your labor and delivery. Making a birth plan can help a birthing parent feel empowered and informed. Research shows that such plans can reduce the number of medical interventions administered, such as oxytocin/ Pitocin or an epidural. However, they do not appear to reduce the frequency of cesarean births, and the research shows that moms with a birth plan *can* be less satisfied with their birth experience than those without.[8] It is not uncommon for mothers with a strict birth plan to be stereotyped as type A or controlling and treated with bias or disregard by their medical providers.

Even so, I encourage you to embrace birth planning, but with the knowledge that as with the rest of your leave planning, the thinking through and educating yourself is its own reward. The benefits you gain may have nothing to do with following your original plan to the letter.

Here are some tips to help you make a birth plan that works for you.

- **Come from a place of partnership.** The fastest way to alienate your birth attendants is to be condescending, rude, or demanding. Remember, they have spent their lives learning how to do the work they do *because they want to help.* You may find that you need to advocate for yourself, but that happens best when you can show mutual appreciation and respect. (Learn more about how your birth plan can be a tool for self-advocacy in Chapter 10.)
- **Keep it simple.** With a straightforward, to-the-point birth plan, health care providers are more likely to understand your preferences and take them seriously. *If all your birth plan says is that you expect to be the decision-maker in your care and then you build trust with your medical team so you work well together, you will be in good shape.* A plan that is too fussily detailed is unrealistic and can send a message that you might be hard to

(continued)

(*continued*)

work with. This type of assumption can start your relationship with your birth support off on the wrong foot.

- **Make it visual.** A clear and visual birth plan will make it easier for everyone to follow. This is a win-win for all involved, especially for you, because it will help you feel more comfortable in their caring hands. (It doesn't have to be fancy. Use pen and paper, or get a free visual birth plan template here: https://www.mamanatural.com/birth-plan-template/.)
- **Stay flexible.** Birth is innately unpredictable and requires you to be open when extenuating circumstances mean a course change or safety needs to take priority.
- **Share early and often.** You will have spent hours thinking through all the details of your plan, but to your team it may be one of many they see each day. Do not expect them to remember every detail. A friendly gentle reminder at each visit can help them know what is important to you.

Note: If you are Black, Indigenous, Asian, Latinx, or a person of color and also a birthing mother, you will want to review the resources in Chapter 16 to inform your birth planning and to gain additional support.

Phase 3 Planning: Returning to Work

Though you may not anticipate your return to work with the same excitement as when preparing for parenthood (though many do!), it is worth your while to take equal time and care in drafting the third phase of your action plan: how you would like to off-board from your leave and your full-time parenthood role to enter your new dual role of working parent (or working parent of additional children).

One purpose of this section of your plan is to get you thinking about what you'd like your reentry to work to look like even before you go out on parental leave. Doing this means visualizing the future you are working toward and putting the practical parts of that plan in place so that it will actually happen. Without this, it is much easier to doubt yourself and sabotage your own return. Plus, in the absence of details

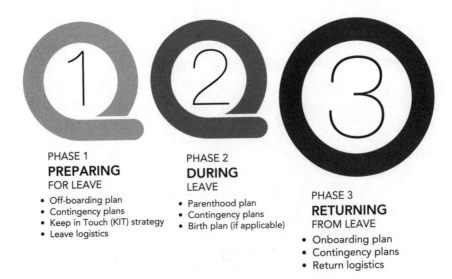

PHASE 1
PREPARING
FOR LEAVE
- Off-boarding plan
- Contingency plans
- Keep in Touch (KIT) strategy
- Leave logistics

PHASE 2
DURING
LEAVE
- Parenthood plan
- Contingency plans
- Birth plan (if applicable)

PHASE 3
RETURNING
FROM LEAVE
- Onboarding plan
- Contingency plans
- Return logistics

about what you want when you return, your manager and team might make assumptions that may or may not be in line with your wishes, such as ruling you out for a big project or an assignment that would include travel when you'd prefer to be involved.

This section of your plan will also serve a very practical function as your ideal proposed return to work plan. Similar to your Phase 1 plan, you will want to share this with your manager and team. Later, in Chapter 11, the touchpoint about return arrangements, I'll go into detail about what to do to revisit this ideal plan when you are about to return to work. Many people find that they need to make adjustments to their ideal return plan once their child has arrived.

Phase 3 of your plan is designed to help you think through ways to integrate your new (or expanded) role as a parent with your previous work role to create a cohesive working parent role that feels authentic to your priorities, manageable in the day-to-day, and sustainable over the long term. Use this planning to consciously think about how you would like to build your skills and integrate your work and home roles.

The third phase of your plan should include these elements:

- *Onboarding plan:* how you'll pick your work back up from your cover team and how you'll get help and support as you head back to work

- *Contingency plans:* back up plans for the unexpected.
- *Return logistics:* the little details that will ease your return (I'll cover this in Chapter 11)

Supports for Returning to Work

In this section of your plan, you'll detail all the supports you think you will need to move back into work smoothly after your leave. Start by taking a moment to review your list of parenthood supports you created in Phase 1 of your plan. Is there anyone you need to add to that list as you think about your return needs? If so, add those contacts into the supports section of your return plan. Identify whom you would like to designate to act on your behalf if you are unable to for whatever reason (we'll touch on this more in the chapter/touchpoint on advocating for yourself). Be sure to share your plan with anyone you've included.

Thinking through your support system now will save you a lot of stress in the future, when you will have few resources to devote to researching and thinking about who you would like in your corner. Talk to people who you know have a similar situation to you but are further along. Ask them what worked for them and what supports they were glad they had or wish they had put in place. Then ask yourself what you want for your own support system. Do you need someone to help with childcare pickup? Someone to clean your house? Someone to bring meals for the first few weeks, or a meal preparation subscription kit? Can you start getting your groceries delivered to help free up some time? Or put bills on autopay? What other supports have you seen others use or can you imagine you might need? Remember, you can download a spreadsheet template of our *Next Steps: Action Plan* (which includes this section) for free at http://www.cplleadership. com/playbook.

SUPPORT

WHO?	WHAT?	WHEN?	WHERE?	HOW?
Support source	Description of support and need	Times when support is available to help	Contact information for support	Specific ways support will help

Use this same *who, what, when, where, how* structure to revisit the support list you made in Phase 1 and build it out considering any new support help you need as you transition back to work and for the next three to six months. Be sure to share it with anyone who might need the information and to post it somewhere easily accessible. One client put her whole plan in a binder on her dining room table so she could leaf through it and remind herself she had people to reach out to when she felt like she was in solitary confinement on the days she was home alone with her toddler and her sweet, needy newborn.

Planning to Pick Up Where You Left Off at Work

Once you've planned what supports you need and outlined their roles in your plan, you can begin to imagine what heading back to work could look like. This next section of your return plan is where you will outline your explicit plans for *how tasks will be handed back to you.*

It will be helpful to start by looking at the plan you made to off-board your tasks when you were preparing for leave (where you used the TASCARS method) and consider all of the tasks and roles you included there as shown in the figure.

Your onboarding process is not necessarily the inverse of your off-boarding plan, because you might have additions or deletions, but that plan can inform your return preparations in useful ways.

TASCARS: Returning from Leave

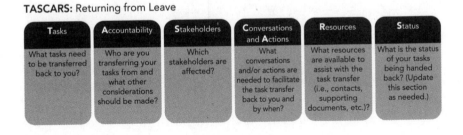

Tasks	**A**ccountability	**S**takeholders	**C**onversations and **A**ctions	**R**esources	**S**tatus
What tasks need to be transferred back to you?	Who are you transferring your tasks from and what other considerations should be made?	Which stakeholders are affected?	What conversations and/or actions are needed to facilitate the task transfer back to you and by when?	What resources are available to assist with the task transfer (i.e., contacts, supporting documents, etc.)?	What is the status of your tasks being handed back? (Update this section as needed.)

General Considerations for Return-to-Work Planning

- Have you had a chance to familiarize yourself with any internal workplace resources that may be available to support your return? If yes, how can you harness these; if not, how can you find out more? For example, some companies have working parent support groups or new parent resources through HR, an employee assistance program, or insurance plan.

- Is there a certain return date you have to abide by? If not, what date would you like to return to work? Can you schedule your start date toward the end of the work week to ease back in?
- Does your employer offer flexible work arrangements? If so, in what ways (for example, staggered days, longer condensed days, or remote work)? Is there more you would like to learn or understand? Would you like a nontraditional schedule on your return?
- Have you considered a ramping-up strategy that includes a buildup of days on your return (that is, starting back to work two days a week and building up to full time over a few weeks or months)?
- What logistical arrangements should you consider now to ease your return, such as keeping your laptop, phone, or other IT working while you are away?
- Will you be returning to your current role? If your role will be a new one, what can you learn now that will set you up for success? Does that new role involve a new manager and team as well? Are there people you should meet before you go on leave, so you are not returning to complete strangers?
- What do you need your manager/team/colleagues to do or know to prepare for your return to work? This includes the role and task details you described before handoff using the TASCARS tool as well as anything else that may apply to your return but was not necessary to include in your leave planning.
- How would you like your first few days back to be organized to ensure that you have an effective reentry into the workplace? For example, would you like a lot of meetings to reconnect or would you prefer more solitude to catch up on your in-box and reorient to current events?
- Would you like someone to give you an orientation to catch you up on what has happened and changed while you were away? Is there someone who can serve as a return mentor? What is the best way to ask for that support ahead of time so that person can pay attention to things that happen while you are away in order to update you on your return?
- Is there anything you need to coordinate with clients, vendors, or other external stakeholders about your return, such as scheduling recurring meetings?

- Will you be required to travel for work on your return? Consider talking to your manager about easing back into travel or postponing for a couple of months while you get your sea legs under you.
- Have you thought about how you can best use technology to help support your transition back (for example, using calendar or app alerts to send specific messages to your manager or team as your return date gets closer or reminders to yourself of things to put in place on certain days)?
- What support would you like from your manager in the early days of your return? Can you preschedule meetings with your manager to make your first few weeks back go more smoothly as you work to get updates, gain feedback, problem-solve, and monitor how you are doing? (For example, a weekly update with your manager in the first month may be useful for reporting on what is working well and to raise any issues of concern.) Put those on your calendars now, knowing you can always adjust later.
- If breastfeeding or expressing breastmilk at work is part of your plan, are you familiar with available facilities and procedures before going on leave? If not, how can you find out what they are? Some lactation rooms run on a tight schedule, and other situations are more flexible.
- What would be the worst thing(s) you could possibly imagine happening on your return? Is there anything proactive you can do now to prevent or make it less likely?
- Is there any additional planning you need to do now in order to be comfortable onboarding when you return to work?
- Is there anything that was part of your off-boarding plan that you want to be sure does *not* come back to you on your return? On the flip side, are there new things that you want to be sure do get handed to you? Be sure to indicate that in your ideal return plan.

Return Logistics

Look back over the logistics you put in place or on hold as part of your Phase 1 plan. Take a moment and think through which of those logistics need to get reinstated for your return to go smoothly. Common hiccups include not getting security access into the building or access back into your company's computer system reinstated in time.

For some there may be time sheets that need to be created or insurance paperwork that needs to be submitted or adjusted. Whatever yours are, be sure to include them in the return section of your plan.

Contingency Plans for Your Return

As with all sections of your plan, think through and include any contingency plans you can imagine using if your original plan is not what you need when the time arrives. As you get closer to your actual return to work, you can revisit and adjust your return plans. If you've created a contingency plan in advance, it will be simple to put parts of that in place as needed. I will discuss how to revisit your return plan and implement contingencies in Chapter 11.

Final Thoughts on Planning

I recognize this is a *lot* to take in! The most common feeling at this point is one of being overwhelmed. This is a moment where I often see resistance pop up and expectant parents start telling themselves that this is all just a bit too much and they would be better served by simply rolling with whatever comes their way. I understand. I am a *big* fan of flexibility; it is one of the main skills needed for parenthood and I encourage you to keep practicing until you master it.

However, when it comes to your leave plans, I suggest you pause right now and block out an hour or two on your calendar to walk through what we have covered here and document your plans step by step. When you have a finished draft of your action plan, you will be able to meet with your manager, go over it to get feedback, make any needed changes, and ultimately get their final approval. Once you have an approved plan, work with those involved to stick to it, but be aware that life doesn't always go the way you think it will. Contingency planning is important, and revisions may be necessary to ensure your plan stays relevant and useful for all. In fact, you will want to let your manager know that although you have done your best to plan and contingency plan, you will both need to stay flexible as things unfold.

Even if you must adjust your plans (and you will), you will never regret the time you spent thoughtfully considering how to make your transition a smooth one for you, your larger team, and your family.

Leadership Lessons of Parenthood

Action Planning

At first glance, action planning seems to be all head-based leadership. But don't be fooled. Effective action planning also requires the heart, intuition, and the integration of it all, which is a skill mastered by *whole-person leaders*. In leave planning, you have to analyze the entire chessboard, including the current and future needs of all stakeholders (you, your manager, cover team, clients, family, etc.), then draw on your emotional intelligence, strategic thinking, project management, and ability to put a plan into action with as few moves as possible. The key to getting this right is in shifting perspectives. This is not a zero-sum game to win, but rather an opportunity to find win-win solutions.

Here are a few of the *whole-person leadership* skills you'll be practicing during this touchpoint:

- Setting a direction
- Thinking strategically
- Communicating your needs
- Considering the needs and viewpoints of others
- Working collaboratively
- Finding win-win solutions
- Putting a plan into place and enacting it (project management)
- Pivoting to contingency plans as needed (change management)

Chapter
Seven

Touchpoint 4
Acknowledge the Transition to Parenthood

A NEW DAD named Darren crisply summarized a realization most of my clients have at some point: "Everyone told me everything would be different after I had kids, but I didn't realize they meant *I* would be different." It's true: the person you are today, getting ready to leave work, is not the person who will be returning.

We don't talk enough about how we will be different on the other side of welcoming a child (even when it is not our first). Yes, most of us can imagine that our schedule and daily commitments will be different. We know having a child will be a big emotional experience. Too often, however, there isn't recognition of the need to pause our busy lives and take notice of what we are experiencing and how we are evolving in response. This fourth touchpoint is not only about how you want others to acknowledge your leaving work and welcoming a child but also about how you want to do so internally, *for yourself.*

Maybe you want to throw a big party such as a baby shower (or any of the catchy names they're sometimes called for dads) in addition to a quieter form of acknowledgment, like a blessing circle or other ceremony, with those you are very close to. This touchpoint is about your own recognition of the transformation that is unfolding. Who do you want to be as a parent? What are your hopes and dreams? What are your fears? Capturing your feelings in a baby book or journal or creating a box of heirlooms and special items for your child can help everything feel real and will give your future self a nostalgic window to this time. If you have a spouse or partner, what do they want parenthood to be like? By scheduling time to reflect and dream on this monumental shift, you create the space to lead the process rather than be consumed by it.

Let me be clear. Leading is not the same as controlling. If parenting has taught me one thing, it is that you really don't control *anything*. And you don't need to. What parenting requires is *presence*; it is about being able to clear your mind to be able to be fully present for all you are experiencing. Becoming a working parent is about presence on a whole other level. If that's hard to envision, that's OK. It is impossible for you to really know what I mean until you become a parent yourself and have that experience to draw on. As important as it is to envision who you want to be as a parent to this child, you must also recognize that this vision will evolve as you adjust to new information and experiences.

In leaving work and entering leave, you will move from spending your days predominantly focused on work to giving your attention to your new child and your home life. Your priorities may change during this time, and with that shift you might question who you are and what you want and value. Give yourself space and time to have those thoughts and mull over whatever questions arise. Pushing them aside will not make them go away; rather, it may lead to more complicated and conflicted questioning later on.

Inner Work

My coaching experience has shown me that this lead-up before the child comes is anything but calm. Dozens of other concerns may come up at any given time. You may find, when you pause to take time for reflection, that you have a lot of things going through your head—a busy brain with a lot of inner chatter. One expectant mom, Tally, described it this way: "All I want to do is stop and have a moment to think and be with myself, but when I finally do, it is like a tornado in my brain and I don't even know where to begin." If you relate, try moving all that thinking out of your head and onto paper (or into a digital document) for safekeeping. You may need to get your mental to-do list out of your head before you can dig deeper to reflect on your feelings and values behind that list. Maybe you start your reflection process with 10 minutes to write down everything on your mind (later you can translate this stuff into tasks for your leave plan). Or maybe you make a voice memo or ask a friend to take notes while you do a brain dump. Either way, externalizing your mental chatter will free up inner space for room to be present and grounded while you reflect on what you are experiencing right now.

Reflection Questions

* What parts of your transition to parenthood do you feel most strongly about? Maybe breastfeeding is important to you or incorporating traditions from your culture or family.
* Are there parts of your transition to parenthood that you know you are avoiding? Is there a big talk you need to have with your partner or boss, or medical or dental work you haven't attended to?
* Is there something—or many things—that you want to accomplish or finish before this child arrives? Pay attention to what is possible and realistic and which things may need to be set aside, or even let go of. Deciding which are essential (either for practical or emotional reasons) can be hard work and some may even require a bit of mourning as you say goodbye to a path you will need to leave untraveled.
* What kind of parent do you want to be? What are your dreams and goals in becoming a parent to this child?
* If you have a partner or spouse:
  o What are your relationship goals and values to honor during the transition?
  o How do you want to celebrate and mark this time together before the child arrives (for example, some people go on a babymoon)?

(continued)

o Are there things on your relationship bucket list that you would like to do? (I'm outing myself as a lit nerd, but my husband and I read *Anna Karenina* together, two copies side-by-side in bed, before our first child came. We were fairly certain we would never have time to read such a thick book again. And while it might not sound like the most passionate, exciting activity, it gave us a sense of complicity and shared accomplishment, a cozy memory to refer back to when things got more hectic and we needed to connect.)

o In addition to dreams and goals, it can be helpful to research and discuss the concrete decisions you will face. Who will your pediatrician be? Where will your child sleep? How do you both feel about sleep training? Breastfeeding? Immunization schedules? If adopting or fostering an older child, what school will they be attending?

o Who will do what? (See the What Does a Fair Division of Labor Even Mean [and How Can We Achieve It]? sidebar in Chapter 10.)

o How will you tend to your relationship when your new child will demand all of your tending?

Keeping Intimacy Alive

Many new parents are resigned to the idea that romantic relationships suffer after children enter the picture and the bedroom (and that is certainly true for *at least* six weeks for any birthing mom). But with a little advocacy, you can build a different future for your relationship.

Married partners in work and life, Drs. John and Julie Gottman have been researching the habits that make romantic relationships thrive—or take a nosedive—for over four decades. According to their research, the first three years of a baby's life corresponds with a significant dip in relationship satisfaction for 67% of heterosexual couples.[1] Let's make sure you stay in the top third that remains satisfied and content!

Through clinical research started in the 1980s at the University of Washington's famous Love Lab, and now conducted at their own Gottman Institute, they have worked with thousands of couples to help them improve their connection and intimacy.

Here is the secret sauce that they shared with me (which confirms what I have seen in my work): *the best predictor of relationship adjustment after a new child joins the family is the quality of friendship in the relationship.*

They also shared their six-step recipe for preserving your relationship while bonding with your child (which they teach in their spot-on book *And Baby Makes Three*).[2]

1. **Realize that we're all in the same soup.** Sometimes couples turn against each other in the face of the everyday stresses of raising a child. Realizing that you are both in a systemically challenging situation can help ease tension and foster teamwork.

2. **Delight in responding to your baby.** Touch and face-to-face play are critical for your child's healthy development. When both partners aim to be responsive, you can delight not just in your baby but also in your shared experience.

3. **Cool down your conflicts.** This involves some simple techniques, including what the Gottmans call "softening how you bring up a problem," and accepting the fact that you both have valid viewpoints. Compromise is a skill you will be able to practice more than ever as a new parent in a relationship. Often, a fight is a clear indication of a conversation that needs to happen, after you both cool off. Much of *And Baby Makes Three* is devoted to handling conflicts.

4. **Savor each other by building a strong friendship and a zesty sex life.** If you do nothing else, prioritizing your friendship with your partner and making time for sex can do wonders for your relationship.

(continued)

(continued)

5. **Add warm fathering to the mix.** If you are a mother, avoid the temptation to exclude dad from caregiving or make him feel like he is not doing it right. As a father, don't accept anything less for yourself than total involvement. Feed your children, change their diapers, coddle them when they are sick. Be your child's playmate and shower your kid with affection.

6. **Create an enriching legacy.** Adopt an attitude of *we* not *me* and work with your partner to create deeper meaning in your family. What traditions will you create with your partner to bring meaning to your relationship and create a solid, safe haven for your child?

Letter Writing as Reflection

Many of my clients write letters as a thoughtful way to mark this transition. I suggest two: one to your *future child* and one to your *future self*. These do not need to be literary works of art. They are to help you better process everything you're thinking and feeling. If you are self-conscious about your writing, you can even burn them when you are done. However, I encourage you not to. Set them aside to rediscover further down the road and your child or future self will thank you.

If you're not sure how to start, try any or all of these prompts and consider closing with a quote that speaks to you or a world event happening that day:

✎ Dear child,

I can't wait to [specific activities such as: smell your head, stroke your cheek, feed you, fall asleep with you, see you grow up].

I want you to feel [specific emotions you want your child to experience such as: loved, cared for, safe].

Honestly, I'm a little worried about [specific anxieties you may have such as: knowing how to take care of you, finding a way to juggle it all].

I promise to [specific promise you want to keep to your child].

But I know it will all be worth it because [your deepest certainty about why you are becoming a parent].

✎ Dear future self,

There are parts of this whole experience that feel [specific emotion such as crazy, magical, overwhelming], like [specific thing causing this emotion].

I thought it would be [how you expected to feel] but it's more like [how you really feel].

I hope I'll always [something about yourself that you want to retain].

I'm looking forward to growing in new ways like [some area you want to cultivate in yourself].

I'm hoping parenting will mean [something you hope to learn].

At Work

By going on leave, you are launching a new phase of your career as well. You will come back to work with new perspectives, new skills (like taking multitasking to a whole new level), and—in some cases—new constraints.

Your leave launch from work, like any new and exciting endeavor, is cause for celebration and those around you will want to wish you well. For some of us, being the center of attention feels uncomfortable, but know that by accepting congratulations, you give others an opportunity to acknowledge your transition, too.

Don't hesitate to communicate what form of acknowledgment feels right. It could be something as simple as meeting for lunch or as elaborate as a party, but consider that how your team celebrates you may set the expectation for others who come after you. Stopping to acknowledge your transition and enjoy celebrations at work and at home allows you a moment to strengthen your connections with your support network and to recognize and bask in the support you will need during leave and on your return.

Reflection Questions

* How would you like your leave acknowledged at work? Has your team already celebrated something like this for others? Would that format work for you? If not, what do you want to modify?
* Who would you like to celebrate with?
* Would you like to celebrate with them all together or in different ways depending on the person/people? You may want a smaller, more personal celebration with close colleagues in addition to having an organization- or office-wide send-off.
* Beyond the practicalities you need to put in place to go on leave (which you've already considered in your action plan), can you do something for yourself personally to mark leaving the office (or home office) and putting work aside? This may be as simple as pausing on your last day to say a quiet *thank you* that this moment has come.

Making time to pay attention to your own experience will cultivate your ability to hear your own voice and not lose yourself in the process. Taking time for yourself in a purposeful way now will help you set up mindfulness habits for when you're in the thick of it. Meditation or prayer, spending time purposefully doing nothing, or taking a walk alone are all ways to stay connected with yourself and integrate what you're learning. These habits will give you increased grounding to steadily navigate the present and your future. Again, this is not just for first-time parents. Although first-time parents may experience the biggest leap, with each additional child there are continuous shifts in how we think of ourselves and how we interact with the world. Someone may have already told you that your child will be your biggest teacher. I invite you to begin being gentle with yourself as you enter Parenthood University and embark on the greatest learning of your life!

When Fathers Take Parental Leave

When it comes to cisgender heterosexual couples, we have ample data to show that when dads take leave, it is a good thing for everyone. Scott Behson, author of *The Working Dad's Survival Guide: How to Succeed at Work and at Home*,[3] described his experience to me and why he advocates for greater access to paternity leave:

> "My paternity leave fundamentally shaped me as a person, parent and spouse, and it contributed to the strength and resiliency of my family. I think the fact that my wife, Amy [not me the author!], and I worked together so closely after our son, Nick, was born helped set up our healthy, shared-care family dynamic. It allowed Amy to return to work with confidence. Years later, if one of us has to work late, we know that the other has it totally covered, and our son knows too.
>
> I believe all dads deserve this opportunity, and that dads, moms, kids, families, employers, and our society all benefit when dads get to immerse themselves in the lives of their children in such a uniquely intimate and transformative way."

The data support his observations:

- Working dads who take leave report a deeper bond with their child (96%), more confidence in caregiving (92%), greater life satisfaction (88%), and a stronger relationship with their partner (83%).[4]
- Working dads who take leave are more active in their child's life nine months after birth[5] and throughout the first few years.[6]
- Older children report more involvement, a closer relationship, and better communication with their father.[7]
- Paternal engagement is related to enhanced cognitive development, decreased delinquency, reduced economic disadvantage, and reduced behavioral problems in sons and psychological problems in daughters.[8]

(continued)

(*continued*)

- Dads who take leave participate more in household responsibilities and have less conflict about household division of labor.[9]
- Mothers report higher relationship satisfaction.[10]
- The parents' relationship is less likely to end in divorce or separation when dads take leave.[11]
- Mom earns more! A mother's earnings increase nearly 7% for each additional month of leave a father takes.[12]

And in case that wasn't enough, organizations benefit too:

- Men with parental leave benefits report greater loyalty to their employer (27%) and are more likely to experience increased job satisfaction (20%).[13]
- When paid family leave has been implemented, most employers have reported a positive or neutral impact in regards to productivity (89%), performance (91%), turnover (92%), and morale (99%).[14]

The End of Phase 1

Phase 1 is time well spent doing heavy lifting of the practical details of your transition (as well as some of the emotional preparation work). You've taken the lead on your leave transition by thoughtfully announcing it, assessing the particulars of your transition, crafting a plan to position yourself and your team well, and acknowledging what this major life transition may mean.

In Phase 2, during your leave, you'll be focused on becoming a parent to your new child while following your Keep in Touch strategy, advocating for yourself and your child and, ultimately, revisiting your plans and arrangements for your return to work.

Leadership Lessons of Parenthood

Acknowledging the Transition to Parenthood

Pausing in your busy day-to-day life to give yourself the space to explore your heart and what you are experiencing emotionally is a key part of *whole-person leadership*. Tapping into this different way of approaching your thinking, feeling, and being may be easy for some. For most of us, it isn't. Yet the practice of reflecting and being truly present for yourself will allow you to hear your inner guiding voice (sometimes called intuition or inner wisdom) more clearly. This vital superpower in your life as a working parent is one you will want to tap into frequently, calling on these leadership skills as you navigate a lifetime of decisions and transitions of all sizes.

Here are some of the *whole-person leadership* skills you'll be practicing during this transition:

- Letting go of the past
- Entering new beginnings
- Creating a heart-led vision
- Tapping into your inner wisdom to steer your leadership
- Making space to nourish your emotional life

PHASE TWO
During Leave

* * *

Parent Focus

Chapter
Eight

Phase 2: During Leave Overview

PHASE 2 IS when your whole world changes. Even if this isn't your first child, the addition of another child means everything is different now: your relationships, your roles, your mornings, your evenings, and everything in between. This second phase, while you are on leave, is when you get to exhale as you walk away from work, then settle into the home sanctuary you have been working to create with all your careful tone-setting, planning, and acknowledging in Phase 1. The touchpoints in this phase, as shown in the figure, focus on communication, self-advocacy, and flexibility to maintain that safe space where you can focus on and explore your new role as parent.

Your main objective for Phase 2 is to care for your new child and yourself, especially if you're recovering from childbirth, and to bond with your expanded family. This will include learning how to be a parent to this child and turning new practices into habits and family norms. When you think about planning for this phase, think about all the ways you can set yourself up to actually remember to inhale and exhale—repeatedly.

10A Transition Touchpoints Framework™ Phase 2

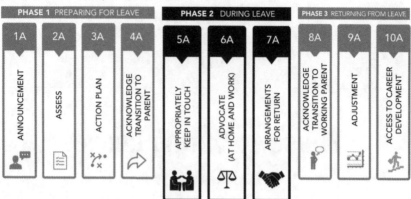

Prepare for All the Feels

Terrence and his wife Saoirse had spent five years struggling with infertility when they found out that they had been chosen to adopt two siblings. They had been eagerly awaiting this moment for years and flew out that night to meet them. When their new son, aged six, walked in holding his little sister's hand, Saoirse collapsed on the floor overcome with emotions. She told me, "It was like a tidal wave of all the emotions I had felt in my whole life crashed into me and I couldn't tell if I was crying from joy, fear, relief, or exhaustion. I couldn't move and Terrence had to take over."

When your child first comes home, it is natural and normal to feel blissfully happy one moment and terrified the next, or even both at once. This is that messy middle part of your transition that I mentioned; you are reinventing yourself and your family, and it can be disorienting under the best of circumstances. If you gave birth, your body will feel like it's reinventing itself, too. You are still physically recovering and experiencing pain, hormonal adjustments, engorged breasts, and more. Add a lack of sleep and it is perfectly understandable when emotions run to extremes.

This time is emotionally charged for everyone—loved ones, partners, colleagues, older children, and even pets! Anticipating that the boat will rock can help you welcome *all* the feelings you (and others) may experience as a normal part of the process. This is preferable to being caught by surprise and passing judgment on yourself or those around you over the fact that it's not emotional smooth sailing. Instead, anticipate this perfect storm, and you will be better prepared to steer a clear course to calmer waters.

This heightened state also means that any extra hurdles you face can leave you feeling traumatized. If you, your partner, or your child experience any special challenges, please refer to Chapter 16, where you will find more information on dealing with healing difficulties and other health concerns, including loss.

As with every phase of your transition, if you feel like you are having difficulty coping, I recommend completing a perinatal mental health screening (go to www.cplleadership.com/playbook to take one for free) and talking to a mental health provider trained in perinatal mood disorders (see Chapter 16 for information and resources).

Make Connection a Priority

My work has let me witness countless individuals and couples creating families. I have seen that the simple daily actions they take during this time are what form habits and build the foundation for their life going forward. It is easy to think that you can change something down the road when you've caught your breath, but instead you will find that the rules of compound interest apply: *your future return on investment is an exponential calculation based on what you deposit now.*

If you want to have a family culture where you reconnect at the end of each day, start prioritizing regular family dinners now. If you want to ensure your relationship with your partner endures, schedule consistent times to focus on it now. If you want to be sure you don't lose touch with your friends, build time in now. Sow what you hope to reap. One of the great paradoxical gifts of transition is the chaos it brings. With chaos comes opportunity. Use it to decide what you want to build for your future and to create the momentum and excitement to get you there.

You will probably be getting less sleep than you are used to. Your baby may be colicky. You may be breastfeeding or supporting your breast-feeding partner. You may be dealing with health issues for your child or yourself. You might be encountering unexpected tensions in your newly configured family life or having a harder time than anticipated setting work aside completely. Whatever you are facing, you can't go wrong by thinking of this as a time when your main focus is strengthening the connections that support and nourish you. With this in mind, I have structured the next three chapters to guide you through anticipating how to honor your work boundaries through your strategy to **appropriately keep in touch, advocate** for yourself and your child, and cultivate legitimate self-care habits (note: self-care isn't simply bubble baths or beers with the boys).

Towards the end of Phase 2, you'll need to make **arrangements for your return to work,** including reexamining, by the light of your new reality, all the assumptions and plans you made about your return before you went on leave.

Read these touchpoints before your child arrives to help you prepare practically and emotionally. Then revisit them while you are home on leave.

Chapter
Nine

Touchpoint 5
Appropriately Keep in Touch

IN OUR COUNTRY's 24/7 culture, the competing demands of work and home can feel all-consuming. You are now adding to that mix a new child, completely dependent on you for their survival. Something has got to give! During leave is when you put your paid work on the back burner and take time to focus on your new family constellation. That being said, it is still common for companies to pressure new parents to work or for new parents to *want or need* to work at their own discretion during leave.

In retrospect, many parents wish they had set firmer boundaries. Take Nora, for example: "I continued to check in and do work while I was in labor at the hospital. Seriously, what was I thinking?" This is the only time your child is young. Important as your work may feel, keep in perspective that statistically speaking, you will be at another job within five years, while your child, though yours always, will never be new to you again. Your leave is also a short time frame to learn this parenting job, and it is to everyone's advantage for you to learn it well. Part of what you will need to learn, now that you have met your new child and have a better understanding of their needs, is where you want to set boundaries between your home and work spheres and how you will monitor and adjust them along the way. Because of the rare breathing space our culture sometimes permits during parental leave, it is a perfect time to start practicing setting those boundaries and figuring out your own definition of what it means to "appropriately keep in touch" with work.

Practically speaking, the Keep in Touch (KIT) section of your leave plan is the place to document your communication intentions so you can share them with your stakeholders, including your manager and team, and your home support team. If you do this well, you will create a protected space to bond with your family during parental leave *and* set yourself up for a less stressful, more values-aligned future as a working parent.

Emotionally speaking, this fifth touchpoint helps you think through how you want the relationship between work and home to feel, while you're on leave and in the long term. You'll begin applying those values now in how you set up and communicate your KIT strategy. For example, will your spouse or partner stop working for a year to care for your child, meaning the family will rely solely on your income? If so, that may mean you want to keep close ties with work—or you may want to cut away entirely to enjoy this brief time. Or maybe you'll be working part-time and would like to taper off your manager's dependence on you. What you decide will be based on your unique situation.

Your KIT strategy will help define lines of communication while you are on leave and set clear expectations and boundaries for home and for work. Keeping in touch allows you to share your new experience as a parent with colleagues and stay updated on the parts of work you want to stay connected to. Once your child arrives, it is time to revisit your plan. Did you agree to what now feels like too much contact? Too little? Keeping in touch on your own terms can also ease the shock of reentry.

You will want to include a KIT section in your leave plan that communicates your information in a format others can refer to when they need to know if it is okay to reach out. I will go into detail next, but briefly, if you are planning a long leave, you will outline the frequency and purpose of contact—if any—you would like through the leave transition. If you are not taking a long leave, you can use this as an opportunity to outline work-life boundaries going forward. For example, perhaps you currently accept calls and respond to emails after your official workday ends and on weekends, but after your child's arrival you would like that to stop. Or maybe you want to limit travel in the first year of parenthood. What specific instructions can you provide to your colleagues to protect your time after you begin your leave? This may mean no contact at all. You decide the level of contact you are comfortable with.

In either scenario it is *always* better to under-commit. If you are unsure, your best bet is to say you won't be in touch at all, except to let them know your new child has arrived and again before your return in order to revisit your plans with your manager for a smooth reentry.

In the United States, if you work for an employer who is required to provide unpaid job protected leave under FMLA, they cannot legally require you to work while on official leave. However, nearly half of all new parents are ineligible for FMLA and can be fired if they do not work as their boss demands. (This is one of the reasons why a staggering 23% of moms in the United States are back to work within two weeks of giving birth.)[1]

There are at least four ways your KIT strategy can help you. First, deciding where to set boundaries between work and home during this time away lets you be in control of your schedule and not at the whim of others. Second, the way you create, communicate, and maintain healthy boundaries now will model how to do so for your family and team and will pay dividends far into your future working parent life. Third, colleagues will be happy and grateful that you have given them a clear road map. It helps them know what to expect and takes the guesswork out of how to communicate with you—or not—during this important time when they may be respectfully wary of disturbing you. Finally, keep in mind that staying connected with work, although not everyone's preference, can significantly decrease anxiety for some people—so do not feel guilty if this is you. I've also seen it help deepen work relationships, which can aid new parents in feeling more supported when they return.

One of my clients, Tao, experienced this. He did not want anyone to contact him unless there was an emergency at work (according to the clear definition of an emergency in his KIT strategy). However, he made it a point to send his team cute pictures and updates every couple of weeks, things like, "Sam is growing like a weed. He hates bottles and loves snuggles." Or a picture of Sam with their large dog watching and on high alert: "The dog is not sure if Sam is to protect or eat." When he returned, he found that his teammates were now emotionally invested in Sam: they had come along on his fatherhood journey and wanted to hear more about Sam (and his relationship with their dog). By sending these updates, Tao had sent the message to his team that he was welcoming them into his life, which made for a friendly atmosphere when he went back to the office (and made it easier to explain when, even after Tao's return, Sam's care needed to take priority).

It can be tempting to cave to pressure, whether real or perceived, to stay in frequent contact with work. Some parents worry that if they are not needed while out on leave, their company will realize they can be laid off. Some parents worry that if they try to draw a firm boundary around contact, they'll be fired for lack of commitment. Still others worry that if they maintain the amount of contact they truly want with work, their friends and family will see them as less than an ideal parent. Fear of being judged negatively at work or at home seems to be the number one reason people don't ask for what they really need. So, get really clear with yourself first: if you had a guarantee that no one around you would judge your choice, what would you ask for?

Now, ask for that.

Yes, you invariably *will* be judged and not by an "independent panel of experts," but by many highly invested, inexpert individuals. You cannot possibly please all of them. *You* are the expert here. And because the fact that you will be judged is beyond your control, you may as well focus on getting what you truly want during your transition.

General Considerations for Your Keep in Touch Strategy

As you create your KIT strategy, here are some things to consider:

- If you have decided (or you are required) to hand back your work communication equipment (phone, tablet, laptop), what alternative contact details will you include?
- How do you want to alert people when your new child arrives?

- It can be helpful to set up a KIT partner, a gatekeeper of sorts, who will take responsibility for staying in contact with you during leave. Although this may be your manager, consider whether it makes sense to set up a separate or additional KIT partner who handles the less official but sometimes equally important information that you usually get around the water cooler.
- Are there any important dates or milestones that occur during your leave (such as planning days, conferences, team activities, holiday functions, performance or bonus reviews)? How would you like to include them in your KIT?
- On a related note, are there dates when you need to set a reminder to submit paperwork (including leave compliance forms, time sheets, sending a birth certificate to your health insurance company, etc.)?
- Would you like to differentiate between standard versus emergency KIT communication methods? For example, you may choose to have people email you at your work email address for regular updates and send a text if urgent.
- Beyond the practical, how can you find meaningful ways to stay connected to your team (for example, sending them regular updates on your growing child, an article or meme that made you think of them, etc.)?
- Do you want to be updated on any important changes while you are on leave? If so, how and about what?
- Will you use your social media accounts while on leave? If so, how and to what extent—both work and personal ones? List them out and make a decision on professional and personal accounts for each platform, if applicable.
- Are there any important stakeholders or sponsors with whom you want to stay connected? If so, who and how?
- Do you need to make explicit the difference between personal and professional contact boundaries? (Maybe it is fine for someone to comment on a baby picture you sent, but not to ask you about a work matter.)
- Would you like to be considered for and contacted about any career development activities or promotion opportunities that may come up while you are on leave?

- Do you want to build time into your KIT strategy to use during the end of your leave to help prepare for your return (like a meeting with your manager or lunch with your team)?

Contingency Considerations for Keeping in Touch

What will you do if one the following situations occurs?

- Confusion comes up at work about the amount, method, or content of contact. (This is one area where a KIT point person can be useful.)
- Organizational changes occur during your parental leave (for example, change in manager, team, or a restructure). What are some alternative contacts and/or dates and milestones when people would be able to contact you if such changes occur?
- Your KIT strategy is not followed or not working once you go on leave. How will you manage the expectations for this? Do you have someone who can advocate for you?
- You realize after being on leave that you've changed your mind and you want different parameters for your KIT contact—less contact, more contact, or different contact?

Keeping in Touch with Your Personal Support System

However you choose to keep in touch with work, you will also want to keep in touch with your personal support network, reaching out for help if needed and accepting support when it is offered. These relationships also benefit from clear communication about your boundaries. You can reach out to evolve those boundaries at any time.

Many parents welcoming a new baby via birth find it challenging to decide who to have accompany them, whether in a hospital or birthing center or during a home birth. Some want lots of support. Others would prefer that only their partner or one trusted person be present. Even when new parents are clear on their needs, this moment can be highly charged for them and their extended families, and communicating those needs to loved ones without hurting any feelings can be an added hurdle. Find ways to let loved ones know you value them, then clearly outline when and how their love and support will be most welcome. You know your situation best, but if this feels like a tricky area for you and your family, I recommend reaching out to a coach or therapist. It is not uncommon for lifelong family wounds, even feuds, to begin with an argument about who can be in the birthing room or visit the baby first. New parents who communicate with love, compassion, and empathy—rather than getting bogged down in petty exchanges—are the ones I see able to use this time to deepen extended family bonds rather than strain them.

Once you're home and settled, set further parameters for contact and support as needed. For example, let your support team know not to contact you during nap times, or past a certain hour, or on certain days. One client shared a spreadsheet with time slots for visits, phone/video conferencing calls, and tasks that needed doing around the house, such as laundry, cleaning, baby holding, sibling care, and cooking. She asked people to sign up for what worked for them. I have rarely seen a happier new parent.

You and everyone around you will enjoy your transition more if you're clear about your needs and wants.

Revisiting Your KIT Strategy After Your Child's Arrival

Planning how you want to stay in touch with work before your child enters your life is important for setting expectations and starting the conversation. It is also an exercise in wishful thinking, not yet rooted in experience of your upcoming new reality. I see many parents rush to modify their KIT plan once their child arrives; sometimes circumstances arise that make a change of KIT strategy necessary, but often it is simply a change of heart. Your plan was based on what you *thought* you would want. Be kind to yourself: using a contingency plan—or creating an entirely new KIT plan—does not mean you have done something wrong or failed but is a normal part of any transition as you adjust to evolving information and feelings and discover what works best for you and your newly expanded family.

Jay was a project manager at a prominent engineering firm. He and his partner, Robert, were expecting a baby via a surrogate. They had planned that Robert would be the primary caregiver for the first few months. Jay planned to take off one week and then head back into the office to avoid a cut in pay and getting a reputation as "not committed" to his job. But as soon as that baby landed, Jay realized how badly he wanted to share in the experience for longer than a week. He put in a call to his boss and successfully negotiated a month-long leave and then a few days per week of remote work for another two months. He was able to build his confidence in baby care, share this once-in-a-lifetime experience with his partner, and bond deeply with his new child.

Modifying Your KIT Strategy During Leave

Once you have decided exactly how you want to adjust your initial KIT plan, it's time to communicate those changes. Start by checking in with your manager. Simply propose the modification you are seeking in a matter-of-fact way. Though you may feel the need to justify your changes, resist the temptation to strike an apologetic tone. Remember, if you have FMLA coverage, you cannot legally be asked to work during your approved leave.

Here is a script for adjusting your KIT strategy during leave:

> "When I was planning for leave, my best guess about the frequency of communication with the office was X. Now that I'm out, I can see that Y would work much better for me. If this works for you, let's discuss how to communicate the change with the wider team."

Honoring Your KIT Strategy

Once you have made and communicated any desired adjustments, it's time to follow the plan. This means avoiding temptation to communicate in ways that deviate from your plan. Don't answer an email on Thursday when said you'll only check email on Fridays. Don't comment on a work project when said you are not working. Your actions speak louder than your written plan, so if you don't follow it, you cannot expect that others will. Especially if you have a management role, be aware how your actions will serve to shape the norms in your organizational culture. How leaders keep in touch or not sends a clear message to other workers about what is appropriate. When leaders (especially male leaders) actually take their leave and detach from work for as long as they can, it gives permission to other men and models good "detachment behavior" for women employees.

Leadership Lessons of Parenthood

Appropriately Keeping in Touch

It can be confusing to prioritize home life when the message our culture sends is that work is primary. Taking ownership over how you use your time has the power to sustain you as a working parent. Embedding your values in the choices you make now and being thoughtful about how you communicate your KIT strategy (in ways that make those around you feel heard, included, and supported) is a key skill of *whole-person leadership*. Mind reading is not a skill most people possess. Your colleagues and friends will thank you when you set expectations through clear, healthy boundaries while remaining flexible and open.

Here are a few of the *whole-person leadership* skills you will be practicing during this transition:

- Taking ownership over your time
- Modeling healthy boundaries by setting, keeping, and adjusting them
- Considering the needs of others
- Communicating your own needs
- Setting expectations
- Facing an ever-changing landscape with flexibility

Chapter
Ten

Touchpoint 6
Advocate

So OFTEN, OUR default as new parents is to make sure we take care of our family and work commitments first. Although these are important, if we don't take time to also care for ourselves, our capacity to show up for others is unsustainable. If self-advocacy has been a weak point for you in the past (this may have surfaced as a liability during your 6-S assessment back in Chapter 5), know that parenthood will present *many* opportunities to work on this skill. Look through your assets and see if there are any that would help your advocacy efforts. For example, if you have supportive coworkers, perhaps you could enlist them to go to bat for you with your supervisor.

Advocate sits in Phase 2 because you will be doing lots of advocating for yourself in real time as you welcome your child—at work, at home, and potentially with your health care team. Read this chapter before your child arrives for maximum benefit in applying advocacy to all phases of your transition and beyond.

Self-advocacy is about understanding your responsibilities and needs, then managing those responsibilities and protecting those needs in the face of external pressures by developing healthy boundaries. As a new parent, you will also frequently need to advocate on

125

behalf of others, including your child(ren) and family members. If you find it easier to advocate for anyone other than yourself, that protective instinct is normal and admirable; just remember that you serve the ones you love best when your own needs are met through good self-care and self-advocacy.

The good news is, advocating for yourself does not have to involve conflict. Most of the people around you want to be helpful, but they don't always know the best way. Jessica, a consultant, was the breadwinner for her family and was unable to take a long parental leave. She asked for and was given permission to bring her newborn to work. "When I was in meetings, I hired an intern to babysit. Otherwise, she was with me, being worn or sleeping in my office. I converted half of my office to a nursery—crib, changing table. My coworkers were so welcoming to my baby. One stopped by regularly on his lunch and would feed her so I could rest or get work done. I am so grateful that I was able to have that time with her."

Speaking up for your needs can strengthen your relationships and give you the support you need to thrive now and far into the future. You will, however, have to make your needs clear. One way to do that is to set boundaries that feel healthy and right to you. Self-advocacy and boundaries, such as those we touched on in the touchpoint on creating your KIT plan, are intertwined. (More on boundaries in Chapter 14.)

Having Difficult Conversations

One of the themes I see when I look at parental leave transition assessment results from our clients is a general discomfort with difficult conversations. Always tricky to do well, this can be harder during your big transition due to heightened emotions and worries of being cast into a negative working parent stereotype, disappointing your colleagues, derailing your career, hurting your partner's feelings, and more.

One of the challenges of this transition is that the significant internal changes involved are usually invisible—especially at work, where the role you return to might not have changed and where colleagues tend to expect the same old you to come back. This means that you need to take the lead in having conversations about the impact of this transition.

An interesting effect of the coronavirus pandemic is that the lines between work and home, which were already getting blurry, disappeared almost overnight. One of the silver linings is that this makes a traditionally invisible transition more visible. Notice where you can use your environment to facilitate those difficult conversations—both at home and work. For example, it may be easy to ignore a breastfeeding mother's need to pump and schedule back-to-back meetings when she is working in the office, but it is a lot harder to ignore a baby crying to nurse during a video call!

Exercise: Preparing for Difficult Conversations

In this exercise, I will ask you to identify some difficult conversations you need to have. This can be something you have been avoiding or something you know you should discuss before it becomes an issue. Make a plan for what you would like to cover in the conversation and examine your preconceived notions about how things will go. If you are confronting an especially tough talk, consider practicing with a trusted friend or family member before tackling the real conversation. Also, this does not have to be a face-to-face meeting; conversations can happen by phone, video call, or email. Consider what format will bring you the most ease and success.

A simple, useful model for framing difficult conversations is the Center for Creative Leadership's Situation-Behavior-Impact™ (SBI™) model, originally designed for performance reviews. Each word in its title describes an element or building block that helps make up a productive, straightforward conversation. All you need to do is define your building blocks and string them together.

- **Situation** describes what has occurred (or needs to).
- **Behavior** describes the observable behavior of those involved (including you).
- **Impact** describes what you thought or felt in reaction to the behavior.

For example, let's say you need to address a communication issue with your manager. Of the situation, you could say, *"Now that I'm working from home with no childcare,"* then move into behavior, "*when you send me an email at 11 p.m.,*" and finally, the impact, "*I feel unclear about when you expect me to reply and worry that if I don't reply right away you will think I'm not committed.*" You have worked all three building blocks into one very effective sentence.

You can then offer a new behavior as a solution and show the impact it would have: "*If you could please add when you need to hear back from me [behavior], I won't worry and can prioritize my tasks to be most efficient [impact].*"

You can use this to describe a behavior you are worried about occurring too. For example, imagine this conversation with your manager: "*When John came back to work after his daughter was adopted [situation], I noticed that it was hard for me and all of us on the team to know how to include him with tasks we'd been working on while he was gone [behavior]. It was awkward for all of us. If that happened to me, it would make me feel like I wasn't part of the team anymore [impact].*" Then offer your solution, "*I'd like to make a clear plan for how I will pick my work back up on my return and share it with everyone before I go [behavior]. I think that will make everything explicit and clear [impact]. Would that be OK with you?*"

If you'd like to try this now, grab a notebook and follow along.

1. Name a conversation you have been putting off having—a situation where you need to advocate for yourself.
2. Write down your desired outcome.
3. Write down your worries about what could go wrong in the conversation or the outcome.
4. Now identify what behaviors need to change (or what boundaries need to be created and/or communicated) to address your worries and get to your desired outcome. Another word for boundaries is *clarity*; think of them not as barriers but as you having integrity with your words and thoughts. (For more on boundaries, see Chapter 14.)
5. Now bullet out the main points you want to cover in the difficult conversation using the SBI model. This may seem like overkill, but doing this a few times helps you not forget a point and gives you practice in the model. Before long you will internalize it and clear communication will be a natural habit.

Self-Advocacy at Home

When her child was about two months old, Tamara found herself on her knees on the cold kitchen tiles, screaming at her partner, "I can't do it all anymore!" Stunned, he picked her up off the floor. He had not realized she was stretched so far by home tasks while recovering from childbirth. Although we all sometimes wish our partners could be mind readers, what is more realistic is to advocate for ourselves rather than taking on more than we can realistically handle until we sink under.

Advocacy is rarely a one-time conversation. Think of it as many small conversations to plant the seeds of what you need throughout your transition. It is unlikely you will get it right on your first try, and neither will whoever you are talking to. Advocating is as much about listening to the needs of others as it is about telling someone what you need. Consider the whole picture and be clear on your guiding values in order to understand how to prioritize your needs, given limited resources.

Advocating for yourself at home could be as simple as asking for help from a trusted friend so you can get some uninterrupted sleep or a shower, or it could be something more difficult, such as a conversation with your partner to work out who does what at home. Let's explore some of the self-advocacy you'll need on the home front.

Self-Advocacy with Your Partner

If you have a partner, bringing a child into the relationship has the power to make all the best parts of your relationship even better and all the stressful parts of your relationship even more challenging. Good communication is absolutely key in working together to figure out how you'll both get enough sleep, exercise, nutrition, and other basic self-care that will keep you healthy and mentally fit during a challenging time.

Use the following checklist to go over the elements of your day that will need to be covered and divvy up who will do what and when. Many couples disagree about what is critical and what can get pushed off. Determine where you can compromise and save your energy to advocate for your non-negotiables. (Don't forget you can always change your mind; just own up to the change and communicate it.)

In many areas you may need to re-prioritize (for some this means lowering standards!) for a while as you adjust to your new normal. It is not critical that the floor be vacuumed every day. It *is* critical that you eat and sleep. We are lucky that the pandemic pushed us into a new normal where many remote services are now widely available. Don't hesitate to use any services that will make your life easier. If you are in a position to hire out tasks on this list, I highly encourage you to do so, particularly in the early months. If you fear being judged for outsourcing (as many of my clients do), remember that often the judgment we think we will get from others for doing something a certain way is just an old voice in our head. Even if it is real, the sting of that judgment will likely pale in comparison to the relief you will feel with the added support.

Sample Checklist: Things To Do In A Day ✓

- Cleaning
- Laundry
- Getting groceries
- Preparing meals and snacks
- Feeding your child(ren) and self
- Bathing child(ren)
- Bathing yourself
- Setting up appointments
- Running errands
- Handling paperwork/bills/banking, etc.
- Cleaning breast pump supplies and parts
- Stocking up on things you know you will need, such as diapers, wipes, or formula
- Gathering/packing supplies for childcare
- Sleeping
- Exercising
- Alone time (to do whatever you want, even simply sitting in a room alone!)
- Bonding time with baby
- Bonding time with partner

What Does a Fair Division of Labor Even Mean (and How Can We Achieve It)?

If you are part of a couple, one of your tasks in this touchpoint is to embrace that you are a team and advocate for equitable distribution of new responsibilities. This means making choices about how you want your partnership to evolve. Being reactive will damage, rather than strengthen, your bond. When one parent is doing more than the other (or feels like it), resentment is almost inevitable. A survey conducted by Equality at Home shows that over one-third of respondents thought their relationship could be transformed by learning how to better share the mental load (35%) and household chores (33%).[1]

Couples who figure out how to communicate well and work together *fairly* to tackle the demands of working parenthood are more successful overall and are less likely to separate or divorce. That's a *big* deal. Lack of equality creates resentment and is a major driver of divorce. In heterosexual couples, the mother most frequently carries the extra work parenthood brings. This extra is called many names—mental load, second shift, emotional labor, invisible work—but they all mean the same thing: *doing more*.

Eve Rodsky is the first thinker I've seen move beyond simply naming this entrenched situation to figuring out a way to literally game the (messed-up) system. Rodsky found herself being what she brilliantly dubbed the "she-fault" parent. She told me, "I was about to lose the one thing that held my family together, my marriage. Yes, I was slightly resentful that I had to be the one to figure out a way to create a systemic shift for us, but that was nothing when compared to the growing resentment I felt for being the one whose work on behalf of our family wasn't being valued."

She turned her personal experience into *Fair Play*,[2] a revelatory book and accompanying card game for couples to play together. A series of conversation starters lets you prioritize which of the 100 specific tasks required to support a healthy family are important to *your* family, and enables you to explore each other's values to determine which jobs are better suited for whom. Then

(continued)

(*continued*)

you divide these tasks up with clarity and ease and walk away knowing who will take the lead with every chore—from diapers to laundry to dinner. (*Pro tip: play this game as you prepare to fill out the second phase of your leave plan.*)

Rodsky shared a few ground rules with me to help you get started:

The Four Rules for Fair Play

1. **All time is created equal.** You might get paid differently at work, but at home your time is equal. Dad's time is not finite, nor mom's infinite. The sooner you start valuing each other's time equally, the faster the division of labor will shift toward parity.

2. **Reclaim your right to be interesting.** Many people, both men and women, fear they will lose themselves when they have kids. This only makes it more urgent that you and your partner make time to do the things we don't feel permitted to do as busy parents—which are often the very things that have the depth to keep us interested in, and interesting to, ourselves, our partners, and our communities. One second-time mom got back into snowboarding. Another who wished she'd gotten an MFA started volunteering as a docent at her local art museum.

3. **Start where you are now.** You cannot get to where you want to go as a couple without first assessing more about who you are, who your partner is, and what your specific intention is for playing this game of life together. This assessment shows each partner what it looks like to take on full ownership of *conception, planning,* and *execution* of each card item. (I recommend you build this part of the game into the work you do for the second touchpoint in this book, *Assess.*)

4. **Establish your values and standards.** Every community has a shared set of values and traditions that guide them. You and your partner should be no different. First, define your guiding values and standards (see Chapter 13 for a values exercise to help with this and read *Fair Play!*), then draw on them to collaboratively divide the tasks that your family values.

Self-Advocacy with Your Family

Maggie gave birth early in the coronavirus pandemic when there was little information about how severe or easily transmitted the virus was or what the effects would be. No visitors were permitted in the hospital. When it was time to bring their baby home, she and her partner had to decide whether to let their closest family members come meet the new little one. Prepared for hurt feelings and judgment, they drew the line anyway and asked for no visitors. In the end, their families were gracious. "They reassured us that they would be there ready and willing as soon as a visit was possible," Maggie said.

If you're lucky enough to have a great relationship with your immediate and extended family and you cannot imagine welcoming a child without them being involved, that's truly wonderful. Many people have complicated relationships with their families and sometimes big life events like welcoming a child can add stress and strain to those relationships. Remember that this is *your* child and *your* transition. Think through the role you would like your family to play and be clear about it. This may mean a few difficult conversations, but in having them, you will ultimately strengthen those relationships.

Self-Advocacy with Your Birth Team

When you considered your birth plan back in Chapter 6, that was a form of self-advocacy. If you are welcoming a child through birth, a birth plan helps you think through your vision of how you'd like your birth experience to go. As with all the plans you make here, remember that it is only a draft and that life will invite you to learn and grow by bringing you to places you did not expect. Remember, too, that deviations from your plan are not failures on your part but the unique character of your own story asserting itself, like the irregularities in the patterns of the Navajo weavings we spoke about in Chapter 6.

A birth plan prompts you to do your research about your various birthing options (midwife, doctor, hospital, birthing center, home delivery), learn about the common practices for where you plan to deliver, and make sure you and your birthing team are on the same page philosophically well before labor begins. One client, Merriah, planned a vaginal birth after cesarean, at home with a midwife, for her second child. She spent time describing to her midwife the type of birth experience she wanted and contracting with her about what to do if they needed to deviate from her plan. Merriah did not see birth as something that would happen *to* her, but as something that was going to happen *because of* her. She was clear that she expected to be included as the primary decision-maker and treated as the powerful birthing woman she was—throughout the entire process. She spent time defining the energy she wanted the midwife to ground herself in, rather than the specifics of her plan. When they came to an aspect of her birth that was not in her plan and could have gotten scary, the advocacy and clarification Merriah had done kicked in: "At a moment when it all could have gone really wrong, the midwife instead contained the fear and worry on the side and didn't let it take away from the power of my experience. I really feel like she heard me."

As Merriah's experience shows, having a birth plan can help, though it creates no guarantees. I have heard many stories about how rigid adherence to a birth plan by the parents can contribute to their experience being unsatisfactory or even traumatic. This should not preclude you from making a plan; just keep in mind that expectations are made to be broken, and babies (and medical professionals) do not always cooperate. Create a few backup plans in case your ideal birth isn't possible due to circumstances. Think of your birth plan as a way to communicate how you want your birth to look and feel, and coach yourself in welcoming (or at least accepting) having to pivot to your backup plans or a new plan altogether. If you feel yourself tightening or getting angry or defensive in response to your birth not going to plan, that could be a sign that it is time to take a breath and reevaluate, or in some cases, it could be a sign that you need to step up and advocate more for yourself. This can be tricky because sometimes you need to let go of the plan and be flexible in the moment and other times you need to increase your self-advocacy efforts. This is the type of complexity that parenthood will give you lots of practice with. Clear conversations ahead of time will help you navigate intense moments like these.

Self-Advocacy with Your Doctor or Pediatrician

Doctors and other health care providers, like all humans, are imperfect and vulnerable to being swayed by biases (unconscious or not). Women in general and individuals from underrepresented and marginalized communities are all statistically more likely to get inferior treatment than men, particularly cisgender, straight, white men—including waiting longer for pain medication, having pain classified as psychosomatic, or having symptoms ignored that turned out to be serious.[3]

Even fame and money cannot shield you from potential bias, as the harrowing birth story of Serena Williams shows us. In 2018, the day after giving birth to her daughter, she began feeling short of breath. She alerted the medical staff that she had a history of pulmonary embolisms and advocated for very specific diagnostics and treatment (a CT scan with contrast and a blood thinner delivered by IV), but her request was initially dismissed. The nurse assumed she was confused due to her pain medication. Eventually, doctors arrived at the same conclusion as Serena: she had a pulmonary embolism.[4]

Advocating for yourself may mean asking about specific guidelines that should be followed for what you (or your child) are experiencing, requesting further explanation for a care plan (or lack thereof), and seeking a second opinion. It may mean repeating yourself until you are taken seriously.

A smart precaution is to appoint someone ahead of time who can advocate on your behalf, in the unlikely event you are not able to do so for yourself due to a mental or physical health challenge (see Chapter 16 for more information on additional challenges) related to pregnancy or birth, or even well afterward.

Self-Advocacy with Your Childcare Provider

Finding high-quality, consistent care for your child while you work is one of the most important and anxiety-provoking parts of parenthood. You and your childcare provider should be on the same page about the type of care your child is to receive. For example, if you want to make sure your child gets lots of touch, such as being worn in a baby carrier, make sure that is in line with that provider's policy or philosophy. Or if you want to make sure your baby is fed when hungry, make sure you say so (some providers are rigid about feeding according to a set schedule). Be clear and specific about your expectations.

You know yourself and your child better than anyone else in the world. Learning to trust your own gut instinct is one of the fundamental leadership lessons of this experience. You may make missteps from time to time, but working on your self-advocacy skills is never a waste of energy.

Self-Advocacy at Work

It comes as a shock to most expectant parents when they learn that their manager (like nearly all managers in the United States) is not trained on how to support their parental leave transition. Even if you have a great working relationship, this is likely unfamiliar territory for both of you, and it's up to you to advocate for yourself about your needs.

My client, Kellen, had taken just a few weeks off after the birth of his son. When his son was three months old, his partner was ready to head back to work. They had a childcare hiccup, and the timing was not lining up. Kellen was hesitant to ask for more time off, but he put together a plan that would mean no one would have to pick up his work while he remained on leave for another two weeks. His manager readily agreed.

Time and again, I see clients afraid to ask for something that would make their transition smoother and more productive because they have decided in advance that something is "against policy" or that "no one else has ever gotten that." And, time and again I see clients get exactly what they need—and more—when they muster the courage to respectfully and thoughtfully ask for it. Decide what would work for you and then build a case for why it would also work for your manager, your team, and your organization.

At work, advocating could look like reminding your manager and colleagues of your KIT strategy or letting them know you need to use a contingency plan.

Sample Scripts for Self-Advocacy at Work

Thoughtfully approach any conversation when you are advocating for yourself using the SBI method discussed previously to form your strategy. Consider ahead of time what solution will serve both parties and propose a solution based on mutual wins. Remember, striking a non-confrontational tone does not mean you come in apologizing. Self-advocacy won't automatically be taken as adversarial.

Example: meeting adjustments to accommodate breast pumping:

"I know we have that big half-day meeting coming up, and I'm really excited to see what comes out of it. I wanted to suggest that we build in a few extra breaks so I can stay on my pumping schedule. I don't want to miss any of the content, and I think such breaks will keep everyone fresher during the meeting."

Example: request to work remotely for part of the week:

"Being back at the office has been great. Everyone is really welcoming. At the same time, I have a lot to catch up on. I think I could concentrate better and clear some backlog if I could work from home on Thursdays and Fridays. Here's my plan of what I'll get done on those days [insert plan]. Can we try it for a month and see if it helps my productivity?"

Recruiting Others to Advocate for You

Sometimes, putting all the advocacy work on yourself is too much. Where it seems helpful for your circumstances, I recommend enlisting professional support. Before becoming a parent you may want the support of an adoption or fertility specialist. To support a birth, you may wish to have a midwife or birthing doula in your corner. After the birth, you may want to hire a postpartum doula to take care of household chores and the baby so you can get enough support. Some people love hiring night nurses to ensure they get enough sleep. If you are facing discrimination in a workplace or health care setting, you will want a lawyer (see Chapter 16 for resources related to discrimination and see the sidebar about childbirth advocacy). A good therapist can be a wonderful advocate at any point in your transition, especially if you experience perinatal mental health challenges. I also recommend a parental leave coach, such as my company provides, who has been trained in executive coach, doula, therapist, and consultant skills and can help you think through and advocate for yourself during all phases of your transition.

Dealing with Unsolicited Advice

Know that, for the most part, the people around you want to help you during your transition, but they don't always know the best way to do that. You will be flooded with well-intended information and advice. Learning how to navigate and distill this down to what is useful to you is an important skill. Many of us resist being told what to do. Your core values (see the values exercise in Chapter 13) can help ground you in the patience and perspective to see advice as an attempt by others to connect with you over a shared experience. *Advice is almost never about the person on the receiving end; rather, it is about the giver.* Ask yourself what difficulty they must have encountered to have feelings strong enough about the topic to offer advice, and then you can meet them in a place of gentle care and gratitude. Sometimes a simple exploratory question is the best response to unsolicited advice: "Would you be willing to tell me about the experience you had where you learned about this?"

How to Advocate for Yourself During Childbirth

Your birth experience will have a profound impact on your parental leave transition. Sadly, for many, birth doesn't always go "as planned" and in some cases can become traumatizing, especially when basic rights are violated.

Attorney Hermine Hayes-Klein became interested in how women are treated during childbirth while working overseas and giving birth to her two sons in the woman-centered Dutch maternity care system. Hayes-Klein soon learned that women's fundamental human rights are routinely violated in maternity care systems around the world. In 2012, before moving back to the United States, she organized the first global Human Rights in Childbirth conference at The Hague University. Over the next five years, she organized five more international, multi-stakeholder conferences on human rights in childbirth. A premiere expert in maternal health and childbirth law around the world, she has worked to make a foundation for herself and others to practice this emerging focus area of law.

(continued)

(*continued*)

Hayes-Klein and others advocate for the recognition of human rights in maternity care, including the right of every pregnant person to be:

- Recognized as the decision-maker about their health care throughout pregnancy, childbirth, and postpartum;
- Provided with the evidence-based information and support necessary to exercise informed consent in maternity care; and
- Treated equally, regardless of skin color, gender presentation, age, or any other quality that may cause a health care provider to manifest bias (unconscious or not) in the provision of care.

Hayes-Klein shared the following tips to help you advocate for yourself in childbirth:

1. **Know your rights.**
   a. You have the right to make all of the decisions about your care on the basis of information, advice, and support from your providers. This includes the right to refuse any offered intervention.
   b. You have the right to non-discriminatory treatment. Let your providers know at the beginning of care that you plan to exercise these rights. Get more information on your rights during childbirth at: https://www.nationalpartnership.org/our-work/resources/health-care/maternity/the-rights-of-childbearing-women.pdf.
2. **Make a birth plan.** The main message of your birth plan should be to let your providers know that your plan is to make *all* the decisions about your care *even if the birth doesn't go as planned.* The rest of your plan can outline the types of decisions you are likely to make in certain scenarios, understanding that you may change your mind in the moment. (For more on birth planning see Chapter 6 sidebar.)
3. **Hire a labor doula.** Make sure the doula you choose is willing to help protect your right of informed consent. Some labor doulas consider this outside of their scope because they wish

(*continued*)

(*continued*)

to avoid conflict. One of the main roles of a doula should be to advocate for the birthing mother. (If cost is an issue, contact a school for doulas near you. You may be able to hire a student or new doula at a reduced rate.)

4. **Interview different providers.** Trust your gut: hire a provider that makes you feel respected and safe. You are looking for someone who believes in your right to make your own decisions about your care and who will work to ensure you have the information and support your need to make those decisions.

5. **Deal with your own fear of confrontation.** If you need to, find someone you can role-play with to practice advocating for yourself in a medical setting. Remember, it is not rude to ask for what you need regarding *your* health care.

Advocate for Others by Providing Feedback on Your Leave Experience

Finally, I encourage you to share feedback with your organization about the policies, practices, and processes you experience during this time as a way to advocate for new parents who come after you. If this feels dangerous, it can be done anonymously or through a group feedback mechanism, such as an anonymous survey or a simple anonymous note to someone in HR.

Leadership Lessons of Parenthood

Advocating

Many people avoid conflict at all costs, so the idea of advocating for themselves can feel dangerous. Becoming a parent will present you with countless opportunities to shift your mindset

(*continued*)

(*continued*)

toward understanding that advocacy is not conflict; rather, it is *integrity* and *clarity*. Being able to recognize when to take a stand and having the courage to initiate difficult conversations, all while staying steadfast and calm, is a gift to yourself and those around you. Mastering this skill will also help you maximize your assets, minimize liabilities, and ensure your needs are understood and prioritized. Advocating will protect you from derailment and sabotage that might stand in the way of your successful parental leave transition and future as a working parent.

Here are a few of the *whole-person leadership* skills you'll be practicing during this touchpoint:

- Honoring your needs (and the needs of your loved ones)
- Modeling integrity
- Regulating emotions
- Initiating and engaging in courageous conversations
- Communicating clearly and calmly
- Taking a stand

Chapter
Eleven

Touchpoint 7
Arrangements for Return

In CHAPTER 6, I walked you through how to plan for your return to work as part of your original leave plan. I love to say: *the best way to prepare for leave is to plan your return.* Planning for your return reminds everyone that you do, in fact, intend to return. When you create an *ideal* plan with clear expectations and transparent intentions prior to your parental leave, all parties will be better positioned for your smooth reentry.

Now we are going to leap forward in time and talk about what to do when it is actually time for you to return to work, enriched by the new information and experience that comes with the arrival of your new child. You may find that you want or need to do something different from what you outlined in your original plan, or you may find your plan still works perfectly. Either way, this touchpoint highlights the importance of noticing your new circumstances and thoughtfully reconsidering (and, for many, rewriting or renegotiating) your return arrangements through the eyes of a new parent.

Sometimes clients get confused when I tell them they may need to throw out all the careful planning I urged them to do in the first place. This is not a contradiction, but a paradox that I urge you to embrace.

When I introduced this concept to a client whose background is in the military, he understood immediately. He shared an insight from former president Eisenhower, who was also an Army general: "In preparing for battle, I have always found that plans are useless, but planning is indispensable."[1] Planning before your child comes prepares you to adapt deftly and quickly when those plans won't actually work.

Revising Your Return-to-Work Plan

As we all know, even after a long weekend—let alone weeks or months—it can be hard to get one's head back into the work world. An extended time away can be unsettling for everyone. You will make version 2.0 of your return plan a couple weeks before you go back to work, once you have a clearer idea of what you need with your new child in your life. This update should include any adjustments, clarifications, or necessary changes to the plan you submitted prior to going on leave—such as doing a phased-back return, working reduced hours, or working remotely. If you are proposing substantial changes to the original plan, consider framing your return arrangements as an experiment, something to try for a number of weeks or months and then revisit with your manager and team.

Just as you had the right to change your mind about how to communicate while on leave, you can adjust the details of how you will return. During the planning stage, my client Stacey was planning to take her maximum (unpaid) leave time as allowed by FMLA. However, after several weeks at home with her baby, two things became apparent to her. She was running out of money, and more important, the upcoming shift from being home every day with her baby to working 40 hours per week away from her child for over 9 hours per day was more than she could bear to think about.

A quick call to her boss ironed it all out. She would return to work sooner than planned but would work only Mondays, Wednesdays, and Fridays, taking her FMLA intermittently until her leave hours were used up. "I figured that no matter how bad a day was for either me or my baby, we'd always have the next day to recover together." This worked beautifully for Stacey and allowed her to ramp back up to full time—and her boss was delighted to have her back early.

You may want challenging projects immediately on return from leave, or you may prefer to transition back in with less critical assignments. Don't assume you do not have a choice in the matter. If you can make the case that your wants are consistent with organizational needs, you should feel comfortable asking for them. (This is a harder ask if that synergy is not there. However, keep in mind that ultimately, suppressing your own needs is never good long term for the organization as a whole or you.)

As with all changes, talk to your manager and then update all your stakeholders with your new return plan. (And, don't forget to make sure your chosen childcare provider has availability for your new plan, too.)

Your revised plan will need to be shared, prior to your return, with the same people copied on your original plan. Keep in mind your return will be a transition for your family, manager, and team as well. This is an opportunity for you to model a thoughtful, gracious, and professional return to work that is considerate of your needs and also the needs of those around you.

Where to Start?

An easy place to start is by dusting off your original return plan and taking a look at how you outlined picking your work back up using the TASCARS method. As you read it, think about anything that has changed (at work or home) during your leave and how those changes might affect the tasks and role transfer back to you. In the same way you did before your leave, use the TASCARS method to update how and when work tasks should be transferred back to you, the stakeholders affected, and the conversations or actions that need to happen.

TASCARS: Returning from Leave

Tasks	**A**ccountability	**S**takeholders	**C**onversations and **A**ctions	**R**esources	**S**tatus
What tasks need to be transferred back to you?	Who are you transferring your tasks from and what other considerations should be made?	Which stakeholders are impacted?	What conversations and/or actions are needed to facilitate the task transfer and by when?	What resources are available to assist with the task transfer? (i.e., contacts, supporting documents, etc.)	What is the status of your task handover? (Update this section as needed.)

I gave you a hypothetical example in Chapter 6 to explain how to use the TASCARS process for off-boarding. I created an imaginary teammate named Alex who was taking over your team's yearly report update for you. Let's pick it up again here and say that even though in your off-boarding plan you set it up that you would go back full time right away, you have now decided you would like to ease back in on a flexible schedule. Given that adjustment, you will not have the bandwidth to take back that full task you had given to Alex of compiling the yearly report. Today you identified a solution when you looked at the task breakdown on your TASCARS grid: ask your manager if it would be OK for Alex to keep the information-gathering part of that task, and you resume the actual writing and submitting of the update. This is a way to reduce your tasks while keeping your contributions visible. It also enables you to mentor and set Alex up to take the full yearly report task over completely someday when you are promoted.

Being part of a new parent's coverage team can be hard. Most likely your colleagues will be adding your work to their already-full plates. Let them know how much you appreciate their support. A handwritten card or small gift can go far to show you mean it.

Include any changes or adjustments to your ideal return plan from Chapter 6 into your revised return plan. Then schedule time to share the finalized plan with your manager and team roughly a week before your return. If that is not possible, set up a time on your first day back.

General Considerations: Arrangements for Returning to Work

- Are your return date and working hours still acceptable to you? If not, what would you prefer?
- Do you need to reconsider any decisions you made about flexible work arrangements for your return? For example, a ramping-up strategy that includes a buildup of days in your return (like starting back two days a week and increasing gradually) may look more attractive than it did when you made your original plan. Remember, just because something was not specifically offered does not mean it is out of the question. Make the case and ask for it.

- Are there any internal workplace resources that you can research more or tap into, now that you are about to return to work?
- If you learned during leave that you are returning to a different role, do you need clarity about its responsibilities or parameters before your first day back? If so, whom should you talk to about this?
- If you were on leave during your annual review process, alert your manager. Review your goals and objectives and set a time for your discussion.
- As it gets closer, should you reconsider what you arranged for your immediate reentry support? Think about what would enable you to have an effective reentry to the workplace and then put those supports in place. For example, would you like to take back your work in phases?
- Is there anything you'd like your manager/team/colleagues to do or know that is different from when you left to help them prepare for your return?
- Now that you are getting closer to your return, in what ways can you make any new details of your reentry and reuptake of your tasks explicit?
- Think carefully about how your return may affect those who have covered for you while you are on leave. How can you honor the extra work they did to support you while you were away?
- Is there anything that needs to be set up or adjusted before your return to notify clients, providers, or other external stakeholders of your return?
- Consider asking your manager for a "return-to-work buddy" to get you up to speed on any work changes. Decide if you would like that to be someone with or without children. A fellow parent will understand what you are going through. A non-parent who gets a close look at what working parents are up against may become an ally.
- How can tech help facilitate your reentry? For example, if you will be working part time or partially from home, does your email signature clearly express your working days or indicate when you are working from home?
- Do you need to reschedule any meetings you put on the calendar with your manager to support the early days of your return? Should you add some manager meetings in your first few weeks back to gain feedback, problem-solve, and/or monitor how you are doing? (I recommend short weekly meetings the first month back.)

- Have any new regular meetings been put in place at work that will conflict with any of your new routines or boundaries? Have you thought about what strategies you would like to put in place to handle early-morning or late-afternoon meetings, group outings, and so on?

- If applicable, schedule time on your calendar for pumping. Identify the lactation room and/or request a lock for your office door or other private space.

- If you need to work off-site, are there lactation facilities at regular client sites, or do you need alternative solutions?

- If breastfeeding and leakages occur, do you have a spare top and bra packed up that you can change into?

- If applicable, have you reviewed your work wardrobe? If your body shape has changed, you may need to find new clothes for work. If you have given birth, check your work shoes—feet often change sizes.

- Do you know whether you will need to travel for work? If so, what arrangements are in place for the overnight care of your child(ren)? Have you done a test run or two? The value of test runs cannot be overstated.

- If you are pumping and need to travel, the logistics can be tough. Test your travel pump, research options to ship milk home to your child (try www.milkstork.com), and see if your airport or destination has a nursing room or pumping pod (such as those found through https://www.mamava.com/find-mamava).

Return Logistics

When you made your ideal leave and return plan (Chapter 6) I asked you to think through all of the little things that you needed to include in your plan to make things run smoothly. For some people that may have involved actions such as deactivating cell phones or security cards. For others it might have meant putting certain certifications or registrations on hold. It may have meant handing over access to a company car or turning in your laptop. Save yourself stress on your first day back by thinking through everything that you put on hold or deactivated during your leave that needs to be put back in place.

Tips for Breastfeeding at Work

If you've chosen breastfeeding (also known as chestfeeding and bodyfeeding, terms that recognize trans and nonbinary parents as well as the whole-body experience it is to provide human milk for a baby), you know that like parenting itself, it can be a source of joy and stress. Most of my clients feel that stress most at two points: when establishing breastfeeding and when returning to work.

Jada Shapiro is a reproductive health expert in New York City and the founder of *boober* (www.getboober.com), a company through which expectant and new parents can access virtual lactation support and find classes and on-demand care providers from pregnancy through postpartum. She shared these tips with me to help make your back-to-work breastfeeding more successful and less stressful.

Before You Return

- Begin building a stash of milk three to four weeks before your return.
- Make sure you introduce a bottle to your baby well before the day you go back to work. You may have to try a few!

When You Pump at Work

- During the hours they spend at work, lactating parents should pump about as many times as they would during that interval if they were nursing or pumping at home. For most people, this means two to four times in a workday.
- Give yourself 15–20 minutes to pump, plus at least 5 minutes to set up and 5 minutes to clean up.
- Invite relaxation and think about your baby right before you pump. Smelling a baby blanket and/or watching a cute video of your baby can help.

What to Watch Out For

- Know your workplace rights for your state. You can find them here:
  - https://www.dol.gov/agencies/whd/nursing-mothers/faq
  - http://www.usbreastfeeding.org/workplace-law

(continued)

(*continued*)

- You do not have to do this alone! A lactation consultant can help prepare a nursing/pumping/feeding plan that works for you and your baby.
- Sometimes babies will want to nurse more at night when their parent returns to work. Called reverse cycling, this is a great way to keep milk supply and cuddles up, but it can be exhausting!
- Skipping pumping sessions or not pumping for as long as you need to is the quickest way to reduce your milk supply. Both could lead to clogged ducts and mastitis (painful inflammation or infection of the breast tissue). If you are often on the go or in lengthy meetings, consider a wireless, wearable breast pump.

Arrangements at Home for Your Return to Work

There are also many moving parts to consider at home. Although taking this first step toward your return can feel hard, your new beginning is an opportunity to (re)define your working parent self. How do you want this next phase of your life to look and feel?

General Considerations: Arrangements at Home for Your Return to Work

- Do you have a childcare provider and strategy in place for your return? Don't forget to make contingency plans, too.
- Put your childcare plan in place and do a few practice runs, including time at the provider to ensure it is a good fit before finalizing your plans. Remember the impact on any older children as well.
- If applicable, have you agreed with your childcare provider and partner on a plan to manage drop-offs and pickups of your child(ren)? Be sure to familiarize yourself with any late fee policies.
- Do you have an emergency backup plan in place for when your child is sick? In two-parent households it can work to alternate who leaves work if the child is sick or determine which parent has a more flexible situation. Whatever you choose, make it explicit.
- Have you scheduled "getting settled" days for your child to start getting used to the care arrangements and care provider before you return to work?

- Have you considered questions about routines, including nutrition and behavior management, to ensure consistency for your child(ren)? This will be especially important if care is being provided by family members or a nanny, rather than a daycare, which will follow a consistent protocol.
- Have you scheduled some "me time" into your calendar, incorporating exercise, relaxation, creative work/practice, or hobbies?
- Have you had a conversation with anyone sharing in household/ domestic duties about rebalancing of roles and responsibilities? As mentioned in the last chapter, it may be helpful to determine which tasks are critical *and* which can be done by someone else.
- Have you thought about how you can consolidate work and home calendars in a way that works for you, your family, and those supporting you at home (scheduling apps, synced calendars)?
- If you move frequently between work and parenting time, it can be useful to think about ways to disengage from work to be wholly present with your child. This might mean planned activities or simple rituals to mark the start of your time together (a secret handshake with an older child, a nose nuzzle and forehead kiss with your newborn, etc.).
- If applicable, have you planned for some quality time with your partner, such as scheduling date nights? Your calendar can be a useful tool to ensure consistent focus and attention on cultivating what matters most to you as well as ways that you want to grow. (We will delve into this and a specific values exercise in Chapter 13.) Remember, you need to practice the habits you've chosen to focus on in order to sustain the life you want to build.
- Are there any areas that may need extra planning? (For example, if your child is not sleeping through the night, and now you will be working, how will you cover nighttime caregiving? Are there any weaning issues that should be considered?)
- Sometimes the transition to work and away from a child can create separation anxiety (for the child and also for the parent). What support do you have in place to help you through this time (friends, relatives, colleagues, therapist, parents' group, extra buffer time, etc.)?
- Is there any additional information you need in order to be comfortable disengaging from full-time parenthood and returning to work?

Helping Older Kids Through Their Own Transitions

If you have older children, it is important to make time to help them adjust to this transition. Notice signs of distress and engage in conversation and play activities to help prepare them to be an older sibling and to separate from you more easily when you return to work.

Start by being aware of your *own* worries about returning to work and separating from your children. It can help to notice all the parts of your transition you are looking forward to and follow these tips:

- **Listen.** Children may be aware but unable to articulate the worries they feel, first about meeting their new sibling, and then later when you return to work. Make time to listen— feeling heard helps ease anticipatory anxiety as they adapt and embrace their exciting new family life and their new big sibling role.

- **Communicate in an age-appropriate way.** Once you understand their concerns about going back to school/childcare, it can help to walk them through a play-by-play of what their day will be like. Point out things that will be different and emphasize things that will be the same to build in some reassurance.

- **Choose quality over quantity.** Dedicate time exclusively focused on older children each day (even just 10 minutes). This one-on-one time maintains a direct connection when your attention is scattered, so emphasize quality time when you cannot afford quantity.

- **Let them know they are important and needed.** Give your older child opportunities to help with their new sibling *and* the transition back to work. Role-play ways they can participate. Put them in charge of something they can be proud of, such as putting diapers in the bag or lining up coats at the door. Acknowledge their contribution to

(continued)

(continued)
   let them feel needed and valued as the big sibling and big
   helper they are.
- **Stay steady, knowing this moment will pass.** Be flexible and
   patient with your older child as they adapt to their new situation. Older kids can experience a full range of emotions over
   the arrival of a new member of the family. They may act out
   or experience behavioral regression such as tantrums or sleep
   issues while finding their fit within the new family structure.
   Try not to give these new behaviors too much attention; just
   move on matter-of-factly. If they continue, enlist the help of
   a parent support specialist.

Arrange for Self-Care

Self-care can look different for everyone. At its core, self-care is about
doing things that strengthen you. It could mean that instead of *adding*
something to your plate you are *removing* things that are unimportant
or don't align with your values. Self-care is about being authentic to
yourself and your needs. You will be better able to know what you need
when you get enough sleep, so make sleep your top self-care priority—
especially if your new child is an infant (more on sleep later). Self-care
is not a substitute for the systemic change that is needed in our country
to properly support new parents. In the meantime, however, nobody
wins at work or at home if we don't get decent sleep, good nutrition,
exercise, and some time to think our thoughts uninterrupted. Self-care
is *not* selfish, it is a basic requirement for a healthy life.

General Considerations for Self-Care

- How can you make home care help a priority (such as asking family and friends to bring nourishing food, get some help cleaning,
   automate bills, have groceries delivered, etc.)?
- How can you put in place and use any working parent benefits
   you have access to through work and other avenues (employee
   resource group, online parenting group, therapist, religious community, lactation consultant, etc.)?

- Do you have any health and hygiene appointments that can be scheduled in advance (dental, ob/gyn, exercise, hair, nails, massage, etc.)?
- Where and when can you carve out time to be alone in whatever way recharges you: tinkering on a project, meditation, journaling, reading, and so on?

To help you keep track of all of the moving parts of this time, use the new parent checklist available at https://www.cplleadership.com/playbook.

Leadership Lessons of Parenthood

Arrangements for Return

Effective *whole-person leadership* requires understanding that plans are made to be changed—so try not to get too attached to them. The developmental opportunity of this touchpoint is to practice letting go of the desire to control, which is based in fear, and welcoming, with a curious mind, whatever comes to replace your "perfect" plan. This release and acceptance are the opposite of giving up; they are a form of courage that demands agility rooted in faith that things will work out. Letting go of the desire to control may also require you to ask for help and will likely entail juggling competing demands.

Here are just a few of the *whole-person leadership* skills you'll be practicing during this touchpoint:

- Taking a leap of faith
- Letting go of the idea of perfection
- Practicing agility
- Acting with courage
- Pivoting to contingency plans
- Asking for help
- Juggling competing demands

PHASE THREE
Returning from Leave

* * *

Working Parent Focus

Chapter Twelve

Phase 3: Returning from Leave Overview

WHEN LAILA AND her wife welcomed a baby girl, her wife returned to work after just a few weeks. Laila maxed out her leave and planned to place baby Rae at a daycare center a few blocks from her office building. The week before she went back to work, Laila brought Rae into the center for a tour and orientation. Afterward, the manager of the center suggested that Laila leave Rae in the infant room while she went across the street to get a cup of coffee. Laila froze. The thought of leaving her baby, even for the time it took to go to Starbucks, filled her with dread. The manager gently persisted, and Laila successfully left Rae for 20 minutes to get a latte. She worked out a system with the manager to leave Rae for longer and longer increments, until soon Laila was able to leave her in their capable hands as she returned to work (though she never missed a lunchtime visit).

The experience of moving out of your leave and back into work is a life-changing transition of similar magnitude as when you began your leave. Although it is rarely given that same level of recognition in our culture, you will benefit from giving this phase equal care and attention.

The first touchpoint of this phase focuses on the self-reflection and inner work required for you to **acknowledge** all that you have learned in your transition so far and how that growth has influenced who you are and what you want now, as you head back into work. In the second touchpoint of this phase, I will ask you to think about how you will put what you have learned into action as you prepare for the twists and turns of your **adjustment** over the months after your return. In the last touchpoint of this phase (and of this book), you will turn your attention to your long-term career goals and how to build in **access** to ongoing career development to successfully and sustainably continue building your career.

10A Transition Touchpoints Framework™ Phase 3

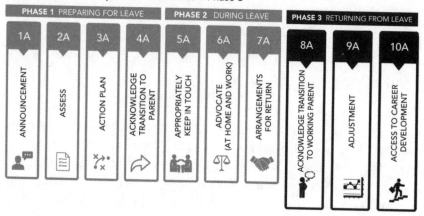

There are a few concepts that are important to outline as we begin this phase. We will start with what is often referred to as *work-life conflict* or *interference*. In preparing for leave during the first phase of their parental leave transition, many working people believe that they will be able to successfully combine work and family with little or no difficulty. However, the transformative change inspired by this major life transition, coupled with a lack of understanding and support at organizational and societal levels, can threaten many new working parents' assumptions about their place in the world. As you return to work, your preconceived ideas about working parenthood will likely be tested.

Your One Whole Life

The language we use for the interplay of the various elements of our lives—terms such as *work-life conflict* and *work-home interference*—can make it sound like work and life are two separate things, destined always to be at odds with each other. I find it more accurate and useful to think of our lives as being rich and full of various spheres of interest that are fluid in terms of size and importance. At times they take the shape of a Venn diagram and the spheres overlap, enhance, and build off each other. Sometimes, they are more like a bouquet of balloons, touching up on each other and sharing space or moving around in the bouquet but not combining. Our lives are not made up of perfectly separate spheres—what happens in one part can often spill over into or move in front of another. This often creates competition for our limited time, energy, and resources, which can feel like a conflict or an interference. Prolonged interference can take a toll on individuals, organizations, and society as a whole. When our spheres are integrating well and supporting each other, we can find harmony and use our energy for better things than dealing with conflict. Unfortunately, finding that sweet spot of integration and support is not a given for working parents.

Recent research shows that the conflicts and costs of parenthood are rising and catching many people off guard—particularly college-educated women who have worked hard to have a career and expected and planned to be able to become a mother without too much impact on their work lives.[1] They set these expectations in large part because they grew up being told that equity was coming and that they would be able to have it all by "balancing" work and home life.

The unrealistic expectation that parents give their all both at work and at home affects all families. At the same time, these expectations have an outsized impact on single-parent households (predominantly run by single moms) and female same-sex couples. Men face narrow, gendered role expectations in our society as well. They are still expected to bring home the bacon at the expense of being the involved caregivers many of them want or need to be and they may be stigmatized for choosing an alternate route. Until we allow and expect dads to take their full parental leave, and do the work of long-term caregiving on equal footing with women, moms will continue to shoulder that burden. Under those conditions, women cannot achieve equality in pay or level of role and authority.

Work-Life Conflict

Work-life conflict (sometimes called *work-life interference* or *work-family conflict*) is defined in the academic literature, roughly, as *the pressures from work and life demands being mutually incompatible to the point that meeting the demands in one area makes it difficult to meet the demands in the other.* More colloquially: when you have something going on at work or at home that makes it feel impossible to get done what you need to in the other sphere.

Take a moment to think about where you experience work-life conflict. Frequent examples include missing children's school activities for work commitments, not having time to cook the nutritious meals you want to feed yourself and your family, missing out on social events, or passing up that interesting project because it requires more travel than you can handle.

Symptoms of work-life conflict include stress, mental and physical exhaustion (for some to the point of complete overwhelm, even burnout), an inability to switch on and off between work and home, and for many, a loud and critical inner voice. Researchers are citing a relatively new contributing factor to this increased interference between work and home: *telepressure*, or the inability to stay away from your work-related emails, texts, voicemails, and other notifications no matter what you are doing and who you are with. I'm sure you have experienced it, because let's be real—who hasn't?

Pressures can spill over from any of our various spheres of life to interfere with the others. After a rough day at work, we take that bad feeling home with us and end up snapping at our partner. Or, going through a rough patch or up all night at home, we find ourselves dozing off in a meeting or being scatterbrained because we have taken that distraction and exhaustion to work with us. The interference most people experience between work and home can increase dramatically in Phase 3.

These issues are so massive and systemic that they will not be solved in your child's early years. However, you can learn to navigate better and buffer yourself and your family as much as possible from the impacts of this larger societal issue. One way to do this is to deliberately focus your attention on the places where you can have a positive impact. Touchpoint 9, which is all about adjustment, offers some ideas about how to do that.

Work-Life Enrichment

The flip side to work-life conflict is work-life enrichment (also called *work-family integration* or *work-home enrichment*). Research in this field explores the extent to which your experiences in one role *improve* the quality of life in your other role(s).

Work-Life Challenges & Opportunities

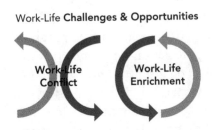

Although much of the academic and public press focus has been on work-life conflict and its negative spillover, a growing body of research suggests that fulfilling a variety of roles can also have many benefits (positive spillover). There are emotional elements of negative and positive spillover; a good mood from a great day at work can come home with you and a good night's rest can make everything easier at work.[2] Focusing on framing your experience on positive spillover and the leadership lessons you are accumulating will make every day feel easier and more meaningful.

The late Supreme Court Justice Ruth Bader Ginsburg illustrated this point beautifully: "My success in law school, I have no doubt, was due in large measure to baby Jane, my daughter. . . Each part of my life provided respite from the other and gave me a sense of proportion that classmates trained only on the law lacked."[3]

In other words, her ability to excel and her professional success came *because of* insights and strategies she gained as a parent, not *in spite of* having to split her time between family and her studies. Anything you learn in one sphere of your life has the potential to apply and enrich your experience in another. This is one of your biggest areas to leverage as a working parent!

In the next two chapters, I will help you acknowledge the realities of work-life conflict and where you may be affected. I'll ask you to notice whether you like to integrate or separate your work and home spheres or prefer a middle ground that has both happening at once. Then I'll focus on ways to create healthy boundaries between work and home that increase positive spillover.

Self-Efficacy and Self-Evaluation

During this returning to work phase of your transition, it is important to cultivate your skills in self-evaluation and self-efficacy (your belief in your own ability to succeed at accomplishing specific goals and tasks). Having an appreciation for your own unique perspective, skills, and talents will help you form your new working-parent identity (your 6-S self-assessment from Chapter 5 will guide you here). Your ability to assess how your transition is going will help you make the macro- and micro-adjustments that will be continually needed throughout Phase 3 and beyond, as your child reaches new developmental stages and you progress in your career.

You may not know what kind of parenting identity you want to embody (free-range or attachment parenting, strict or permissive, etc.) and perhaps you may not pick just one or simply don't want to attach a label to what you do. While you are figuring yourself out as a parent, you will also be reestablishing your professional identity, and these two aspects of your life can have spillover effects on each other. However, having to figure out "who you are" in several areas of your life at once can feel like a genuine identity crisis. In response to this identity "threat," you may feel the need to prove your value as an employee and strive ever harder to conform to the image of an "ideal worker." Self-evaluation and a growth mindset can help you avoid experiencing this transition as a crisis state.

Phase 3 can feel a bit like the first day of school—challenging and exciting. I'll guide you through ways to ground yourself in your values, make use of your assets, and create boundaries that will set you up to thrive in this next phase of your life. I recommend that you read the next three chapters before your child arrives to help you prepare both practically and emotionally. Then come back to them when you are about to return to work, revising the plans you made through the lens of your new role(s) and expanded life experience.

Chapter
Thirteen

Touchpoint 8
Acknowledge the Transition to Working Parent

JUST AS WHEN you paused in Phase 1 to acknowledge your transition *out* of work and into parenthood, this touchpoint exists to remind you of how important it is to pause again as you *return* to work. You are moving to the next phase in your transition: becoming a working parent. This is the counterpoint of the self-reflection and life prioritization work you did in Touchpoint 4, and you will benefit in direct proportion to the attention you give it.

Although congratulations are in order with your return to work, this can also be an incredibly emotional time—remember the ups and downs of the emotional journey in Chapter 3, as you left work? Whether you are a new mom or dad, walking through those (figurative or literal) doors again is not always simple.

Taneka was just a few days away from returning to work when she woke up in the middle of the night, not because her baby needed to be fed but because she was sobbing in her sleep and it startled her awake. Another client, Jim, found he was angry that returning to work so soon meant that he felt less skilled about caring for his baby than his wife and he found himself acting out in ways that were harming their connection (and which he expected would leak out at work as well).

163

Just so you don't think it is all tears and anger, another client, Isabel, found so much joy and fulfillment in her work (and loved the predictability of her workdays) that she literally threw herself a going-back-to-work party. She invited her best friends to a celebratory brunch. She had a cake decorated with tiny briefcases, laptops, and "Congratulations Isabel!" She even gave herself two wrapped gifts: a new work bag and shoes. She was so excited to get back to a part of herself she missed that she wanted to sing it from the mountaintops.

Wherever you land on this spectrum is normal. Your emotional journey to parenthood won't follow any script—you get to write your own. That said, this momentous life change means a wide range of human emotions (positive and negative) that can only be stuffed down for so long before they leak out, one way or another. Although our impulse is often to try to put emotion aside and get to work (either "grin and bear it" or stay professional and not let our joy shine), allowing yourself space to experience the full range of feelings that come up when returning to work can help you process them faster and ease your transition.

It is a good time to put your emotions in context. Most every emotion is healthy, even those that feel unfamiliar or big. Keep in mind that being sad does not necessarily mean you have postpartum depression (which can affect women and men, birthing or not), being worried does not necessarily mean clinical anxiety, and experiencing something that goes differently than the way you planned does not always equal trauma or create PTSD (though it can). That said, if you are questioning whether your emotions are normal, that is the only justification you need to reach out for support from an expert (and be sure to schedule and attend all of your health care visits). Good self-care includes regular perinatal mental health screenings, so you can give clear information to your health care provider and advocate for yourself if extra support is warranted. (See Chapter 16 for more information on perinatal mood and anxiety disorders and places to get help.) I ask all my clients to take this screening monthly (and sometimes more frequently), regardless of how they *say* they are doing. Outsized feelings are par for the course, suffering is not.

You Are New and Improved

Phase 3 is all about integrating your old and new roles into your working parent identity, and this touchpoint acknowledges that this change is a big deal. Although you may look much the same to others, you likely *feel* very different. One client echoed what I hear from many others: "I was definitely emotional after having my baby and that was unfamiliar to me. In so many ways, I feel like a different person now." It's important to find ways to process everything you have been through—even the good stuff—whether that means journaling or talking with a friend or therapist.

The emotional challenges waiting for you when you get back to work might include lack of confidence, resentment of new constraints, guilt about being away from your child (and maybe even guilt about *not* feeling guilty!), and feeling overwhelmed.

You will encounter many opportunities as well. How will you redefine yourself as a working parent? What have you learned from parenthood that you can bring to your work world? What can you learn from working that you want to bring back to your parenting?

One of the gifts of this unpredictable time is that everything is thrown up in the air and you get to choose which new habits you'd like to form. First, however, you need to be clear on your values so you can create habits that will help you live them.

Exercise: Identify Your Guiding Constellation of Values

As you pause, however briefly, to acknowledge your transition to working parenthood and all the changes it has brought in your life, getting clear on what is most important to you will help you navigate your return from a values-led place, rather than being in reaction mode. Ideally, you will identify your guiding values *before* you make your three-phase action plan prior to going on leave. Doing so will enable you to ensure your values serve as the foundation for that plan and beyond. I invite you to grab a notebook or use the worksheet at www.cplleadership.com/playbook.

Imagine the five values that guide your life (or that you wish guided your life). Maybe compassion, loyalty, success, teamwork, and adventure are most important to you. Or maybe you value truth, tradition, family, financial security, and authenticity. Write down the words that come to you. (For inspiration, review the list of possible values in Appendix 1.)

Now, circle your top three values and brainstorm some ways to honor them and integrate them into your daily life. For example, if family is a value, your daily life may include dinner together, story time, and, if you share parenting with a partner, time with them once your child is asleep.

The most powerful part of this exercise is being conscious about your values and intentional about how to live them in your daily life. Put them in writing and post them somewhere you can refer to often. Urgent things will always arise to crowd out important things. This is one way to remind yourself of your key values and find ways to advocate for and prioritize them.

Identify Your Shadow Values

Sometimes, a value may be important to us and affect our behavior and choices even though we don't admit it or even realize it. In her book *Optimal Outcomes: Free Yourself from Conflict at Work, at Home, and in Life,* Dr. Jennifer Goldman-Wetzler defines the concept of *shadow values* as those we implicitly learn and often hide because society gives us mixed messages about them.[1] They vary from person to person according to upbringing, home life, cultural influences, and other factors. Frugality or competitiveness might be a shadow value for you but an overt, ideal value for someone else. These values can conflict with our explicit, expressed values and cause us to act in ways that increase conflict in daily life.

For the purposes of setting up your new life as a working parent, your shadow values can be as important to identify as your ideal values. Much of the work-life conflict my clients feel comes from tension between (and guilt over) their values about parenting and their values about work.

Goldman-Wetzler told me, "Becoming aware of your shadow values is not particularly difficult to do. Think of what you value but are not comfortable *saying* you value." Once you have identified some values you hold but are not proud of, Goldman-Wetzler recommends spending some time exploring tensions that exist between your ideal values and your shadow values. Maybe you have an ideal value of honoring family time and a shadow value of loving recognition at work. This may cause tension if a big project creates an opportunity for recognition but interferes with family time. Now you can deploy what Goldman-Wetzler calls the *both/and* principle. Look for ways that these two values can coexist. Desire to shine at work doesn't mean you cannot also honor family time, though perhaps you'll need to make some temporary adjustments to meet the needs of your big project.

If you have a partner, it can help to think about and discuss their shadow values and how your set of shared values—both ideal and shadow—might play out during this transition (this is a great complement to the *Fair Play* discussion from Chapter 7).

Reframing

The number one thing you can ask yourself to help reframe the challenges and difficulties of working parenthood is *how can I make this an opportunity to learn and grow?* This question helps release work-life conflict and shift to work-life enrichment.

When Sharone went back to work she quickly became frustrated that she had to pick up her baby before a daycare late fee kicked in, which meant leaving the office at five p.m. Yes, she really wanted to see her baby, but she missed her old role of office savior when she could stay late to address urgent issues. We worked on reframing this limitation. "What will happen if you're not there to save the day?" I asked. "Someone else will have to step up," she said. "Is there any benefit to that?" I asked. "I guess it will make the team stronger if it's not just me cleaning up messes." She was able to recast her frustration as an opportunity to improve her team dynamics. She also admitted to herself that workplace heroism wasn't as fulfilling as being present for her family.

Some of my clients find it useful to track their growth in a way they can easily reference. Take a moment and divide some paper (or a spreadsheet) into two columns: *Learning* and *Rocking*. In the left column track your emerging lessons from your transition and in the right column list all the things you are doing well. Move things from the Learning column to the Rocking column as you gain confidence in that area. When the going gets tough you can go back over this list and feel the tangible benefits of what you are going through as you develop and grow.

Other Tips to Help You Acknowledge the Transition

Here are a few more ways you can slow down and acknowledge your new role as a working parent:

- Adopt a growth mindset that focuses on learning as you go while you figure out what works for you. Be gentle with yourself as you find your way in your dual role of working parent to this child. Nobody is an expert right away.
- Commit to ongoing self-care during this major personal and professional adjustment. Decide what is restorative for you and schedule it.
- Add buffer time into your day as you transition between work and home. This can help you move between roles without bringing any unintended emotional carryover with you and be present where you are.

Reflection Questions

The transition to working parenthood can be exciting and overwhelming. Pausing for a few moments to acknowledge the significance of this major life and career transition—the practical and emotional pieces—is an important part of leading your leave.

Reflect on how you can use this time to start fresh and define the future you want. For most people, becoming a successful working parent requires the mindset shift that I have been referencing throughout the book. I've seen a pattern among my clients: those who take up the inner work and adopt a growth mindset approach to working parenthood buffer themselves from getting locked into outdated or undesirable positions and identities. They embrace the complexities of new roles with curiosity and excitement and can see possibilities instead of getting stuck. This is crucial because it is the human condition to freeze in the face of the unknown and work from our lizard brains, which are good at *either/or* and *yes/no* thinking but not evolved enough for the *both/and* thinking that will serve you as a working parent.

(continued)

* How would you like to define yourself going forward?
* Have any of your core values or priorities shifted now that you are a parent to this child? If so, how?
* What have you learned during your leave transition that you can bring with you as you develop your skills as a working parent?
* What assumptions do you hold now? Reflect on them and rewrite them as fact-based statements. Example: *I assume that my boss would not be open to me working a more flexible schedule. In fact, I haven't asked her yet, so I don't know.*
* What are your current assets and liabilities? (It can help to run through another 6S assessment as you did in Chapter 5.)

Another Letter (or Two or Three)

Just as you wrote a few letters to acknowledge the transition to parenthood, it can be helpful to write a few more now, as you prepare to head back to work. Many of my clients write another letter to their child to share how they are feeling about the impending separation. If something about your recent experience is wonderful, troubling, or you simply keep thinking about it, take pen to paper and write a letter or journal about it.

One woman wrote, "I was questioned often about postpartum depression following my daughter's birth. What they didn't understand is that I was mourning the loss of my ideal birth. It was a traumatic birth experience followed by weeks of complications. I knew from the start that this would be my only child, and I would never get the birth experience I wanted." She shared that once she wrote it down it felt like a weight lifted, and although she was still sad, she was no longer in mourning. Another client told me that one of his favorite things to do when he was waiting for his second child to arrive was to go back and read his journal from the same time frame for his first. He was interested and delighted to see how far he'd come and where he still worried. His only regret was that he'd been inconsistent about writing and wished he had written more. He said, "I did this for myself, but reading these I'm excited to put them in her baby book so she'll see a part of me that I've outgrown so she'll never know." (I had to gently remind him to not just read them but write some for his second child, too!)

Whatever your experience has been in the transition into being a parent, writing a letter to express your hardships, your joys, and even your hopes for moving forward can be a potent part of your transition process, as well as a way to set your intention for your working parenthood.

Leadership Lessons of Parenthood

Acknowledging the Transition to Working Parent

By once again pausing and reflecting as you enter the final phase of your parental leave transition, you are further cultivating your capacity to hold the complexity of all that you are juggling—and becoming—as a working parent.

Here are a few of the *whole-person leadership* skills you will be practicing during this touchpoint:

- Identifying and deepening your guiding core values
- Embracing the complexities of your combined working parent role
- Moving from binary *either/or* thinking to *both/and*, which centers curiosity, embraces contradictions, and expands possibility
- Further cultivating a growth mindset
- Practicing patience (again) with yourself and others

Chapter
Fourteen

Touchpoint 9
Adjustment

WHEN YOU RETURN from leave, it is not uncommon to experience that transition shock I mentioned in Chapter 5 as you reintegrate into the team, take back your duties, and learn how to navigate the dual roles of worker and parent. If you have a new manager or role change, recognize that your double or triple adjustment will take some time. This touchpoint reminds you to be kind to yourself as you acclimate to your new normal and make both macro- and micro-adjustments to maximize your work-life enrichment and minimize the work-life conflict I talked about in Chapter 12. It can be helpful to think of adjustment like the various controls on a radio that allow you to change the volume, bass, and treble. Think about how you can finely tune the music to give you the exact sound that brings you the most enjoyment. One effective way to adjust to your working parent role is through boundary management techniques such as examining and redrawing or redefining what you want your boundaries to look like between work and home. In this chapter we'll spend time exploring what boundaries are and aren't and how you can get them to work for you as you adjust to working parenthood.

I've Still Got My Raising Kids Head On

Source: Betsy Streeter/Cartoonstock.com

Identify Your Integration Points

The first step to maximizing work-life enrichment is identifying where work and home intersect. Ask yourself these questions:

- Where do your job skills enhance or support your home life?
- Where do your parenting skills enhance or support your work life?
- What are some of the tangible ways that work and life overlap for you in the course of a normal day?
- How can you get creative about your use of time to better attend to all of your priorities? Examples might be incorporating time with your baby and exercise by doing a stroller workout or visiting/feeding your baby during lunch breaks.

Communication

Now that you are back, it can help to schedule regular meetings with your manager and be clear about your needs. Do you want extra feedback or flexibility as you adjust? Or would you prefer to be treated as if you were never gone? Is there an accommodation you would like your manager to consider? Although your manager may not be able to grant all of your requests, having open dialogue and remaining focused on solutions will improve your relationship as well as your return experience.

Communication helps prevent misunderstandings and hard feelings. I have had clients who were upset that their position changed when they returned to work and assumed it was some sort of punishment. Although this is unfortunately sometimes true, more frequently that is not the intention. Workplace needs can change during an employee's extended absence, and management may feel that because your work has already been reassigned, you are more easily available for a new project, or perhaps more amenable to change. This is a perfect opportunity to shift your mindset and communication approach into curiosity. Rather than assuming ill intent, ask your manager to share their thinking behind the change.

When you need to recalibrate workplace expectations about what is possible for the new you, present your requests as solutions serving the interests of your team and organization. If you are not getting the adjustment support you need from your manager, continue reaching out to them directly (refer back to Chapter 10 on self-advocacy). Remember the other resources you can tap into if needed—including HR, employee assistance programs, colleagues, a parental leave coach, friends, health professionals, and employee advocates and lawyers.

Adjusting at Home

Understand that your home life and child are also in the midst of a major adjustment, affecting everyone at many levels, from the big picture of family identity down to mundane details. Keep a lookout for major and minor ways you can change the way your home life runs. Solve your biggest pain points first. For example, if you are completely exhausted, solve for how to get more sleep. If you crave time alone with your partner or a friend, solve for that. Depending on their own schedule and work/home juggling act, perhaps your partner (if you have one) can cover for you while you sleep uninterrupted in another room a few nights per week. Maybe you can afford a night nanny. Another obstacle can be an unsatisfactory childcare situation. Finding a remedy for your biggest problems will help make all the smaller problems feel more manageable.

Fixing smaller issues can also have a big effect in your day-to-day enjoyment of work and family. I once had a therapist who called small annoyances "windshield wiper problems," like when your wipers need to be replaced and they make it so you can't *quite* see clearly when it rains, which makes driving more stressful. These little problems can add up to big irritations; solve a few and your days go more smoothly. Buried in laundry? Ask for or hire help or get a diaper service. Constantly cleaning breast pump supplies? Get an extra set or buy steam bags that will let you quickly clean them in the microwave. Hate cooking and would rather spend that time snuggling with your family? Consider consolidating meal prep to a set time for the week or get a meal kit service if it is in your budget.

If you can, build downtime (even a little!) into your days off, and again, remember your self-advocacy skills from Chapter 10. Adjustment is about the long game. After about three months back at work, the adrenaline of your return can wear off. As reality kicks in, consider scheduling a long weekend or "staycation" that you can look forward to amidst pressures at work and home. Build in time to recharge and assess how your adjustment is going.

Adjusting Your Boundaries Instead of Attempting "Balance"

Balance means many things in our culture, including the false perception that all the varied parts of your life are distinct from each other, yet if you somehow figured out how to give them equal time, you would be able to balance demands from all the spheres of your life without conflict. Balance has positive connotations of serenity, as if you might walk out of the office and straight into the spa or a long nature walk. Who doesn't want that? But mostly what I see with my clients is that failing to attain an unrealistic, misty ideal of balance creates another layer of self-judgment.

To release yourself from the expectation that you can reach an unreachable bar, it is worth asking a seemingly simple question: *what is balance, anyway?*

In Australia I had the pleasure of working with organizational psychologist Sarah Cotton, PhD, who did work on balance and boundaries for herself and her clients. I trained Sarah and her team in my

How Sleep Affects Your Career and Family Life

Sleep is a critical resource to sustain the energy required for activity and engagement[1]—things like raising a child and performing well at work. Sleep deficits influence your ability to self-regulate,[2] affecting attitude and emotions as well as your ability to process information. Sleepiness at work impairs your ability to complete tasks, to be adaptive, and to be an engaged team member, while increasing your likelihood of being late or absent or failing to observe safety procedures.[3]

Lack of sleep can affect your health and home life, too. You are more likely to feel stressed and enjoy your time with your family less. Sleep is highly correlated with perinatal mood disorders.[4] Although a new child makes getting adequate sleep a challenge, it is not impossible, and making sleep a priority will serve you well at work and at home.

Research shows that work can have a big impact on duration and quality of sleep. Leslie Hammer, PhD, and Ellen Ernst Kossek, PhD, are a trailblazing duo in the academic world of work-life research known for their research pinpointing the family-supportive behaviors managers need to adopt to increase health and successful work-life integration of employees.

They have found that when supervisors provide empathy and resources for managing work and family demands, employees sleep better.[5] Supporting employee sleep can include giving them more control over their work schedule, teaching them about healthy sleep practices, and offering concern by asking if they slept well.[6] A study of grocery workers conducted by Hammer and Kossek showed that supportive leadership creates a positive group culture that benefits entire teams.[7]

Because your manager is likely not being trained in this information, it will be up to you to put these things in place for yourself or to choose jobs that offer such flexibility to begin with. Ask for more schedule control if you need to, and suggest boundaries for work times, such as off-hours email etiquette, that can help everyone be productive at work and enjoy their time

(continued)

(*continued*)

off. This is an opportunity for you to manage up and teach your entire team about the importance of sleep leadership. If everyone sleeps better, you will look like a process improvement rock star!

Interactions at home make a difference in sleep quality and quantity as well. Hammer's research has shown that sharing positive news about your day with your partner and getting a supportive response correlates with better sleep.[8]

So, in addition to following good sleep hygiene practices like making ample time for sleep and taking turns getting up during the night to care for your baby, you can add good communication at work and home to your plan for getting the rest you need and deserve each night.

RETAIN parental leave coaching program and supervised them as we piloted RETAIN at the largest retail employer in Australia. We spent years working together across continents to improve the support available to expectant and new parents. I learned a lot from our work together, and I particularly appreciated the deep dive we took into this question about balance. Elements of this section are inspired by our shared inquiry and a workshop she offered called *Balance to Boundaries*.

One thing that became clear in our discussions was that finding a single definition of work-life balance is far from easy. Described in many ways across the academic literature, work-life balance can be about whether you spend equal time on your various roles, whether you find those roles to be equally satisfying, how well you feel you fulfill different roles relative to each other, how much control you feel over various roles, and how comfortable you are with whatever tension naturally exists between roles.

The fact that there is no single, clear definition is an indication this idea will not be very useful for you going forward. There are a few other *big* problems with the ideal of balance.

1. There Is No Societal Infrastructure to Help You Balance

The first problem with balance as an ideal is that our culture is not set up to help you achieve it. By becoming a working parent, you have unwittingly signed up for a system that in large part sets you up for balance failure. Your best chance is to reject those expectations by creating your own systems and healthy boundaries unique to your needs. There are many pressures on parents today, coming from all angles: from the dominant culture of our country, from our employers, managers and teams, friends and family, and even, especially, from ourselves.

The way we parent today doesn't look anything like the parenting many of us grew up with. In the 1980s and 1990s, parenting was defined by latchkey kids, an absentee parenting style if ever there was one. Today we have veered to the other extreme, with the emergence of helicopter parents and even guerrilla warfare helicopter parents. (For more analysis on why the western way of parenting isn't the only, or best, way read *Hunt, Gather, Parent* by Michaeleen Doucleff, PhD.)[9]

Beyond cultural expectations, we face mounting financial burdens that did not exist in the same way for previous generations of parents. Since the early 1980s, childcare costs are up by 65% or more, depending on where you live; at the same time, real wages have not increased at nearly the same rate. The costs of housing and health care have also been steadily rising out of proportion to wage increases, and these costs can hit working parents particularly hard, making work-life balance seem that much more out of reach.

Caregiving time burdens have also increased. For example, 80% of women breastfeed now, up from 50% in the 1980s.[10] Breastfeeding is time consuming, usually taking a half hour to an hour per session, with at least six sessions required a day! A recent popular meme calculated that one woman spent 1,848 hours breastfeeding in a year, or 35.5 hours a week (not including the mental load involved ensuring she drank enough water and ate well). That represents another full-time job, one that does not give you a break on the weekends! Breastfeeding beyond parental leave, for the parents who choose to, can be a real stumbling block and require emotionally difficult decisions, adjustment, and a lot of support.

2. Aiming for Balance Creates Conflict Between Work and Home

The second problem with expecting balance between opposing spheres is that the dualistic mentality it creates sets you up for conflict. Author and speaker Elizabeth Gilbert talks about how the idea of balance has been turned into a weapon that too many women use against themselves. Increasingly, we see it harming men as well. Gilbert suggests balance is not something we find once and arrive at. Rather, we should seek to let our values guide us when planning different parts of our lives to ensure that our commitments and needs are met. It is in doing so that we make our lives as purposeful and rewarding as possible.[11]

Work-life theory considers the intersection of our work and non-work lives, along with any issues that may arise at that intersection. Work-life conflict is when the demands of participation in one role make participation in the other role more difficult.[12] For the parental leave transition, we focus particularly on work-life conflict, theories related to work-life balance, and theories that explore how the business world is responding by creating policy and service changes designed to make the workplace more "family friendly."

The notion of work-life balance has long been an elephant in the room for parental leave discussions, and since the pandemic, that elephant has trampled the makeshift workspaces we have carved out of our living rooms, kitchens, and closets. It's become apparent that perfectly balancing all of our work and home responsibilities is laughable. (Though if you weren't laughing, you would be crying, right?)

Balance sets up a **Home versus Work** mentality

The transition shock often experienced when a first-time parent returns to work after welcoming a child is closely tied to work-life balance. This touchpoint, along with the RETAIN pedagogy behind it, helps you to think of this as an adjustment period rather than expecting things to be the same at work as they were before your leave. By recognizing that it is normal not to feel like everything is business as usual, you can mitigate any shock.

3. It's Not Your Fault

I want you to know that if you are not feeling balanced when you get to this part of your transition, it's not your fault. For all the reasons I have cited, the idea of work-life balance as something to strive for has been largely debunked by experts. Your "failure" to achieve balance is completely normal. The parental leave transition is a complex time. Throw in whatever is going on in your environment (such as a global pandemic, recession, social justice reckoning, etc.) and if it is hard for you, that doesn't mean you are doing it wrong. It means *this is hard!* The truth is that what our culture sets us up to expect of ourselves and each other is impossible. But at least that impossibility is increasingly clear: *this is a structural issue, not a personal failing.*

I want to show you the concept of boundaries and boundary management as an alternative to the unattainable ideal of work-life balance. We will look at how understanding your relationship with boundaries and being able to create and communicate healthy, flexible boundaries are critical tools in your working parent toolbox that you can use to make adjustments for yourself and the needs of your family going forward.

Types of Boundaries

It is easy to read the word *boundary* and imagine an impenetrable barrier, but that is not the only type of boundary I'm suggesting. There are other ways to compartmentalize so we can concentrate on and enjoy *one thing at a time* and not lose ourselves to distraction. Ed Batista, an organizational behavior and management professor at Stanford and expert executive coach and author, puts it this way: "While balance requires an unsteady equilibrium among the various demands on our time and energy, boundaries offer a sustainable means of keeping things in their proper place."[13]

I love that distinction and advise you to choose sustainable over unsteady any chance you get. So, what kinds of boundaries is Batista talking about?

- **Time boundaries** enable us to carve out pockets of time for things that are important to us.
- **Physical and behavioral boundaries** involve a physical barrier or removing ourselves from a place or situation.
- **Mental boundaries** help us distance or remove ourselves in our mind.

There are also different intensities or strengths of boundaries. A boundary can be too weak or permeable, or it can be too strong, meaning nothing gets through. Neither extreme is a healthy boundary. What is most effective is a semipermeable boundary—not too strong and not too weak. I call this perfect boundary a "Goldilocks boundary." It's just right!

To illustrate, Batista tells us about his colleague, biologist Michael Gilbert, who has advocated that healthy boundaries should replace the notion of balance, saying, "Just as functional membranes (letting the right things through and keeping the wrong things out) facilitate the healthy interaction of the cells of our bodies, so do functional personal boundaries facilitate the healthy interaction of the various parts of our lives. Bad boundaries lead to either being overwhelmed or withdrawal. Good boundaries lead to wholeness and synergy."[14]

The cell biology model is useful for this idea of organic permeability and how even if *boundaries* sounds solid, harsh, and unwavering, a healthy, permeable boundary enables us to respond to our environment, changing needs, and demands through real-time give-and-take.

Let's say you need a fence to keep your dog in your yard. If you build a thick, high wall, the dog cannot even see out, and guess what—neither can you. The dog is safe, but at what price to both of you? If you build a fence without any fence posts, it won't stand up for long. The dog will knock it down and happily run off chasing cars, perhaps to be run over by one. This is not an effective barrier. Now, imagine you build a picket fence with proper posts. You and the dog can see out, and your dog can stick her nose through and get some attention from a passerby or even "chase" cars along the inside of the fence. You have not changed your dog's nature—you have just protected her from danger with a just-right boundary. The best boundaries allow for the needs—and nature—of everyone involved.

Exercise: Establishing Healthy Boundaries

Practically speaking, how do we move away from the false notion of balance and toward supporting ourselves by setting, then managing, healthy boundaries? First, look inward to uncover and confront your inner monologue and address any lingering bias about boundaries. For inspiration, consider the words of Brené Brown, whose research focuses on courage as it relates to vulnerability and shame. In *Daring Greatly*, she said, "Daring to set boundaries is about having the courage to love ourselves, even when we risk disappointing others."[15]

Fear of disappointing or upsetting others is a big part of the emotional baggage that comes with boundary setting. We must overcome that fear and lovingly take those risks if we want to build a life where work and family peacefully coexist.

Take a minute to write down your default notions on boundaries. Following are some common thoughts I hear from clients.

- o *"I will hurt someone's feelings if I say no."*
- o *"I'll lose my job if I say I won't check email on the weekends."*
- o *"I don't want to set a boundary and then have to undo it."*
- o *"I'm great at boundaries, it's my [boss, mom, partner, friend] who is bad at them."*
- o *"Only women are bad at boundaries."*

In this exercise, you may have exposed some received ideas about boundaries that do not serve you and prevent you from setting boundaries that could improve your well-being and help you live the values you identified in Chapter 13.

Take a moment now to remind yourself of those values. They will help you decide what boundaries will help you stay focused on what is essential for you as a working parent—and give you the courage to enforce them.

Next, for practice, take a moment to reframe one of your thoughts about boundaries and come up with a conscious alternative.

For example, if your current thinking was "*I will hurt someone's feelings if I say no,*" then you might reframe it as "*Saying no and setting a boundary here will make space for me to say yes to something more aligned with my values.*"

Once you have reframed any attitudinal roadblocks about boundaries, you can move toward identifying ways to set and hold them.

Steps to Setting and Holding Boundaries: Checklist ✓

- **Uncover** old notions that could stop you from setting healthy boundaries.
- **Decide** what boundaries are needed and communicate them.
- **Uphold** them over time and in the face of competing demands on your time.
- **Tweak** them when you come to information that you determine changes them (permeability!).
- **Observe** their impact on helping you live your values.

Enlist Boundary Guards

Setting and communicating boundaries is an art. Soliciting support to uphold them over time at work and home is an important strategy for making them sustainable for as long as you need to keep them in place.

One client, Talia, wanted to leave work every day at 5:00 p.m. Her first week back from leave, she mentioned this to her manager. For two weeks she stayed on course, but midway through the second week she started to waver. She would stay until 5:15. . . 5:20 . . . 5:30. The third week her manager said to her "Talia, it's 5:30, didn't you say you wanted to leave by 5:00?" The next day she struggled to leave on time, too. But on Wednesday at 5:00 p.m., her boss packed up and came out of his office and said, in front of Talia's whole team, "Talia, it's 5:00. Ready to go?" And he waited while she packed up and walked out with her.

He did that for the next three weeks, not once making her feel bad about that boundary. Not everyone has as fantastic a manager as Talia's, but most of us have a colleague or spouse or friend who can act as an accountability partner. If you work from home, this may mean you have to be even more strict with, and creative about enforcing, your boundaries. One client who was struggling with turning off from work got a child-control app and had their Wi-Fi turn off at 6:00 p.m.

Know Your Boundary Management Style

There is no universal right or wrong way to manage your boundaries between work and home. Ellen Ernst Kossek, PhD, and Brenda Lautsch, PhD, discuss three work-life boundary management styles in their book *CEO of Me: Creating a Life That Works in the Flexible Job Age.*[16] Each style has pros and cons. *Integrators* enjoy and get value from quick switching and permeable boundaries between work and home but can lose focus if they integrate too much. *Separators* prefer to keep strong, unchanging boundaries between work and home but sometimes don't benefit from positive cross-domain spillover. *Cyclers* go back and forth, sometimes having firm divisions and other times, such as during a big project, acting more like an integrator. Cyclers need to ensure their stakeholders understand their current priorities or they risk burnout. Determining which style you prefer, and working to mitigate its downsides, will support your goals and foster well-being.[17]

Boundary Management at Work

As you adjust to your return to work, I encourage you not to bring your work home with you unnecessarily, no matter how strong the temptation. Here are some boundary-management techniques I've seen work well:

- Control your time in ways that are effective for you (for example, use the Pomodoro Technique for bursts of productivity, block certain hours when you know you are most fruitful).

- If meetings are not productive in your work unit, suggest process improvements that limit meeting frequency or duration. Be mindful that some colleagues may work best with frequent meetings, so a little give-and-take may be necessary.
- Limit electronic notifications and interruptions (turn off alerts, schedule when you respond to email, etc.).
- Set up autoresponders to protect your concentrated work time.
- Take your breaks and make sure to eat lunch!

Boundary Management at Home

Home relationships are often where we have the poorest boundaries, especially if we have internalized the idea that boundaries are selfish. It can be helpful to look at them not as barriers between you and those you love but as a supportive framework holding everyone up.

In a perfect world, it would be easy to have serious boundary discussions with our loved ones, but that is not always the case. Emotions can run high on topics like these. Try communicating your core values as a way to open the discussion, especially if they are shared values. *"Because family time is so important to me, I've been thinking about some changes we could make to help create more time for that."* Then discuss potential boundaries:

- Schedule sacred family time where work is off limits.
- Be explicit about household chores (who will be responsible for what and when).
- Strengthen your support network (augment with caregivers, even remote ones for older children; get food delivered; automate or outsource bill paying/laundry, etc.).
- At the start of every week, schedule in free time, priority tasks, and time with your family. Block off annual holidays, getaways for recharging, and important days like birthdays.
- Prioritize your annual health check-ups.
- Decide if there are times when work and home can overlap (for example, clean out work emails via your phone while watching a mindless show).

Exercise: Boundary Management for Transitioning Between Work and Home

Transition time is an overlooked coping tool. It can act like a decompression chamber between the various areas of your life. Think about what rituals you can create to make your transition times more enjoyable and let you be your best self when you enter a new space.

Take the example of Matt, father of two and very introverted by nature. He found that when he drove home from work, he felt immediately overwhelmed by the noise and activity of his family, but when he rode his bike home, he was able to use that transition time as a meditation and could more easily handle his bustling household on arrival. Meghan, who worked from home, created a "shutting down work ritual." She noted what she'd done that day, planned her to-do list for tomorrow, closed her tabs and browser, then shut her computer, took three deep breaths, and walked upstairs to her family.

- Create start and stop rituals for the workday.
- Develop a physical or mental routine to transition between work and home, even if they are in the same physical space.
- Try not to overschedule yourself. Build in time between appointments and tasks.
- If working from home, avoid the temptation to constantly switch focus between work and home demands (multitasking can be unavoidable at times, but mostly it is fool's gold: shiny and alluring, but full of false promise).

Now that you have thought through some ideas about how and where to create boundaries and some examples of what that can look like in general, it is time to get specific. How will you actually make the shift from work-life conflict to work-life enrichment through the use of healthy boundaries?

Start by identifying your pain points. Take two minutes and think about sources of conflict between your work and home spheres right now. Once you have identified a few that feel important to your happiness moving forward, consider how you will address them and with whom.

Addressing your pain points is the last step and it is the hardest because you won't be doing it as an exercise in your notebook—you will be doing it out in the world. It requires you to identify where an important boundary needs to be established or modified, determine exactly what you want that boundary to look like, and then do what it takes to communicate it. Usually, being simple and direct works best. Revisit Chapter 10 for tips on handling difficult conversations.

Where Boundary Adjustment May Be Needed

Because situations evolve continuously, we must periodically revisit our boundaries if we want them to serve as supple supports in our lives rather than rigid constraints. Adjustment might be necessary when you realize you no longer need a certain boundary you've set or when a boundary is consistently being sabotaged—either by someone at home or at work or by yourself. Here are some examples of places where you may need to use your imaginary radio dials to adjust a boundary to just the right setting and volume for you:

- Your boss is scheduling meetings back-to-back, leaving you no time to check on your child between them.
- Your extended family is habitually dropping in unannounced on weekday evenings when you are trying to unwind with your partner and child.
- Your spouse/partner expects you to make dinner and watch kids at the same time.

Adjusting to your new normal as a working parent is big work. Your routines and priorities are undergoing a serious reshuffling. Being patient with yourself and those around you, determining how to make your boundary management style work for you, setting and communicating boundaries, and seeking innovative ways to create work-life integration will enable you to carve out a fulfilling, well-rounded life while expanding your family and maintaining your career.

Leadership Lessons of Parenthood

Adjustment

Adjustment requires maturity and a willingness to be patient and accept yourself and those around you with loving kindness. You also need to engage wholeheartedly in the face of the unknown. Through experimentation, you can find what works, what doesn't, and where you need to try again. This takes courage, creativity, and the tenacity to stay flexible.

Here are a few of the *whole-person leadership* skills you will be practicing during this touchpoint:

- Experimenting/failing fast
- Practicing flexibility/going with the flow
- Adjusting expectations in the face of ever-changing realities
- Harnessing creativity
- Re-contracting to ensure healthy boundaries
- Showing up authentically as your full working-parent self

Chapter
Fifteen

Touchpoint 10
Access to Career Development

ONE OF THE most powerful experiences I see many new parents go through during their leave is an internal reorientation or realignment with their values and purpose in the world.

One client, Lyn, told this story:

My dad was a small-town architect and I grew up side-by-side with him on the drafting table. I loved helping him make the models out of balsa wood and imagining the lives that would happen in the buildings he designed. When I went to grad school for architecture, I really thought I was going to be making that kind of life for myself and my future son. Instead, I found myself in the big city, working around the clock so the celebrity architect of the firm could get more famous. I told myself that if I could make a name for myself there as his protégé I could leave and start my own firm and have more flexibility. When my son was born it was the best day of my life and leaving him to go back to work broke me. I felt like I had seriously gotten off track somehow. Here I was with this perfect kid, and I couldn't even spend time with him because I was at work all the time, and it wasn't like they would ever let me bring him in to draw next to me. That's when I knew I had to move, both cities and jobs. I'm working for a small design-build company now and I love it.

Becoming a dad forced Lyn to face something he had been avoiding for a long time—his career was turning out to be incompatible with the life he wanted to build, and so, for his son, he did something about it.

Cherrie, a graphic designer for a publishing company, came at this realignment another way. In her words,

Those first two months at home I stared at him. His tiny fingers, the way his ear was crumpled on one side, how his lip curved up into a smile when he slept. I started to sketch him, and the more I did the more I thought about how when I was a kid, I wanted to be a comic book illustrator. I'd even become a graphic designer thinking that might help me get there, but somewhere along the way I stopped drawing. Sketching him reminded me how much I loved it. Making him in my body felt like a miracle and reminded me that life is short, and that I'd been given a talent. When I went back to work, I asked my manager if I could start working on some hand-drawn designs. He must have seen the spark, because he moved me onto a project as an illustrator. Now when I look at my son, I always notice something. It could be a color or a line his blanket left on his cheek. There is always something that I can bring back to a design. I love working so much more than I ever did before I had him.

This tenth touchpoint exists to draw your attention to the opportunity you have at this point in your transition to reevaluate your career trajectory and do what it takes to make sure you are the one driving it, and in the direction you want. You might find that you need to incorporate a new training or have a talk with your manager about taking on new projects. Or as Lyn and Cherries stories illustrate, you may need to pivot in the face of new information or circumstances. Either way, becoming a parent means that you will constantly be pushed to the edge of what you thought your capabilities to be. You will always be learning and growing, forever iterating as you try to keep up with the developmental milestones of your child. Your career is one more place where you will benefit from thinking of yourself as a lifelong learner.

Modern Career Development Models

The traditional career development theories of the 20th century are epitomized by the American Dream of the young man starting out in the mailroom and, with hard work and determination, working his way up the ladder until he runs the company. This dream is all but gone, and with it the social contract that had employers offering a lifetime of job security in return for company loyalty and job dedication. Contemporary career development theories instead offer an individual level of focus that has employees working as their own brand manager to successfully navigate across a number of careers over their lifetime. According to Bureau of Labor Statistics research conducted from 1979 to 2017, the average number of jobs in a career span is 12—with many employees spending five years or less in any one job.[1] With increasing movement toward a freelance or gig economy, many people are managing different new clients (or jobs) each week—which makes a dozen jobs in a lifetime seem incredibly stable.

A number of more contemporary career development models tell a different story, with implications and applications for working people becoming working parents. The kaleidoscope career model, for example, acknowledges that people carefully evaluate their options when deciding on career next steps such as whether to accelerate, slow down, or even pause their advancement.[2] We seek an equilibrium among many competing factors, including career responsibilities, barriers and opportunities, relationships, nonwork roles, and personal values and interests.[3]

Subsequent research using the kaleidoscope career model revealed striking gender differences across career spans pertaining to the importance and prioritization of three values: *authenticity*, *balance*, and *challenge*. For women, work-life balance varied significantly across career stages while the importance of interesting and challenging work remained somewhat consistent. The reverse was seen for men, who placed consistent (and lesser) value on work-life balance throughout their career, while fluctuating about their need for authenticity and challenge. The importance of balance was highest for everyone during early career stages, but at mid-career (prime parenthood time), women placed significantly more value on work-life balance than men did.[4]

With your move into working parenthood, navigating your career path becomes much more complex. It will be up to you to assess your current parameters and determine if you need to look for different opportunities. In your new role as a working parent you have fresh insights and skills you can tap into to help you find your way through the added complexity. Not everyone initially welcomes this idea that there may be a new career path or direction opening in front of them. Yet for some, the unexpected detour their career takes around this time becomes one of the most exciting and rewarding things to come out of their parental leave transition. I encourage you to embark on any new paths with curiosity and your learning mindset—and never beat yourself up for not having made it down a path that was open to you before becoming a parent but that seems less available or aligned with your needs now.

Parental Leave as a Career Development Opportunity

Even with the unpredictability of today's career paths, becoming a parent does not mean your career plans *have to* change. Nor does it mean they *can't* change. New parents have a wide diversity of preferences and needs when it comes to work-life integration and career ambition. This tenth and final touchpoint reminds you to continue to build in access to ongoing career development opportunities for yourself, now and in the long term—whatever that looks like for *you*.

In my experience, this final phase of the parental leave transition is a huge—and often overlooked—career development opportunity. You can leverage the personal growth you have experienced during your transition to parenthood and bring your new wisdom and skills back to your workplace—like Cherrie did, using her creativity in a way that felt more authentic to her. I've worked with many parents who found that the passion, efficiency, and productivity superpowers they acquired in adjusting to parenthood set them up for big advancements and a more rewarding life in the workplace.

Let this touchpoint nudge you to revisit your life and career plans and envision your future, given how your parental leave transition experience has changed you. Being a working parent is easier when you get a similar amount of enjoyment from your work as you do from your home life. Use your transition to make more room for the work you love doing and ensure you are on the path of your choosing.

Career Development Isn't Always a Straight Line

Twelve to 18 months after returning to work, it is not uncommon for new parents to question their intention to stay (and for some this happens much sooner). Be aware that this is normal and that you may need to seek extra support at this critical time. The fact that for most working parents, prime childrearing years coincide with critical years for career advancement can lead to wondering whether you really want the career track you have been working toward—or in the time line you had planned for it.

Ellie, a university professor, had her second child in the year before she was up for tenure. She loved the flexibility and autonomy that the research and writing gave her and had more than the number of publications she needed for promotion. But as she got closer, with a newborn and three-year-old, she realized that the things that attracted her to her field were not the focus of a tenured professor's job.

> "The further I go the more I see that once you move past junior faculty, your job really becomes about bureaucracy. I love research and teaching, but that's not where I'm going to be spending my time. The thought of investing the amount of energy and time as I did before kids but focusing that time on making charts for a meeting or chairing committees is a lot less attractive. I'm not sure I'm willing to sacrifice my time that way. I want to be able to have dinner with my kids. Part of me wishes I could just put tenure off for a few years, but I spent years getting my PhD, and not going for tenure would be viewed as a demotion. It'd be way less prestigious and everyone would wonder what happened to me."

If you find yourself struggling with similar thoughts, take time to investigate your options. It can help to reach out to someone who is further along in your same career path and ask them what they wish they could tell their younger self when they were at your stage. Slowing down or even pausing your career growth while your children are young does not mean you have failed—rather that you are able to reexamine your circumstances in the face of evolving demands and make tough decisions (an adult life/leadership skill). At the same time, it is useless to pretend that there are no real-world implications to making that choice. A little further on in this chapter I will cover some potential implications of putting your career in overdrive, downshifting, or even opting out for a bit. Ultimately, I encourage you to choose what's right for you and your family, setting aside how that choice may be interpreted or judged by others. Not to be a broken record, but it is a working parent truth that you can't please everyone and that you *will* be judged for whatever choice you make. If you double down on your career, some people around you will think you are a bad parent. If you decide to put your career on hold, others will think you are throwing away your education, opportunities, and hard work. Making the choice based on what works for you and your family takes courage, but it will enrich your life far more than the (fleeting) good opinion of others.

Reflection Questions for Career Development

Use these prompts to reflect on where you want your career and life to go:

* Are your career goals the same as before you became a parent or have they shifted?
* Reflect on the last year. What have you learned about why you love your work?
* What aspects of work feel draining, tedious, or frustrating, and how can you minimize them?
* Where do you want to be in your career in one year, three years, five years?
* How will your chosen career path affect your home life, now and at various stages? How can you minimize any potential liabilities or sabotages? (Consider running a 6-S assessment to update your assets and liabilities for any possible career path, as you did in Chapter 5.)

(continued)

(*continued*)

* What might be holding you back from pursuing your desired career path? What are you putting off to do later when things settle down?
* What training or education do you need to get to your career goals? Can something temporarily be shifted at home or at work—or both—to let you phase this in?
* Does your employer, or other organization, offer any career planning resources, programs, or educational reimbursements?
* Would you like a mentor to help you plan your career next steps? How can you get one?
* Consider scheduling a one-on-one meeting with your manager to discuss short-, mid-, and long-term career goals.

Shifting Between Career Gears: Pedal to the Metal, Downshift, Park

Many working parents take a serious look at their careers during Phase 3 of their transition. The decision to opt out, opt in, or something in-between is fraught with hand-wringing and (even more!) sleepless nights. For some, such decisions can be made in a methodical and level-headed way, but for others who encounter a parental leave transition experience that was unexpected or even shocking, the decision-making process can be reactive and rushed. Wherever you find yourself, the reflection and exploration you do here will help guide you through these important, life-changing, decisions in a way that holds your long-term goals—for career and family—in perspective. For those who know they want or need to work and parent, the objective is simple (though getting there may take time): find the career trajectory that lets you be happy and engaged at *both* work and home.

Accelerating Your Career

Whether you work in an office or a classroom, on an oil rig or an airplane, you need to be confident that your career or line of work will continue to grow alongside your family. The best way to ensure this is to get clear about what you want your path to be, then make your own opportunities and carefully weigh any that come your way.

For eight years, Ben had owned a restaurant famous for its incredible hummus. His first parental leave coincided with a glowing review and an uptick in business that demanded his attention. During his leave, investors approached him about expanding. Ben had not planned to change his predictable and steady career, but here he was, presented with the unexpected potential to position his family better in the long term. It would also mean that after parental leave, Ben would need to work around the clock to set up a new partnership with his investors and launch three new restaurants in his child's first year.

He did not accept or reject this new option blindly. He and his spouse made time to sit down and conduct the 6-S analysis we discussed in Chapter 5 to see what truly worked for them. They looked at their *situation*, their current abilities (their *selves*), their *supports*, *strategies*, and potential *sabotages*. They carefully weighed pros and cons and decided to go for it. They knew it would be demanding and set up their plans and home supports accordingly. They asked Ben's mom to spend every other month with them to help with caregiving. His spouse agreed to take on minimal shifts at work, and they made a commitment to each other that they would both take off every Monday and Tuesday together, *no matter what*, for uninterrupted family time.

The complicated family decision-making algorithm unique to them indicated that this was a risk worth taking. They jumped in knowing where they needed to be careful and excited about a choice that ultimately helped them create the infrastructure and financial foundation to support the larger family they had always dreamed of.

Downshifting

Grappling with the decision to downshift your career is a common theme with clients—and for good reason. Sorting through the kaleidoscope of competing options that could have life-altering ramifications is hard. If you have spent the bulk of your life working toward a specific career goal with drive and ambition, this choice can be excruciating. For some people, however, it feels right.

Chris was an ER nurse who loved the thrill and speed of his job. He came alive in a crisis, and in calmer moments he got to use his genuinely caring and friendly nature to soothe countless frightened people. On the days it went well he felt like a superhero, but on days it went poorly, he had to use all his resilience resources to not go home in a puddle of sadness and defeat. His work was a high-stakes roller coaster and he was considered one of the best on his team. When he became a dad for the first time, he took a three-and-a-half-month leave while his wife had six weeks of leave. That put him in a primary caregiver role for two months before his return to work. As the day of his return approached, his doubts increased. He discovered that he loved using his skills to nurture someone he had a relationship with and saw every day. It gave him joy to see progress in a way the revolving door of the ER did not. He knew his wife would need to focus even more than usual on her career in the coming year. He also worried that he would no longer be able to keep up with the ER's fast pace and need for instant solutions to complex problems as he adjusted to being the sleep-deprived working dad of an infant.

Through soul-searching and detailed conversations, Chris and his spouse decided it would support their short- and long-term plans for him to downshift his career for one year. They wanted to avoid losing his benefits and he loved his colleagues, so through talks with his manager and HR they set up a temporary plan for him to work in a less demanding department for one year. This choice balanced Chris's needs with his family's, all while setting him up for continued career fulfillment.

Parking Your Career: Things to Consider Before Deciding to Leave the Workforce

Many of my clients, like Chris, feel a loss of confidence in their abilities or temporarily lose interest in their career aspirations after an extended leave. Some new parents consider leaving their job or the work world altogether while their children are young.

For many new parents, financial constraints mean that leaving the workforce is not an option they can entertain. For others, their calculations may work out so that they can afford a short or long career break. Still others may be forced to make the decision to leave the workforce altogether due to caregiving needs or any number of unexpected circumstances. If you find yourself in a position where you are considering leaving the workforce, do not make your decision impulsively or without a clear understanding of what your choice could mean for you, your career, your finances, and your family. Understanding that situational and mindset adjustments are possible enables you to explore more creative ways to make it work before taking the drastic action of leaving a job.

- **Crunch the Numbers**   Before coming to any decision, consider your ultimate career and financial goals and how a career break might affect your ability to attain them. Taking a significant career break (beyond your parental leave) may have an adverse impact on your chances for reentry and advancement. It can also reduce your financial readiness for retirement. For the time you are not receiving a paycheck, you are not making Social Security contributions, and for many people it also means no employer contributions or matches to a 401(k) or other retirement accounts. Leaving can also affect your health care costs, if you are covered through your employer. When making big decisions like this, it can quickly pay for itself to meet with a financial consultant to help you crunch the numbers from every angle. (Some EAPs include a visit or two with a financial advisor, so check your plan if you have one.) Having a clear picture of what you are giving up and what you are gaining should you decide to leave work is invaluable.
- **Brainstorm Alternate Solutions**   In times of stress, we often think in very binary terms: *"Either I stay in my current role full time or I quit altogether."* Before making a decision to leave, identify your biggest pain points and then brainstorm at least 20 ways to mitigate them without completely bowing out of the workforce. What changes could you make, at work and at home, that would bring some relief? Get creative (and if you are not feeling creative, bring in a friend known for their out-of-the-box thinking)!
  On the work front, can you ask for any of the following changes?

- A reduced schedule
- A job-share arrangement
- A short sabbatical
- A different assignment
- The option to work remotely
- A change of employers
- Freelancing

On the home front, can you ask for any of these changes?

- Hire help for childcare, cooking, or cleaning. (If this is outside your budget, get creative with other parents and set up childcare or dinner exchanges. I know one family who did "rotating responsibility days" with five other families. Each had one day a week when they took care of all the kids and made family-size meals that were sent home with each kid at the end of the day.)
- Find ways to get more sleep so you can better manage an energetic child and stress.
- Get a coach or therapist who can help you reframe your challenges and explore options you may not have considered.
- Radically change your living arrangements to save time, money, or both. (I have seen clients downsize to save money on their mortgage so they could switch to part time, while others move closer to their workplace to eliminate long commutes that suck time and energy, and many move closer to family.)

You may find that by using some combination of ingenuity and mitigation strategies, you are able to stay in the workforce while still creating the type of home life you desire. If you decide to take a career break after trying other options, you can take comfort that you did not make a hasty decision. You know the trade-offs you face, and you are willing to accept, even embrace, them.

Damned If You Do, Damned If You Don't: Four Reasons to Reject Working Parent Guilt

We are bombarded with images of the perfect working parent who puts on their crisp white shirt (seriously?), kisses their smiling angel on the top of the head, and calmly walks out the door with their work bag. In reality, you are much more likely to have to gently tear a screaming child off of you while holding in your emotions, grab a protein bar while wiping up your spilled coffee, and get to the office only to notice—while in a meeting with your boss—that you are wearing mismatched shoes and have spit-up down your entire back (true client story). Many of us feel guilty

(continued)

(*continued*)

when our reality fails to match our imaginary parental ideal. Guilt will ruin the day-to-day enjoyment of your working-parent existence faster than just about any other emotion. Fortunately, changing how you think about the trap of parent guilt can keep it at bay. Remember these tips:

1. **Guilt does not fill your cup.** Guilt is draining. However, paying attention to when we feel guilt can point us to areas of our life where slight course corrections may be genuinely useful. It is normal to feel guilty for not spending enough time at work or home, or for using media as a babysitter, but we live in a world of constraints and often have to make the least bad choice. Commit to your values and priorities, and then make an active effort to get your life closer to that alignment.

2. **Little eyes and ears are always learning.** Taking care of your own needs, both personally and professionally, teaches your child the value of taking care of themselves as a whole person. You do not want them growing up thinking they are supposed to handle it all by themselves, too, do you? Show them everyone is just right exactly the way they are, no guilt needed. Teach them that there are a lot of unrealistic expectations we all have to sift through to find what works for us. Let them see you show up best for your family when your needs are met, too.

3. **Embrace *good-enough* parenting.** Children do not require your unrelenting time and attention every waking moment. Many experts advise focusing on *good-enough* parenting. There is a nearly endless list of things that you *could* do, but for healthy and secure parent-child attachment, research shows that parents simply need to be emotionally present, comfort their child, attune to their child's feelings, and show delight when seeing their child. Five focused minutes doing these things can go a long way.[5]

4. **Your family is a small herd of magical unicorns.** Working parenthood is a constant opportunity for development and

(*continued*)

(*continued*)

growth, which means you will always be at your learning edge and rarely feel entirely confident. Parenting is tough no matter what else you are doing. No family has the same set of circumstances, and as I said at the beginning of the book, there is no manual you can follow to the letter for *your* child. Let go of comparing your family to someone else's and redirect your attention to appreciate what is special about your herd.

Your Career Need Not Be Your Calling

For many people this concept and the reevaluation their parental leave transition brings can make them question if they are staying true to their purpose or calling in life. If this is you, I invite you to explore what it would mean if you untangled your purpose from your work. For some, their work is their calling. But for the majority of people, work *can* just be a job. Author, Coach, and leadership expert, Tara Mohr, put it this way: "I never met a calling that asks to also be the thing that pays your bills." You can still find ways to bring the essence of the thing that is calling you into your daily life, no matter what your job.

The late writer Toni Morrison wrote along similar lines in the *New Yorker*: "I have worked for all sorts of people . . . geniuses and morons, quick-witted and dull, bighearted and narrow. I've had many kinds of jobs, but . . . I have never considered the level of labor to be the measure of myself, and I have never placed the security of a job above the value of home."[6]

Seven Tips to Grow Your Career as a Working Parent

Becoming a parent requires enormous mental focus, problem-solving, and adaptability—all things that you can bring back into your career to fuel your development and advancement. It does not require you to compromise your career goals by taking a step down or forgoing a promotion (unless you want to). Use this big

(*continued*)

(*continued*)
moment of internal and external change to set new behaviors in motion to benefit your career and your home life. You can be a great parent *and* a great employee if you manage your time and energy deliberately.

Here are some ways to bring the growth you have realized in your transition to parenthood back to your career.

- **Overcommunicate.** Many new parents find themselves narrating their every move to their child to teach them new words and how to be in the world. Use that skill at work. Share your plans, goals, and priorities with your manager and team in a way that demonstrates your excitement and commitment (repeat as necessary!).

- **Use constraints to be hyper-efficient.** Many people are astonished at how fast they can skillfully complete their work when they are motivated to be home in time for a snuggle. Find the inefficiencies in your schedule—the things that are not moving your goals and tasks meaningfully ahead—and consolidate tasks where you can.

- **Be a model of healthy boundaries.** Don't be sheepish about your boundaries and continually apologize for them. Instead, strike an attitude that healthy boundaries are a secret sauce whose recipe you're willing to share.

- **Realize that a *yes* in one place is a *no* in another.** Be discerning about what you take on and how it will fit into your schedule and affect your goals. This is closely related to boundaries.

- **Seek out training opportunities that excite you.** There are so many excellent remote learning options these days. No need to waste your time with ones that feel like a grind. Get creative about where you look (think globally) for training and advancement opportunities that you can do on your schedule—and that are fun!

- **Tap your new network (other working parents).** You just gained the biggest and most powerful network in the world! Put yourself out there and build trust and connection with others who understand the challenges you face by joining

(*continued*)

(*continued*)

parent groups, employee resource groups, playground meet-ups, baby classes, and so on. Don't be afraid to lean on those relationships for support and to access interesting opportunities. (Introvert tip: Online parent groups can be at least as effective as in-person ones because of their broad membership scope and range.)

- **Create a deep bench of support.** Build and nurture your daily support network for when things come up at home or at work. You will be more confident to take on last-minute opportunities to advance your career when you have your team in place, ready and committed to your success.

You Can Always Change Your Mind

As you plot the course for your career as a working parent, it can be helpful to remember that all decisions can be revisited and most can be reversed or redirected. Be thoughtful, be deliberate, and be willing to change your mind based on what the future holds.

The End of Your Transition

The "end" of your transition to working parenthood is likely to slide right past your awareness. You will be busy, and time will fly by. So open your calendar right now and make an appointment for about six months after you plan to return to work to remind yourself that you are now a tried-and-true working parent. Schedule a moment to appreciate and celebrate how far you have come, like a birthday for the new you born of this transition. (It can be the perfect time for a date night or a weekend away with friends.)

You honed your planning skills in Phase 1 by taking charge of your experience, assessing your unique circumstances, and creating a thoughtful exit plan—as well as acknowledging the enormity of the transition.

In Phase 2, you held your communication boundaries so you could devote time to forming your family, and you had ample opportunity to practice advocating for yourself and your child, not to mention how to pivot your plans to address new realities.

In Phase 3, you again paused to acknowledge the massive challenge that is working parenthood. You were gentle with yourself as you adjusted to your new normal, incorporating the lessons of this transition in order to look at your short- and long-term career goals in a way that makes your life meaningful.

The lessons you have learned during your leave will serve you well for all of the many and varied life events to come—job changes, your child hitting milestones, moving, maybe even taking care of your aging parents and welcoming another child. I hope our time together has helped you feel both practically well equipped and emotionally empowered throughout your journey. Every new parent struggles at some point. However, I've rarely met anyone who didn't grow stronger and wiser during their transition to working parenthood. My wish for you, in writing this playbook, is for you to chart a confident course and navigate as smoothly as possible through this unpredictable, yet exhilarating, life transition.

Leadership Lessons of Parenthood

Access to Ongoing Career Development

Long-term career planning while managing a bustling family life takes agility, resourcefulness, and the ability to balance competing demands toward a strategic end goal. Harness what you have learned and leverage your assets to use this opportunity to thoughtfully redefine your course. When all your options feel not quite right, careful deliberation and honest evaluation will help you make the best choice for you.

Here are a few of the *whole-person leadership* skills you will be practicing during this touchpoint:

- Pivoting in the face of new information; staying agile
- Finding equilibrium between competing demands
- Creating opportunities with strained resources
- Harnessing transition as a developmental opportunity
- Making the least-worst choice
- Embracing lifelong learning

Rounding Out the Human Experience

***

Chapter
Sixteen

Additional Challenges
and Resources

IT IS EASY to think we can divide the parental leave experience into two categories: those who have a healthy, "normal" experience of transitioning into working parenthood and those who are somehow inadequate and don't. That binary line of thinking would lead us to believe that a *normal person* could zing along through each touchpoint in this book without any hiccups, and only an *inadequate person* would need this extra chapter addressing what is "wrong" with them. You can probably tell by my tone here how I feel about this all-or-nothing view of our shared and endlessly nuanced humanity.

The entirety of your experience of becoming a parent and negotiating your parental leave is normal *because* it is yours and it is unique. Every person who becomes a parent does so in their own way, within their own circumstances. Your one-of-a-kind experience is by no means abnormal, even if it is an outlier.

A mother who had a late-stage miscarriage said to me, "I am so aware of my experience being treated as if it were a phenomenon, when really, with every person I talk to, I find out how normal it is." Our country is in the early stages of a societal awakening that is allowing historically marginalized experiences to come out of the shadows and be looked at anew, or sometimes for the first time, in the light. With awareness can come better understanding, empowerment, and support.

My purpose in this chapter is to encourage us all to better talk about and appreciate the infinite ways our individual circumstances and challenges contribute to making the complex transition to working parenthood one of the most formidable—and ultimately rewarding—experiences of our lives.

We will name what is often left unacknowledged: the impacts of systemic racial oppression and bias on the parental leave transition, the heteronormativity and prejudice faced by LGBTQ+ parents, and the challenges that can arise during adoption and surrogacy. We'll also briefly discuss lactation difficulties, previous trauma, infertility and miscarriage, perinatal mood and anxiety disorders, infant loss, and health issues for children and parents—substantial topics beyond the scope of this book. However, I have included resources in each section for those who see their experience echoed in this chapter. The resources are by no means exhaustive, but they will connect you to the networks and support communities that exist to lift you up and care for you. You may be affected by more than one of these issues or none of them directly. By learning more about them yourself, you can be an ally to anyone facing additional challenges.

Systemic Racial Oppression and Bias

Underrepresented individuals, especially those in Black, Indigenous, Asian, Latinx, and other communities of color, face myriad additional challenges in their transition to parenthood. The economic and health disparities that exist due to systemic racial injustice are magnified when we look at them through the lens of the parental leave experience.

For example, Black mothers die from pregnancy-related complications at three to four times the rate of white women, regardless of their income or education level, and the death rate of Black infants is twice that of white infants. Linda Blount, CEO of the Black Women's Health Imperative, makes it clear that "race is not a risk factor. Racism is a risk factor."

The wealth disparities faced by the majority of families of color mean that the financial burdens of welcoming a child, including health care costs and loss of income, are even more onerous. A 2018 report from the nonprofit Prosperity Now defines wealth as assets minus debts and shows that the average white family has $140,500 in wealth, whereas the average Latinx family has $6,300 and the average Black family has just $3,400 in wealth. All nonwhite groups have higher poverty levels and less access to health care and credit. As of 2015, 62% of Black adults and 73% of Latinx adults are either ineligible for or could not afford to take unpaid leave, compared to 60% of white adults. Again, this disparity is the result of hundreds of years of systemic racism that prevented many families of color from being able to build wealth at the same rate as white families, if at all.

What's more, the pandemic has disproportionately affected families of color who overwhelmingly comprise the ranks of frontline workers. Many didn't have the choice to stay home, due to economic vulnerability and the impossibility of working from home or the nature of their work.[1] Many have been forced to drop out of the workforce or leave their children at home alone, unable to tap into an extended network for childcare. Ironically, many women of color are providing low-paying childcare to white parents.[2]

This is a slim sketch of a truly enormous problem with no simple solution. There are excellent organizations working on it, though.

Resources

- **Asian and Pacific Islander American Health Forum:** www.apiahf.org
- **Black birthing bill of rights:** https://thenaabb.org/black-birthing-bill-of-rights/
- **Hispanic Federation:** www.hispanicfederation.org
- **National Association to Advance Black Birth:** www.thenaabb.org
- **National Alliance for Hispanic Health:** www.healthyamericas.org
- **Perinatal Mental Health Alliance for People of Color:** www.pmhapoc.org
- **Postpartum Support International in Spanish:** https://www.postpartum.net/en-espanol/
- **Protecting Your Birth: A Guide for Black Mothers:** https://www.nytimes.com/article/black-mothers-birth.html

Challenges Faced by LGBTQ+ Families

LGBTQ+ families face their own set of unique challenges. Most voluntary paid leave policies do not adequately account for non-gestational parents. Access to paid leave is often limited by gender, allowing women more parental leave than men and little to no leave for dual-dad homes or non-gestational moms. Though these policies may go beyond what is provided by law, they shut out gay dads and other LGBTQ+ families. (This is one of the many reasons my company recommends that employers institute a gender-neutral parental leave policy.) Families with two moms also face the gender wage gap with twice the impact. In dual-dad households, often neither parent has leave benefits. Finally, many LGBTQ+ couples face employment discrimination based on their sexual orientation or gender identification and may not want to risk being seen as asking for "special privileges" (which are not privileges at all, but simply equity) for fear of recrimination.

Resources

- **American Civil Liberties Union** (ACLU) works to protect the rights of LGBTQ+ people to become parents and offers anti-discrimination protection and resources: https://www.aclu.org/issues/lgbt-rights/lgbt-parenting.
- **Family Equality:** https://www.familyequality.org/
- **Gay Parents to Be:** www.gayparentstobe.com
- **PFLAG:** https://pflag.org/loving-families
- **Postpartum Support International** offers specific mental health support for LQBTQ+ parents: https://www.postpartum.net/get-help/queer-parents/.
- **Resolve** offers resources for LGBTQ+ families and couples who want to build a family: https://resolve.org/what-are-my-options/lgbtq-family-building-options/.

Adoption and/or Fostering

The adoption journey can entail many ups and downs, and parents and children may face emotional adjustment and challenges along the way. This is exacerbated for anyone already affected by the additional difficulties I've already touched on. It can help to get support from an organization that specializes in supporting adoptive families. Make sure to do your research and choose an organization that aligns with your values.

Resources

- **Adoptive Families:** www.adoptivefamilies.com
- **National Council for Adoption:** www.adoptioncouncil.org
- **Postpartum Support International** offers specific mental health support for adoptive and birth mothers: https://www.postpartum. net/get-help/adoptive-and-birth-mothers/.

Surrogacy

Whether you are serving as a surrogate or welcoming a child through a surrogate, your experience deserves support from those who understand the challenges you are facing.

Resources

- **Men Having Babies:** www.menhavingbabies.org
- **Resolve:** https://resolve.org/what-are-my-options/surrogacy/

Perinatal Mood and Anxiety Disorders

Perinatal describes the time frame from pregnancy through one year postpartum for moms or dads (birthing or not). Although the majority of new parents will not suffer a perinatal mental health issue, such as depression or anxiety, many do. One in 5 moms[3] and one in 10[4] dads experience a postpartum mood and anxiety disorder in the first year of parenthood. It is important to know the signs so you can watch for them in yourself, a partner, or a friend, and advocate as needed (https://www.postpartum.net/learn-more/). One of the biggest potential sabotages to the success of your parental leave transition and the joy of your experience is a perinatal mood disorder—your own, your partner's, or both.

It is not uncommon for new moms or dads to go through a few weeks of the "baby blues" as they adjust to life with their new child. This can be especially common when sleep-deprived or managing the hormone fluctuations of being a birthing mother or nursing. Although this wobble is considered normal, it can be hard to distinguish it from more serious issues like postpartum depression. Be sure to put regular screenings and check-ins with your health care provider or a therapist in all phases of your action plan. It is a good idea to solicit an advocate to check in with you and build that into the support section of your leave plan (your employer may offer help through an employee assistance program).

Part of the sneakiness of a perinatal mood or anxiety disorder is that our brains aren't actually functioning the way they normally do, and so you are not your best advocate, even if it feels like you are. Dr. Wendy Davis, executive director of Postpartum Support International, describes the challenge:

> When depression or anxiety hits, parents usually don't realize that what they're experiencing are actual symptoms; instead, they think they're failing and are mostly afraid and embarrassed to tell anyone, even when their distress is acute. Emotional and mental health complications are common during this transition, and there are many ways for parents to connect, learn more, and find resources for help. The earlier someone reaches out, the more quickly they will start feeling better. That starts with knowing they are not alone.

Resources

- **Postpartum Support International (PSI)** provides free access to perinatal mental health support and resources for everyone in the world. They provide specialized support via phone, text, online groups, individual and group communities of care for birthing and adoptive parents, partners, LGBTQ+ parents, military families, families experiencing loss and grief, and even grandparents: https://www.postpartum.net/get-help/.

Lactation

From bad latches to cracked nipples, breastfeeding—or the more inclusive term *bodyfeeding*—may be natural, but that doesn't mean it is easy. If you are planning to breastfeed your child, please know that challenges are very common, and support is widely available to help you be successful with this choice. You can often get a referral to a local lactation consultant through your health care system, and online help is also widely available. The Affordable Care Act (2010) mandated that most health insurance plans cover the cost of breast pumps as part of women's preventive health services. This rule applies to Marketplace plans as well as private insurance plans (except for plans that were grandfathered in).

Resources

- **Boober:** www.getboober.com
- **La Leche League:** www.lllusa.org
- **Office on Women's Health in the U.S. Department of Health and Human Services:** https://www.womenshealth.gov/breastfeeding

Infertility and Pregnancy Loss

People who struggle to conceive or suffer a pregnancy loss are often doing private grieving while trying to keep up appearances at work. According to the CDC, about 12% of women ages 15 to 44 have trouble getting pregnant or carrying a pregnancy to term. And according to the American College of Obstetrics and Gynecologists, 15% to 20% of known pregnancies end in miscarriage.

Although most new parents will not undergo these difficulties, the numbers are not insignificant. Many who experience these struggles do not get timely support or help to deal with the trauma involved. Instead, they are expected to carry on at work as if nothing were wrong. It can be difficult to communicate that we have suffered this kind of loss or know how to reach out and provide support to people who have. In the event that you or a loved one is experiencing infertility or miscarriage, there is support available; please reach out.

Resources

- **Postpartum Support International** (PSI) offers loss and grief support: https://www.postpartum.net/get-help/loss-grief-in-pregnancy-postpartum/.
- **Resolve** is a national infertility association offering resources and support to those experiencing infertility and pregnancy loss: www.resolve.org.
- **Return to Zero: HOPE:** www.rtzhope.org

Infant/Child Loss

No one wants to entertain the possibility that they may lose a child. Should you or someone you love face this excruciating reality, it is crucial to get support for the grieving process. Like becoming a parent, grief is a transformational transition that doesn't get enough attention, respect, or support in our society—let alone adequate leave time. Employee assistance programs often offer targeted counseling sessions and other support options and will provide direction during a devastating time.

Resources

- **Infant Loss Resources** is a nonprofit whose mission is to promote safe practices that reduce the risk of infant death and to provide grief support for families who have lost babies: wwww.infantlossresources.org.
- **Postpartum Support International** (PSI) offers loss and grief support: https://www.postpartum.net/get-help/loss-grief-in-pregnancy-postpartum/.
- **The Finley Project** is a holistic program that supports mothers who have experienced loss physically, emotionally, and spiritually at no financial cost to them: https://www.thefinleyproject.org/.

Further Reading
- *At a Loss*, Donna Rothert, PhD[5]
- *Empty Cradle, Broken Heart: Surviving the Death of Your Baby*, Deborah L. Davis, PhD[6]

Previous Trauma

Many people have experienced childhood trauma, sexual assault, or medical trauma that resurfaces when they are pregnant or have a child. This can catch you by surprise, and it is important to know that it is normal. Experiencing a reaction to past trauma is one of the challenges that is not accounted for in standard parental leave policies, but like any mental health difficulty, it will benefit you and help you resolve it more quickly if you reach out for support to process your feelings and reactions.

Resources

- **Mentalhelp.net's PTSD hotline:** https://www.mentalhelp.net/ptsd/hotline/
- **Postpartum Support International (PSI):** https://www.postpartum.net/get-help/

Other Health Issues for a Birthing Parent

Many people giving birth experience pregnancy complications or postpartum complications (ranging from minor to major) that compromise their physical health and well-being. Not everyone for whom such complications arise has the luxury of taking time off to recover.

Resources

- Check with your doctor, health insurance provider, and your employee assistance program for specific resources available to help you.

Postpartum Healing

Birthing parents should not underestimate the importance of healing, nor the time it takes to do so, even for an uncomplicated birth. According to a report published by The New America Foundation, for optimal health of mother and baby, paid maternity leave should be a minimum of six months.[7] Birthing people often hide their recovery experience for fear of being perceived as somehow inadequate to the challenges of childbirth. Because it is talked about so infrequently, women conclude others must be managing just fine and that they are in the minority when they experience a slow healing process. Many other cultures are much better at treating birthing bodies with respect and providing postpartum support. If you are welcoming a child through birth, build recovery support into your plan. It can also help to educate your loved ones about what to expect. For example, sex is off the table for a *minimum* of six weeks and the transition back to your pre-baby sex life may bring physical challenges (including impacts on breastfeeding, see https://www.llli.org/breastfeeding-info/breastfeeding-and-sex/) or emotions you will need to work through together.

Resources

- Check with your doctor, health insurance provider, and your employee assistance program for specific resources available to help you.

Health Issues for Your Child

Unfortunately, it is not unheard of for parents to be required to go back to work while their child is still in the neonatal intensive care unit. Welcoming a medically fragile child can add to the emotional and financial burden of family expansion. It is crucial to enlist extra support if this is your situation.

Resources

- **Centers for Disease Control (CDC):** https://www.cdc.gov/ncbddd/birthdefects/families-support.html
- **Hand to Hold** provides support to families with medically fragile babies: www.handtohold.org.
- **March of Dimes:** www.marchofdimes.org
- **National Perinatal Association:** http://www.nationalperinatal.org/fan

Further Reading

- *Just One of the Kids: Raising a Resilient Family When One of Your Children Has a Physical Disability*, Kay Harris Kriegsman and Sara Palmer[8]
- *Eat, Sleep, Save the World: Words of Encouragement for the Special Needs Parent*, Jamie Sumner[9]

Workplace Discrimination

Throughout this book I have encouraged you to assume goodwill on the part of your manager and others in your organization and work to find solutions. However, there are times when there is not simply a lack of goodwill, but downright discrimination. If you feel your employer is violating your civil rights through race, pregnancy, or gender discrimination, contacting a lawyer can help you understand all of your options and get a skilled advocate on your side.

Resources

- **American Civil Liberties Union:** www.aclu.org
- **A Better Balance:** www.abetterbalance.org
- **Center for Law & Social Policy (CLASP):** www.clasp.org
- **Equal Employment Opportunity Commission (EEOC):** www.eeoc.gov
- **National Partnership for Women and Families:** www.nationalpartnership.org

Conclusion

Whether or not you face any of these additional challenges yourself, it is important that the field of parental leave support grows in ways that are inclusive and kind. It will be a better world when we are all aware of the broad spectrum of experiences a working parent may face and know how to offer support.

See the Appendices for more information on the emerging working parent support ecosystem, a link to recommended books and resources that may offer additional support for your unique situation, and other ways to access tools and updated information as you navigate your full transition over the months and years.

Appendix One

Values Exercise List

- ☐ Acceptance
- ☐ Accountability
- ☐ Achievement
- ☐ Adaptability
- ☐ Adventure
- ☐ Altruism
- ☐ Ambition
- ☐ Authenticity
- ☐ Authority
- ☐ Autonomy
- ☐ Balance
- ☐ Beauty
- ☐ Being the best
- ☐ Belonging
- ☐ Career
- ☐ Caring

- ☐ Challenge
- ☐ Choice
- ☐ Collaboration
- ☐ Commitment
- ☐ Community
- ☐ Compassion
- ☐ Competence
- ☐ Confidence
- ☐ Connection
- ☐ Contentment
- ☐ Contribution
- ☐ Cooperation
- ☐ Courage
- ☐ Creativity
- ☐ Dignity
- ☐ Diversity

- ☐ Efficiency
- ☐ Environment
- ☐ Equity
- ☐ Ethics
- ☐ Excellence
- ☐ Excitement
- ☐ Expertise
- ☐ Fairness
- ☐ Faith
- ☐ Fun
- ☐ Fame
- ☐ Family
- ☐ Fast pace
- ☐ Financial rewards
- ☐ Financial stability
- ☐ Focus

Source: Exercise inspired by Sarah Cotton, PhD., Transitioning Well, LLC, and her Building Your Lighthouse exercise. Additional value options sourced from Brown, B (2019) Dare to Lead, and still others created by Author.
https://transitioningwell.com.au/wp-content/uploads/2020/05/Lighthouse-1.pdf
https://daretolead.brenebrown.com/wp-content/uploads/2019/02/Values.pdf

- Forgiveness
- Freedom
- Friendship
- Fun
- Future generations
- Generosity
- Giving back
- Grace
- Gratitude
- Growth
- Happiness
- Health
- Helping others
- Home
- Honesty
- Hope
- Humility
- Humor
- Imagination
- Independence
- Influence
- Initiative
- Integrity
- Intellect
- Intuition
- Joy
- Justice
- Kindness
- Knowledge
- Leadership
- Learning
- Legacy
- Leisure
- Love

- Loyalty
- Making a difference
- Nature
- Nurturing
- Openness
- Optimism
- Order
- Parenting
- Partnership
- Passion
- Patience
- Patriotism
- Peace
- Perseverance
- Personal fulfillment
- Personal growth
- Power
- Pride
- Privacy
- Productivity
- Promotion prospects
- Reaching potential
- Recognition
- Reliability
- Resourcefulness
- Respect
- Responsibility
- Results
- Risk-taking
- Romance
- Routine
- Safety
- Security

- Self-discipline
- Self-expression
- Self-respect
- Serenity
- Service
- Sharing
- Simplicity
- Solitude
- Spirituality
- Sportsmanship
- Status
- Stewardship
- Success
- Teaching
- Teamwork
- Thrift
- Time
- Tolerance
- Tradition
- Travel
- Trust
- Truth
- Understanding
- Uniqueness
- Usefulness
- Variety
- Vision
- Vulnerability
- Wealth
- Well-being
- Wholeheartedness
- Winning
- Wisdom
- Zest for life

Appendix Two

Free Resources from the Center for Parental Leave Leadership

My team and I have put together a number of free resources to support your transition:

Leave Planning Template: Sample Next Steps: Action Plan

In the *action plan* touchpoint in Chapter 6, you are asked to create a comprehensive transition plan. Use this template as an accelerator for that work. It has useful prompts to help you plan out all three phases and document your support team for phases 2 and 3.

Workplace Perinatal Mental Health Screen (and Referral Resources)

I recommend you complete a perinatal mental health screening during each month of your transition or if you're concerned about having a perinatal mood disorder at any point. You can access this screening tool for free on our resources page.

Parental Leave Transition Assessment (PLTA) Sample Report and Worksheet

In the *assessment* touchpoint in Chapter 5, I walked you through the **6-S System for Parental Leave Transition Success.** At my company, we've created a formalized version of this assessment that provides a transition risk score and recommendations on how to improve your asset-to-liability ratio. Viewing the sample report can give you ideas on how to address any liabilities you discovered and how to make the most of your assets. The 6-S System Worksheet gives you a place to work through this exercise and capture your information.

New Parent Checklists and Reflection Workbooks

If you would like a checklist to track all the moving pieces of planning your leave and return, you can download our checklists for moms and dads as well as reflection prompts to help you do the inner work involved in acknowledging your transition.

Manager Checklists and Resources

My most successful clients are those who work in partnership with their managers to plan and execute their leave and return. Feel free to download and share a manager checklist and other resources with your manager so they can better support you.

Values Exercise: Building Your North Star

Identifying your core values and building ways to live them into your day-to-day life will help you ground your decision making in your own unique perspective and help you guide your life by your unique North Star.

You can access all of these free resources, additional recommended readings, and more at http://www.cplleadership.com/playbook.

Appendix
Three

An Emerging Working Parent
Support Ecosystem

ec·o·sys·tem
/ˈēkōˌsistəm/
1. a group of interconnected elements formed by the interaction of a community with their environment: "the emerging parental leave ecosystem is at an exciting time in its development."

IT'S AN EXCITING time in the parental leave space because so many people are rising up to meet the needs of working parents. I think of it as an emerging working parent support ecosystem. This appendix provides an overview of what is quickly evolving to support you and the parents who come after you, as well as a snapshot of the key players at this moment in time.

Because it's an *emerging* ecosystem with much yet to be done, there is overlap among elements as people and organizations influence one another. For ease and brevity, I've consolidated elements wherever possible, but keep in mind that each of these categories carry many subcategories within them.

To the extent you can, draw on help from this system during your transition. If you are inspired to lend your voice to any of these efforts please reach out to them or to me—I am happy to connect you with or point you toward an organization that matches your interests.

Please visit www.cplleadership.com/playbook for updates and expansions of this ecosystem over time.

Today we have never been closer to the promised land for new parents in the United States, even if the impact of the coronavirus pandemic makes it feel further away than ever. Since the pandemic began in 2020, it is increasingly and painfully obvious to everyone that the way we handle leave and support working parents in this country is broken and not sustainable for families, society, or our economy. We cannot continue to ask working parents to bear an untenable financial and mental burden when they bring children into the world. We know what works in other countries from a policy standpoint, and through the hard work of the enterprising people in what I have dubbed the *working-parent support ecosystem*, we are beginning to understand what works in terms of best practices. The collective voices of these (predominantly) female founders and leaders are finally being heard. Their work is being embraced by both sides of the political aisle and within our companies and organizations, guaranteeing change.

Over the years I have watched as many other people whose experience of becoming a parent was, like mine, difficult (even traumatic) decide to turn their negative experience into organizations, products, advocacy, and services to help make the transition better for others.

Today, I am proud and privileged to situate my company, the Center for Parental Leave Leadership (CPLL), as another female-led organization within an emerging ecosystem of organizations and individuals dedicated to providing support to working parents on a number of fronts, from big-picture policy advocacy to hands-on (literally) breastfeeding help. As a futurist, I love to visualize what will be possible when this family support infrastructure is as well funded as our military industrial complex.

Policy Advocacy

Although CPLL provides policy development and consulting to companies, and we devote a portion of our time to pro bono legislative policy work, there are many dedicated individuals and organizations who have been hard at work for years (and decades, in many cases!) trying to pass state and federal legislation, as well as company policies, that come to the aid of working families. These family-friendly initiatives include guaranteed paid time off work to welcome a child and access to affordable childcare, among others.

The National Partnership for Working Families (NPWF) has been at the forefront of these issues, first bringing others into a broad coalition of advocates, starting in 1984, to work to enact the Family and Medical Leave Act (FMLA), which ultimately passed as unpaid job protection in 1993. Their coalition-building and efforts in recent years have focused on passing paid leave bills to make up for the funding that the FMLA lacked. Paid Leave + United States (PL+US), founded and run by Katie Bethel until early 2021, has had an impact at the legislative and company levels, using its advocacy skills to encourage companies to pass paid leave policies while also working toward a national solution. Family Values @ Work, founded by the indomitable Ellen Bravo, has developed a broad and powerful grassroots coalition that has been instrumental in the passage of paid sick days and family leave in cities and states across the United States, and Dawn Huckelbridge is guiding expanded efforts through the Paid Leave for All coalition and campaign. These are just a few of hundreds of organizations that have sprung into action to work on policy advocacy in the last five years.

Thought Leadership and Practice

As the first consulting company in the United States to focus exclusively on parental leave, my company, the Center for Parental Leave Leadership, has a hand in nearly every area of the ecosystem. I chose our name because I wanted to create a central space for learning and leadership focused on parental leave and rooted in the nonprofit ethos of service, while being a for-profit company that could walk its talk. For many years I felt like the consummate start-up, pivoting our work to where it was needed in an effort to both create and serve an emerging market. We bounced among thought leadership, coaching, policy, research, product development, training, practice, and more. In retrospect, that breadth and depth allowed me to understand and influence the intricacies of this new field *and* the deeply personal and individual human needs of families as well.

Because my goal is to fundamentally improve the way our country handles parental leave, I get to pay attention to all of the elements of the ecosystem in order to help others know what is available to them and how to stay ahead of the curve. In practice, as you've read about in this book, this can mean providing coaching to clients or training coaches (our evidence-based RETAIN parental leave coaching certification program is the first to exist). This can also mean we are helping companies train their managers so everyone can make the most of this overlooked leadership and personal development opportunity.

Other times it means our research team is leading a client's internal parental leave research or audit, or helping administer the first academically grounded self-assessment tool to help navigate parental leave (called the Parental Leave Transition Assessment [PLTA]), or the first in-workplace screening for perinatal mood disorders.

Thanks to the dedicated work of the folks referenced previously, a national paid leave policy is on the way. However, making sure that state and federal policy works for the individual company (or making a policy in the interim) takes forethought and consideration. Too often companies ignore the careful work that is needed to ensure a policy is successful in practice and help that company reach its goals and provide a family-friendly workplace. We thrive on educating and coaching new parents, managers, and company leadership on how to talk about and support parental leave in a way that engages, develops, and retains parent employees.

Practice is what will set employers apart once the playing field is leveled in terms of policy. And practice is what will make or break the experience for new parents. When companies begrudgingly provide parental leave because they have to, the climate for the new parent is unwelcoming and negatively affects morale, productivity, and retention. When good practice fully supports the parental leave transition, everyone can thrive, including whole teams and organizations.

Research and Communications

Prominent research and media coverage of issues related to the transition to working parenthood is absolutely key to changing the policy, practice, and culture. A strong evidence-based focus is forming in the scholarly literature from countless researchers and centers studying the topic. Their work can be found at the Work+Family Research Network hub and across many well-respected networks and centers within colleges and universities, such as the Work, Family and Health Network at Harvard University and the Boston College Center for Work and Family. Many think tanks and nonprofits are also putting out excellent reports and research on the topic. For example, New America's Better Life Lab, directed by Brigid Schulte with Senior Fellow for Paid Leave Policy and Strategy, Vicki Shabo, continues to bring attention to paid leave policy through data gathering, research, and reporting.

On the popular press side, *Working Mother* magazine, founded in 1979, shined an early spotlight on the issues facing working families. Today, we are seeing an explosion of reporting. In 2015, Fatherly.com increased the gender balance by bringing a dad's perspective to the public press. *New York Times Parenting*, started in 2019 and led by editor Jessica Grose, provides a consistent source of well-researched and thoughtful work by countless writers (too many to name!) who have been instrumental in keeping up the drumbeat of information. And a hat tip to the hundreds of mommy bloggers, podcasters, and social media influencers who are keeping the topic at the forefront.

Compliance and Leave Navigation

As new parental leave legislation has been inconsistently passed across various states, and policies implemented within various companies vary, what has evolved is a confusing patchwork of rapidly changing policies, benefits, and private insurance options that are nearly impossible to follow or understand. Companies, especially those that operate in more than one state, have spent countless dollars trying to sort out how to remain compliant with the various laws. We spend a lot of time consulting with companies to help them find solutions in this landscape.

Anna Steffeney, a working mother who lived in Germany while working for a US-based big-tech company, learned the hard way that the awful stories she was hearing about parental leave in the United States were true. After a positive parental leave transition in Germany with her first child, she moved back to the United States. Her experience with her second child was the opposite of positive, even though she worked for the same company. This experience led her to quit her prestigious job and change the trajectory of her career. She poured her parenthood-inspired innovation and her deep skills and knowledge into a new entrepreneurial venture: building a tech company focused on creating a comprehensive compliance and leave management software solution to navigate all the nitty-gritty details and help employees understand the benefits they had available to them. The company she founded, LeaveLogic, was acquired by Unum, the top disability insurer in both the United States and the United Kingdom. Other insurance companies and leave management providers are joining LeaveLogic and Unum and moving into what had been a largely untapped space before Anna's innovation, offering software solutions that help employers save on the administrative costs of managing leave while providing a uniform compliance navigation and leave experience to their employees.

Parental Health and Wellness

High-quality physical and mental health care is absolutely crucial during the transition into parenthood, and a number of innovative organizations are doing work in this area.

It's easy to forget—and often policies don't emphasize it—but health care should always include mental health care. In the perinatal mental health space, CPLL's partner organization, Postpartum Support International (PSI), is globally recognized for their work providing support and education for emotional complications and perinatal mood and anxiety disorders (PMADs), such as prenatal or postpartum depression, anxiety, and OCD, for both moms and dads. PSI employees and volunteers around the globe are largely drawn to the work through their own personal experience with PMADs and tap into their lived experience as well as their training to support others.

Wendy Newhouse Davis, PSI executive director, described their approach to me:

> *Our objective is to provide inclusive and culturally informed services, resources, and connection for the emotional and mental health needs of pregnant, postpartum, and post-loss individuals and families. We know that pregnancy and postpartum do not always go as planned, and there are times that anyone can be overwhelmed by unexpected mental health challenges. We want families to know that they are not alone, that they are not to blame, and that with help they will feel well again. So many expecting and new parents experience emotional complications, but because people don't talk about it, the individual often ends up thinking they are the only one, and they can't tell anyone. PSI is a safe and informed place to reach out for help; our staff and volunteer support network provide free services through phone, text, email, secure online support groups, private Facebook groups, and local Support Coordinators. We understand what they are going through and provide nonjudgmental support and connection to resources. Many of those we help end up coming back to volunteer. Everything can be found through the website www.postpartum.net. We want parents to know: you don't need a diagnosis to reach out for help.*

Other female founders have chosen to address what was lacking in their own parental health care experience by joining the tech start-up race and creating "femtech" solutions. Ovia, which started as a fertility tracking app, has since moved into health care support for pregnancy and postpartum. Maven, the first to focus telemedicine on mothers, has created a virtual care model built for women and families that delivers better outcomes at lower costs. Cleo, the highest-funded femtech start-up yet, is an employee benefits platform for working families whose clients operate in 55 countries. Another example, Mahmee, was started by mother-daughter duo Melissa Hanna and Linda Hanna, who saw how Black women and women of color were being disproportionately affected by subpar communication among a mother's various care providers. Their platform solution received first-round funding from high-profile investors such as Mark Cuban and Serena Williams. By creating online communities of care within a mobile app, Mahmee aims to give mothers of all races a singular place to book appointments, access information about their health, and link in-network physicians such as their obstetrician or pediatrician with ancillary providers such as lactation consultants, therapists, or nutritionists to ensure that information is shared full circle and that all mothers are given the thoughtful proactive care they deserve.

Supporting Services

In addition to the companies who focus on health and wellness or providing employee benefits, there is a vast web of small and mid-size mother-led companies entering the marketplace with a goal to support new families.

These companies provide vital services such as birth education, midwifery, birth and postpartum doula support, lactation and sleep consultation, night nursing, and more. Although not new, many of these services were historically seen as something only privileged or crunchy moms used, but as their value has been documented they have moved into the mainstream.

Giving birth is not the type of experience that lends itself well to virtual support, but the pandemic has forced new parents and their providers to get creative. For example, lactation consulting, once firmly seen as something that needed to be done in person, is now available virtually through services such as Brooklyn-based *boober*. And previously well-established companies such as Milkstork—a shipping service for breastfeeding working moms to quickly and safely send pumped breastmilk home while they are away—are having to rethink their business models in the face of drastically reduced travel.

And lest you think only moms are being supported, companies are finally realizing that dads are an untapped market, too. A recent internet search for *products for new dads* returned over 12 million hits, while *services for new dads* came in just under at 11.5 million.

Funding and Investment

Investors are beginning to see the support of working parents for the gold rush it will become. I only half-jokingly say that the investment impact and resulting societal change (and ROI) will be "bigger than weed." The emerging parental leave ecosystem will require countless products and services across many sectors of society and over multiple years of transition. With roughly 80% of employees becoming a parent at least once in their career life cycle, and the multiplier effect from their managers, coaches, doctors, families, and more, it is safe to say we are entering the decade of the working parent.

An emerging ecosystem with potential like this needs massive investment from multiple directions. We are beginning to see the money flow in from foundations, government, and tech investors. Although still rare, Series A, B, and C investment rounds are bringing in tens of millions of dollars for some start-ups. Angel and seed funding has been slow to take off, in large part because investment money is still overwhelmingly controlled by men; however, we are seeing increasing numbers of women starting their own funds and committing their investments to women-owned businesses.

Foundation grantmaking is critical to deepen understanding of what works and what doesn't through research, funding of capacity building within existing organizations, and to stimulate innovation. Foundations such as Alfred P. Sloan and Ford are long-time funders of initiatives aimed to support working families. In recent years many foundations have pivoted their grants to focus on parental leave and working parents specifically. Their leadership has inspired countless family firms and larger foundations to join them. For example, eight national foundations recently joined together to launch the Care for All with Respect and Equity (CARE) fund and have pledged $50 million over five years to build a comprehensive, publicly supported care infrastructure.

Speaking of a care infrastructure, government funding has also recently come into play in a big way with Biden's proposed $1.8 trillion dollar infrastructure investment plan designed to support working families.

Legal

We are a nation of laws, so our ecosystem also uses the courts to fight for working parent support and protection, including protection from pregnancy and employment discrimination. For over 100 years, the American Civil Liberties Union (ACLU) has worked "to defend and preserve the individual rights and liberties guaranteed to every person in this country by the Constitution and laws of the United States," always with a goal of winning over hearts and minds toward progress (www.aclu.org). Another long-time champion, the National Women's Law Center (NWLC), was founded by Marcia Greenberger in 1972 and advocates for women's rights through litigation and policy initiatives. Working for equitable policies since 1969, the Center for Law and Social Policy (CLASP) has taken a leading role to ensure that lower income employees are included in leave laws. More recently, in 2006, Sherry Leiwant and Dina Bakst cofounded A Better Balance to "use the power of the law to advance justice for workers, so they can care for themselves and their loved ones without jeopardizing their economic security" (https://www.abetterbalance.org/our-issues/).

These are just a few of the other organizations at the forefront of policy creation as well as pregnancy and employee discrimination protections. Others, such as lawyer Hermine Hayes-Klein, fight for human rights in childbirth and the right for everyone to be treated well when becoming a parent.

Conclusion

I am gratified to see the sea change under way when it comes to supporting working parents. For too long, too many employers have seen the parental leave time frame as a burden and have ignored and missed out on the growth possibilities inherent in this major transition. In addition to being a time of opportunity for employers, it is one of the juiciest times for an employee to learn about themselves while deepening their strengths and mitigating their liabilities—at work and home.

As a new parent, you are now a part of an ecosystem that has the power to transform the lives of millions of Americans and finally leverage the parental leave transition as the asset it will be if parents are properly supported. Welcome to the movement!

Appendix Four

Recommended Reading

And Baby Makes Three: The Six-Step Plan for Preserving Marital Intimacy and Rekindling Romance After Baby Arrives, by John Gottman, PhD, and Julie Schwartz Gottman, PhD

At a Loss: Finding Your Way After Miscarriage, Stillbirth, or Infant Death, by Donna Rothert, PhD

Big Magic: Creative Living Beyond Fear, by Elizabeth Gilbert

CEO of Me: Creating a Life That Works in the Flexible Job Age, by Brenda A. Lautsch and Ellen Ernst Kossek, PhD

Cribsheet: Data-Driven Guide to Better, More Relaxed Parenting, from Birth to Preschool, by Emily Oster, PhD

Dare to Lead: Brave Work. Tough Conversations. Whole Hearts, by Brené Brown, PhD

Eat, Sleep, Save the World: Words of Encouragement for the Special Needs Parent, by Jamie Sumner

Eight Dates: Essential Conversations for a Lifetime of Love, by John Gottman, PhD, Julie Schwartz Gottman, PhD, Doug Abrams, and Rachel Carlton Abrams, MD

Emotional Intelligence: Why It Can Matter More Than IQ, by Daniel Goleman, PhD

Empty Cradle, Broken Heart: Surviving the Death of Your Baby, by Deborah L. Davis, PhD

Expecting Better: Why the Conventional Pregnancy Wisdom Is Wrong—and What You Really Need to Know, by Emily Oster, PhD

Fair Play: A Game-Changing Solution for When You Have Too Much to Do (and More Life to Live), by Eve Rodsky

Fed Up: Emotional Labor, Women, and the Way Forward, by Gemma Hartley

Finding Time: The Economics of Work-Life Conflict, by Heather Boushey, PhD

Head, Heart and Guts: How the World's Best Companies Develop Complete Leaders, by David L. Dotlich, PhD, Peter C. Cairo, PhD, Stephen H. Rhinesmith, PhD

Here's the Plan. Your Practical, Tactical Guide to Advancing Your Career During Pregnancy and Parenting, by Allyson Downey

How Not to Hate Your Husband After Kids, by Jancee Dunn

Hunt Gather, Parent: What Ancient Cultures Can Teach Us About the Lost Art of Raising Happy, Helpful Little Humans, by Michaeleen Doucleff, PhD

Like a Mother: A Feminist Journey Through the Science and Culture of Pregnancy, by Angela Garbes

Making Motherhood Work: How Women Manage Careers and Caregiving, by Caitlyn Collins, PhD

Maternal Optimism: Forging Positive Paths Through Work and Motherhood, by Jamie Ladge, PhD, and Danna Greenberg, PhD

Mindset: The New Psychology of Success, by Carol S. Dweck, PhD

Optimal Outcomes: Free Yourself from Conflict at Work, at Home, and in Life, by Jennifer Goldman-Wetzler, PhD

Ordinary Insanity: Fear and the Silent Crisis of Motherhood in America, by Sarah Menkedick

Overwhelmed: Coping with Life's Ups and Downs, by Nancy Schlossberg, EdD

Overwhelmed: How to Work, Love, and Play When No One Has the Time, by Brigid Schulte

Parents Who Lead: The Leadership Approach You Need to Parent with Purpose, Fuel Your Career, and Create a Richer Life, by Steward D. Friedman, PhD, and Alyssa F. Westring, PhD

Playing Big: Practical Wisdom for Women Who Want to Speak Up, Create, and Lead, by Tara Mohr

Raising the Race: Black Career Women Redefine Marriage, Motherhood, and Community, by Riche J. Daniel Barnes, PhD

Setting the Wire: A Memoir of Postpartum Psychosis, by Sarah Townsend

Steering by Starlight: The Science and Magic of Finding Your Destiny, by Martha Beck, PhD

Such a Fun Age, by Kiley Reid

The 15 Commitments of Conscious Leadership: A New Paradigm for Sustainable Success, by Jim Dethmer, Diana Chapman, PhD, Kaley Klemp

The Baby Owner's Manual: Operating Instructions, Trouble-Shooting Tips, and Advice on First-Year Maintenance, by Louis Borgenicht MD, Joe Borgenicht

The Fifth Trimester: The Working Mom's Guide to Style, Sanity, and Success After Baby, by Lauren Smith Brody

The Mama Natural Week-by-Week Guide to Pregnancy and Childbirth, by Genevieve Howland

The Moment of Lift: How Empowering Women Changes the World, by Melinda Gates

The Mother Dance: How Children Change Your Life, by Harriet Learner, PhD

The Seven Spiritual Laws of Success: A Pocketbook Guide to Fulfilling Your Dreams, by Deepak Chopra, MD

The Whole Person Workplace: Building Better Workplaces Through Work-Life, Wellness, and Employee Support, by Scott Behson, PhD

Think Again: The Power of Knowing What You Don't Know, by Adam Grant, PhD

What No One Tells You: A Guide to Your Emotions from Pregnancy to Motherhood, by Alexandra Sacks, MD, and Catherine Birndorf, MD

Working Dads Survival Guide, by Scott Behson, PhD

13 Things Mentally Strong People Don't Do: Take Back Your Power, Embrace Change, Face Your Fears, and Train Your Brain for Happiness and Success, by Amy Morin, LCSW

7 Habits of Highly Effective People, by Stephen R. Covey, DRE

****

To access our continuously updated list of recommended books, articles, websites, and podcast resources please visit our website: cplleadership.com/playbook.

****

Endnotes and General References

Introduction

Endnotes

1. M. J. Budig. (2014). The fatherhood bonus and the motherhood penalty: Parenthood and the gender gap in pay. Third Way. https://www.thirdway.org/report/the-fatherhood-bonus-and-the-motherhood-penalty-parenthood-and-the-gender-gap-in-pay
2. J. B. Bear & P. Glick. (2017). Breadwinner bonus and caregiver penalty in workplace rewards for men and women. *Social Psychological and Personality Science*, 8(7), 780–788.

Chapter 1) Parental Leave Is A Mess—Let's Fix It!

Endnotes

1. E. Scalia & W. W. Beach. (2020). *National compensation survey: Employee benefits in the United States, March 2020*. Bureau of Labor Statistics, United States Department of Labor. https://www.bls.gov/ncs/ebs/benefits/2020/employee-benefits-in-the-united-states-march-2020.pdf
2. S. Brown, J. Herr, R. Roy, et al. (2020). *Employee and worksite perspectives of the Family and Medical Leave Act: Executive summary for results from the*

2018 surveys. United States Department of Labor. https://www.dol.gov/sites/dolgov/files/OASP/evaluation/pdf/WHD_FMLA2018SurveyResults_ExecutiveSummary_Aug2020.pdf

3. Economic Policy Institute. (2020). The cost of child care in [insert state]. https://www.epi.org/child-care-costs-in-the-united-states/

4. C. Ewing-Nelson & J. Tucker. (2021). A year into the pandemic, women are still short nearly 5.1 million jobs [Fact Sheet]. National Women's Law Center. https://nwlc.org/wp-content/uploads/2021/03/Feb-Jobs-Day-v2.pdf

5. B. C. Tefft. (2016). Acute sleep deprivation and risk of motor vehicle crash involvement [Technical Report]. AAA Foundation for Traffic Safety. https://aaafoundation.org/acute-sleep-deprivation-risk-motor-vehicle-crash-involvement/

6. Office of Advocacy. (2016). *United States small business profile*. US Small Business Administration. https://www.sba.gov/sites/default/files/advocacy/United_States.pdf

7. D. G. Allen. (2008). Retaining talent: A guide to analyzing and managing employee turnover. Society for Human Resource Management. https://www.shrm.org/hr-today/trends-and-forecasting/special-reports-and-expert-views/Documents/Retaining-Talent.pdf

8. Joint Economic Committee. (n.d.). *The economic benefits of paid leave* [Fact Sheet]. United States Congress. https://www.jec.senate.gov/public/_cache/files/646d2340-dcd4-4614-ada9-be5b1c3f445c/jec-fact-sheet---economic-benefits-of-paid-leave.pdf

9. D. Patton, J. Costich, & N. Lidströmer. (2017). Paid parental leave policies and infant mortality rates in OECD countries: Policy implications for the United States. *World Medical and Health Policy*, 9(1), 6–23. https://onlinelibrary.wiley.com/doi/epdf/10.1002/wmh3.214

10. OECD. (2021). Infant mortality rates [Indicator]. https://data.oecd.org/healthstat/infant-mortality-rates.htm

11. Centers for Disease Control Prevention. (2020). *Pregnancy mortality surveillance system*. Department of Health and Human Services. https://www.cdc.gov/reproductivehealth/maternal-mortality/pregnancy-mortality-surveillance-system.htm#:~:text=Since%20the%20Pregnancy%20Mortality%20Surveillance,100%2C000%20live%20births%20in%202017

12. The World Bank. (2019). Maternal mortality ratio (modeled estimate, per 100,000 live births)—European Union [Indicator]. https://data.worldbank.org/indicator/SH.STA.MMRT?locations=EU

13. The World Bank (2019). Maternal mortality ratio (modeled estimate, per 100,000 live births)—Canada [Indicator]. https://data.worldbank.org/indicator/SH.STA.MMRT?locations=CA

14. Centers for Disease Control Prevention. (2019). *Racial and ethnic disparities continue in pregnancy-related deaths*. Department of Health and Human

Services. https://www.cdc.gov/media/releases/2019/p0905-racial-ethnic-disparities-pregnancy-deaths.html

15. J. F. Paulson & S. D. Bazemore. (2010). Prenatal and postpartum depression in fathers and its association with maternal depression: A meta-analysis. *JAMA*, *303*(19), 1961–1969.

16. D. B. Singley & L. M. Edwards. (2015). Men's perinatal mental health in the transition to fatherhood. *Professional Psychology: Research and Practice*, *46*(5), 309–316.

17. C. C. Miller. (2019). Sweden finds a simple way to improve new mothers' health. It involves fathers. *New York Times*. https://www.nytimes.com/2019/06/04/upshot/sweden-finds-a-simple-way-to-improve-new-mothers-health-it-involves-fathers.html

18. R. J. Petts, D. L. Carlson, & C. Knoester. (2020). If I [take] leave, will you stay? Paternity leave and relationship stability. *Journal of Social Policy*, *49*(4), 829–849.

19. R. Bleiweis. (2020). Quick facts about the gender wage gap. Center for American Progress. https://www.americanprogress.org/issues/women/reports/2020/03/24/482141/quick-facts-gender-wage-gap/

20. Catalyst. (2021). Women CEOs of the S&P 500. https://www.catalyst.org/research/women-ceos-of-the-sp-500/

References

Martin, N., & Montagne, R. (2017). Nothing protects black women from dying in pregnancy and childbirth. ProPublica. https://www.propublica.org/article/nothing-protects-black-women-from-dying-in-pregnancy-and-childbirth

Michelson, J. (2021). How small companies can offer great paid-leave programs. *Harvard Business Review*. https://hbr.org/2021/01/how-small-companies-can-offer-great-paid-leave-programs

Popper, N. (2020). Paternity leave has long-lasting benefits. So why don't more American men take it? *New York Times*. https://www.nytimes.com/2020/04/17/parenting/paternity-leave.html#:~:text=Men%20Who%20Take%20Paternity%20Leave%20Are%20Less%20Likely%20to%20Get%20Divorced&text=Their%20research%20demonstrates%20that%20paternity,Unlock%20more%20free%20articles

Rehel, E. M. (2014). When dad stays home too: Paternity leave, gender, and parenting. *Gender and Society*, *28*(1), 110–132. https://www-jstor-org.proxy.lib.pdx.edu/stable/43669858?seq=1#metadata_info_tab_contents

Same Sex Parents. (2019). Gender neutral/non-binary parent titles. https://www.same-sexparents.com/post/gender-neutral-non-binary-parent-titles

Chapter 2) The 10A Transition Touchpoints Framework

Endnotes

1. Pew Research Center. (2017). Modern parenthood: Roles of moms and dads converge as they balance work and family [Report]. https://www.pewsocialtrends.org/2013/03/14/modern-parenthood-roles-of-moms-and-dads-converge-as-they-balance-work-and-family/
2. S. Canilang, C. Duchan, K. Kreiss, et al. (2020). *Report on the economic well-being of US households in 2019, featuring supplemental data from April 2020.* Board of Governors of the Federal Reserve System. https://www.federalreserve.gov/publications/files/2019-report-economic-well-being-us-households-202005.pdf
3. Canilang, Duchan, Kreiss, et al., *Report on the economic well-being of US households in 2019.*
4. Pew Research Center. (2019). Despite challenges at home and work, most working moms and dads say being employed is what's best for them [Report]. https://www.pewresearch.org/fact-tank/2019/09/12/despite-challenges-at-home-and-work-most-working-moms-and-dads-say-being-employed-is-whats-best-for-them/
5. Bureau of Labor Statistics. (2020). *Employment characteristics of families—2019.* (USDL-20–0670). United States Department of Labor. https://www.bls.gov/news.release/pdf/famee.pdf
6. Pew Research Center. (2013). Americans widely support paid family and medical leave, but differ over specific policies [Report]. https://www.pewsocialtrends.org/2017/03/23/americans-widely-support-paid-family-and-medical-leave-but-differ-over-specific-policies/
7. 99designs. (2017). How mompreneurs balance business and family [Infographic]. https://99designs.com/blog/business/mom-entrepreneur-infographic/
8. Pew Research Center, Americans widely support paid family and medical leave, but differ over specific policies.
9. Pew Research Center, Americans widely support paid family and medical leave, but differ over specific policies.
10. Pew Research Center, Americans widely support paid family and medical leave, but differ over specific policies.
11. Pew Research Center. (2019). Despite challenges at home and work, most working moms and dads say being employed is what's best for them [Report].

12. Pew Research Center, Despite challenges at home and work, most working moms and dads say being employed is what's best for them.
13. Pew Research Center, Despite challenges at home and work, most working moms and dads say being employed is what's best for them.
14. E. Barba-Müller, S. Craddock, S. Carmona, et al. (2019). Brain plasticity in pregnancy and the postpartum period: Links to maternal caregiving and mental health. *Archives of Women's Mental Health, 22*(2), 289–299.
15. E. Abraham, T. Hendler, I. Shapira-Lichte, et al. (2014). Father's brain is sensitive to childcare experiences. *Proceedings of the National Academy of Sciences, 111*(27), 9792–9797. https://www.pnas.org/content/111/27/9792.abstract?sid=e3887327–4793–48ef-9f22–7cb7d4c82a33
16. D. L. Dotlich, P. C. Cairo, & S. H. Rhinesmith. (2010). *Head, heart and guts: How the world's best companies develop complete leaders.* Jossey-Bass.

References

Beacom, A. M. (2013). The RETAIN maternity leave transition coaching model: Applying Schlossberg's transition theory to create a new model of executive coaching. Doctoral Dissertation. Teachers College, Columbia University.

Behson, S. (2021). *The whole-person workplace: Building better workplaces through work-life, wellness, and employee support.* Authors Place Press.

Lerner, S. (2010). *The war on moms: On life in a family-unfriendly nation.* Wiley.

Warner, J. (2005). *Perfect madness: Motherhood in the age of anxiety.* Riverhead Books.

Chapter 4) Touchpoint 1: Announcement

Endnotes

1. A. Morin. (2014). *13 things mentally strong people don't do.* HarperCollins.
2. A. Morin. (2017). How mentally strong people deal with snarky comments. *Forbes.* https://www.forbes.com/sites/amymorin/2017/09/08/how-mentally-strong-people-deal-with-snarky-comments/?sh=6bae18381cdb

References

Jones, K. P. (2017). To tell or not to tell? Examining the role of discrimination in the pregnancy disclosure process at work. *Journal of Occupational Health Psychology, 22*(2), 239–250.

King, E. B., & Botsford, W. E. (2009). Managing pregnancy disclosures: Understanding and overcoming the challenges of expectant motherhood at work. *Human Resource Management Review, 19*(4), 314–323.

Little, L., Hinojosa, A., & Lynch, J. (2017). Make them feel: How the disclosure of pregnancy to a supervisor leads to changes in perceived supervisor support. *Organization Science, 28*(4), 618–635.

Chapter 5) Touchpoint 2: Assess

Endnote

1. W. Bridges. (n.d.). Transition as "the way through." William Bridges Associates. https://wmbridges.com/resources/transition-management-articles/transition-as-the-way-through/

References

Alcañiz, L. (n.d.). Bringing back the Hispanic tradition of "cuarentena" after childbirth. Babycenter. https://www.babycenter.com/baby/postpartum-health/bringing-back-the-hispanic-tradition-of-cuarentena-after-chi_10346386

Beacom, A. M. (2013). The RETAIN maternity leave transition coaching model: Applying Schlossberg's transition theory to create a new model of executive coaching. Doctoral Dissertation. Teachers College, Columbia University.

Becerra, M. (2017). From the cuarentena to the faja: Postpartum wisdom from my abuelita. Academic Mami. https://academicmami.com/www.academic-mami.com//2017/07/from-cuarentena-to-faja-postpartum.html

Behson, S. (2021). *The whole-person workplace: Building better workplaces through work-life, wellness, and employee support.* Authors Place Press.

Dotlich, D. L., Cairo, P. C., & Rhinesmith, S. H. (2010). *Head, heart and guts: How the world's best companies develop complete leaders.* Jossey-Bass.

Makhijani, P. (2021). How food traditions nourish new moms. *New York Times.* https://www.nytimes.com/2021/02/25/parenting/postpartum-food-traditions.html?campaign_id=118andemc=edit_ptg_20210227andinstance_id=27536

andnl=nyt-parentingandregi_id=92074131andsegment_id=52466andte=
1anduser_id=f6d842a532d42f904645d294c302c650

Schalken, L. (2005). Birth customs around the world. Parents Network. https://www.parents.com/pregnancy/giving-birth/vaginal/birth-customs-around-the-world/

Schlossberg, N. K. (1984). *Counseling adults in transition*. Springer.

Schlossberg, N. K., & Kay, S. (2003). *The transition guide: A new way to think about change*. Transition Works.

Shatzman, C. (2017). Pregnancy and birth traditions around the world. The Bump. https://www.thebump.com/a/birth-traditions-around-the-world

Chapter 6) Touchpoint 3: Action Plan

Endnotes

1. R. Buehler & D. Griffin. (2018). The planning fallacy. In G. Oettingen, A. T. Sevincer, & P. Gollwitzer (Eds.), *The psychology of thinking about the future* (517–538). Guilford.

2. E. Hetherington, S. McDonald, T. Williamson, et al. (2018). Social support and maternal mental health at 4 months and 1 year postpartum: Analysis from the All Our Families cohort. *Journal of Epidemiology and Community Health*, 72(10), 933–939.

3. M. Ohara, T. Okada, B. Aleksic, et al. (2017). Social support helps protect against perinatal bonding failure and depression among mothers: A prospective cohort study. *Scientific Reports*, 7(1), 1–8.

4. S. Ginja, J. Coad, E. Bailey, et al. (2018). Associations between social support, mental wellbeing, self-efficacy and technology use in first-time antenatal women: Data from the BaBBLeS cohort study. *BMC Pregnancy and Childbirth*, 18(1), 1–11.

5. M. Angley, A. Divney, U. Magriples, et al. (2015). Social support, family functioning and parenting competence in adolescent parents. *Maternal and Child Health Journal*, 19(1), 67–73.

6. R. Small, A. J. Taft, & S. J. Brown. (2011). The power of social connection and support in improving health: Lessons from social support interventions with childbearing women. *BMC Public Health*, 11(5), 1–11.

7. G. T. Doran. (1981). There's a S.M.A.R.T. way to write management's goals and objectives. *Management Review*, 70(11), 35–36.

8. Y. Afshar, J. Y. Mei, K. D. Gregory, et al. (2018). Birth plans—Impact on mode of delivery, obstetrical interventions, and birth experience satisfaction: A prospective cohort study. *Birth*, 45(1), 43–49.

Chapter 7) Touchpoint 4: Acknowledge the Transition to Parenthood

Endnotes

1. E. Lisitsa. (2013). Bringing baby home: The research. The Gottman Institute. https://www.gottman.com/blog/bringing-baby-home-the-research/
2. J. M. Gottman & J. S. Gottman. (2008). *And baby makes three.* Three Rivers Press.
3. S. J. Behson. (2015). *The working dad's survival guide: How to succeed at work and at home.* Motivational Press.
4. B. Harrington, T. L. McHugh, & J. S. Fraone. (2019). Expanded paid parental leave: Measuring the impact of leave on work and family. Boston College Center for Work and Family. https://www.bc.edu/content/dam/files/centers/cwf/research/publications/researchreports/Expanded%20Paid%20Parental%20Leave-%20Study%20Findings%20FINAL%2010-31-19.pdf
5. L. Nepomnyaschy & J. Waldfogel. (2007). Paternity leave and fathers involvement with their young children: Evidence from the American ECLS–B. *Community, Work and Family, 10*(4), 427–453.
6. R. J. Petts & C. Knoester. (2018). Paternity leave-taking and father engagement. *Journal of Marriage and Family, 80*(5), 1144–1162.
7. R. J. Petts, C. Knoester, & J. Waldfogel. (2020). Fathers' paternity leave-taking and children's perceptions of father-child relationships in the United States. *Sex Roles, 82*(3), 173–188.
8. A. Sarkadi, R. Kristiansson, & S. Bremberg. (2008). Fathers' involvement and children's developmental outcomes: A systematic review of longitudinal studies. *Acta Paediatrica, 97*(2), 153–158.
9. A. Kotsadam & H. Finseraas. (2011). The state intervenes in the battle of the sexes: Causal effects of paternity leave. *Social Science Research, 40*(6), 1611–1622.
10. R. J. Petts, C. Knoester, & J. Waldfogel. (2020). Fathers' paternity leave-taking and children's perceptions of father-child relationships in the United States. *Sex Roles, 82*(3), 173–188.
11. R. J. Petts, D. L. Carlson, & C. Knoester. (2020). If I [take] leave, will you stay? Paternity leave and relationship stability. *Journal of Social Policy, 49*(4), 829–849.
12. E. A. Johansson. (2010). The effect of own and spousal parental leave on earnings. Institute for Labour Market Policy Evaluation Working Paper No. 2010, 4. https://www.econstor.eu/bitstream/10419/45782/1/623752174.pdf

13. B. Harrington, T. L. McHugh, & J. S. Fraone. (2019). Expanded paid parental leave: Measuring the impact of paid family leave. Boston College Center for Work and Family. https://www.bc.edu/content/dam/files/centers/cwf/research/publications/researchreports/Expanded%20Paid%20Parental%20Leave-%20Study%20Findings%20FINAL%2010-31-19.pdf
14. E. Appelbaum & R. Milkman. (2015). Leaves that pay: Employer and worker experiences with paid family leave in California. Center for Economic and Policy Research. https://cepr.net/documents/publications/paid-family-leave-1-2011.pdf

Reference

Warren, S. R. (2021). 10 most common reasons for divorce. Marriage.com. https://www.marriage.com/advice/divorce/10-most-common-reasons-for-divorce/

Chapter 9) Touchpoint 5: Appropriately Keep in Touch

Endnote

1. A. Pozniak, K. Olson, K. Wen, et al. (2012). *Family and medical leave in 2012: Detailed results appendix.* Abt Associates.

Chapter 10) Touchpoint 6: Advocate

Endnotes

1. Equality at Home. (2020). Survey shows inequality is an issue at home. https://equalityathome.com/blog/f/survey-shows-inequality-is-an-issue-at-home
2. E. Rodsky. (2021). *Fair play: A game-changing solution for when you have too much to do (and more life to live).* G. P. Putnam's Sons.
3. A. Chiu. (2018). Beyoncé, Serena Williams open up about potentially fatal childbirths, a problem especially for black mothers. *Washington Post.* https://www.washingtonpost.com/news/morning-mix/wp/2018/08/07/beyonce-serena-williams-open-up-about-potentially-fatal-childbirths-a-problem-especially-for-black-mothers/
4. R. Haskell. (2018). Serena Williams on motherhood, marriage, and making her comeback. *Vogue.* https://www.vogue.com/article/serena-williams-vogue-cover-interview-february-2018?mbid=zr_serenawilliams

References

Agency for Healthcare Research and Quality. (2019). *National healthcare quality and disparities report*. Department of Health and Human Services. https://www
.ahrq.gov/sites/default/files/wysiwyg/research/findings/nhqrdr/2019qdr-core-measures-disparities.pdf

Amanatullah, E. T., & Morris, M. W. (2010). Negotiating gender roles: Gender differences in assertive negotiating are mediated by women's fear of backlash and attenuated when negotiating on behalf of others. *Journal of Personality and Social Psychology, 98*(2), 256–267.

Sacks, A. (2017). The birth of a mother. *New York Times*. https://www.nytimes
.com/2017/05/08/well/family/the-birth-of-a-mother.html

Chapter 11) Touchpoint 7: Arrangements for Return

Endnote

1. R. Nixon. (1962). *Six crises*. Doubleday.

References

Basu, A., & Rotter, N. (2020). Preparing children for when their parents go to work. MassGeneral for Children, Massachusetts General Hospital. https://www.massgeneral.org/children/coronavirus/preparing-children-for-when-their-parents-return-to-work

Boehmová, Z. (2020). Mom, can we send the baby back? *New York Times*. https://www.nytimes.com/2020/06/30/parenting/introduce-new-baby-sibling.html

Hirsch, L. (2016). Birth of a second child. KidsHealth. https://kidshealth.org/en/parents/second-child.html

Knight, R. (2019). How to return to work after taking parental leave. *Harvard Business Review*. https://hbr.org/2019/08/how-to-return-to-work-after-taking-parental-leave

Lerner, C. (n.d.). "When is he going back in your belly?" How to help older siblings adjust to the new baby. https://www.zerotothree.org/resources/1798-when-is-he-going-back-in-your-belly-how-to-help-older-siblings-adjust-to-the-new-baby

McCready, A. (n.d.). Bringing home baby: 5 tips to help older siblings adjust. Positive Parenting Solutions. https://www.positiveparentingsolutions.com/parenting/bringing-home-baby-older-siblings-tips

Chapter 12) Phase 3: Overview

Endnotes

1. I. Kuziemko, J. Pan, J. Shen, et al. (2018). The mommy effect: Do women anticipate the employment effects of motherhood? National Bureau of Economic Research. https://www.nber.org/system/files/working_papers/w24740/w24740.pdf
2. J. H. Greenhaus & T. D. Allen. (2011). Work-family balance: A review and extension of the literature. In J. C. Quick & L. E. Tetrick (Eds.), *Handbook of occupational health psychology* (pp. 165–183). American Psychological Association.
3. R. B. Ginsburg. (2016). Ruth Bader Ginsburg's advice for living. *New York Times*. https://www.nytimes.com/2016/10/02/opinion/sunday/ruth-bader-ginsburgs-advice-for-living.html?smid=tw-share

References

Ashforth, B. (2001). *Role transitions in organizational life: An identity-based perspective*. Routledge.

Bandura, A. (1994). Self-efficacy. In V. S. Ramachaudran (Ed.), *Encyclopedia of human behavior* (pp. 71–81). Academic Press.

Ladge, J. J., & Little, L. M. (2019). When expectations become reality: Work-family image management and identity adaptation. *Academy of Management Review, 44*(1), 126–149.

Millward, L. J. (2006). The transition to motherhood in an organizational context: An interpretative phenomenological analysis. *Journal of Occupational and Organizational Psychology, 79*(3), 315–333.

Chapter 13) Touchpoint 8: Acknowledge the Transition to Working Parent

Endnote

1. J. Goldman-Wetzler. (2020). *Optimal outcomes: Free yourself from conflict at work, at home, and in life.* HarperCollins

Chapter 14) Touchpoint 9: Adjustment

Endnotes

1. R. W. Quinn, G. M. Spreitzer, & C. F. Lam. (2012). Building a sustainable model of human energy in organizations: Exploring the critical role of resources. *Academy of Management Annals, 6*(1), 337–396.
2. C. M. Barnes. (2012). Working in our sleep: Sleep and self-regulation in organizations. *Organizational Psychology Review, 2*(3), 234–257.
3. H. M. Mullins, J. M. Cortina, C. L. Drake, et al. (2014). Sleepiness at work: A review and framework of how the physiology of sleepiness impacts the workplace. *Journal of Applied Psychology, 99*(6), 1096–1112.
4. L. E. Ross, B. J. Murray, & M. Steiner. (2005). Sleep and perinatal mood disorders: A critical review. *Journal of Psychiatry and Neuroscience, 30*(4), 247–256.
5. T. L. Crain, L. B. Hammer, T. Bodner, et al. (2019). Sustaining sleep: Results from the randomized controlled work, family, and health study. *Journal of Occupational Health Psychology, 24*(1), 180–197.
6. M. Sianoja, T. L. Crain, L. B. Hammer, et al. (2020). The relationship between leadership support and employee sleep. *Journal of Occupational Health Psychology, 25*(3), 187–202.
7. L. B. Hammer, E. E. Kossek, N. L. Yragui, et al. (2009). Development and validation of a multidimensional measure of family supportive supervisor behaviors (FSSB). *Journal of Management, 35*(4), 837–856.
8. S. N. Arpin, A. R. Starkey, C. D. Mohr, et al. (2018). "A well spent day brings happy sleep": A dyadic study of capitalization support in military-connected couples. *Journal of Family Psychology, 32*(7), 975–985.
9. M. Doucleff. (2021). *Hunt, gather, parent: What ancient cultures can teach us about the lost art of raising happy, helpful little humans.* Avid Reader Press.
10. N. Mohrbacher. (2015). Many moms may have been taught to breastfeed incorrectly: Surprising new research. Mothering. https://www.mothering.com/threads/many-moms-may-have-been-taught-to-breastfeed-incorrectly-surprising-new-research.1623877/
11. Marlo Thomas. (2012). The fallacy of balance, from Elizabeth Gilbert [Video file]. YouTube. https://www.youtube.com/watch?v=1yMHJ6G7Rvo
12. J. H. Greenhaus & N. J. Beutell. (1985). Sources of conflict between work and family roles. *Academy of Management Review, 10*(1), 76–88.
13. E. Batista. (2013). Happy workaholics need boundaries, not balance. *Harvard Business Review.* https://bg.hbr.org/2013/12/happy-workaholics-need-boundaries-not-balance
14. E. Batista, Happy workaholics need boundaries, not balance.

15. B. Brown. (2015). *Daring greatly: How the courage to be vulnerable transforms the way we live, love, parent, and lead.* Penguin Random House.
16. E. E. Kossek & B. A. Lautsch. (2008). *CEO of me: Creating a life that works in the flexible job age.* Wharton School Publishing.
17. E. E. Kossek. (2016). Managing work-life boundaries in the digital age. *Organizational Dynamics, 45*(3), 258–270. https://doi.org/10.1016/j.orgdyn.2016.07.010

References

Barnes, C. M., & Hollenbeck, J. R. (2009). Sleep deprivation and decision making teams: Burning the midnight oil or playing with fire? *Academy of Management Review, 34*(1), 56–66.

Barnes, C. M., Schaubroeck, J., Huth, M., et al. (2011). Lack of sleep and unethical conduct. *Organizational Behavior and Human Decision Processes, 115*(2), 169–180.

Brossoit, R. M., Crain, T. L., Leslie, J. J., et al. (2019). The effects of sleep on workplace cognitive failure and safety. *Journal of Occupational Health Psychology, 24*(4), 411–422.

Greenhaus, J. H., & Allen, T. D. (2011). Work-family balance: A review and extension of the literature. In J. C. Quick & L. E. Tetrick (Eds.), *Handbook of occupational health psychology* (pp. 165–183). American Psychological Association.

Kossek, E. E., Petty, R. A., Michel, J. S., et al. (2017). Work-family subcultures: Workgroup multilevel influences on family supportive supervisor behaviors (FSSB) affecting individual sleep quality and safety performance. In M. Las Heras, N. Chinchilla, & M. Grau (Eds.), *Work-family balance, technology and globalization* (pp. 62–85). Scholars Publishing.

Kreiner, G. E., Hollensbe, E. C., & Sheep, M. L. (2009). Balancing borders and bridges: Negotiating the work-home interface via boundary work tactics. *Academy of Management Journal, 52*(4), 704–730.

Morin, A. (2018). The 3 different kinds of helicopter parents. *Psychology Today.* https://www.psychologytoday.com/us/blog/what-mentally-strong-people-dont-do/201802/the-3-different-kinds-helicopter-parents

Rosekind, M. R., Gregory, K. B., Mallis, M. M., et al. (2010). The cost of poor sleep: Workplace productivity loss and associated costs. *Journal of Occupational and Environmental Medicine, 52*(1), 91–98.

Scott, B., & Judge, T. (2006). Insomnia, emotions, and job satisfaction: A multilevel study. *Journal of Management, 32*, 622–645.

Swanson, L. M., Arnedt, J. T., Rosekind, M. R., et al. (2011). Sleep disorders and work performance: Findings from the 2008 National Sleep Foundation Sleep in America poll. *Journal of Sleep Research, 20*(3), 487–494.

Trefalt, S. (2013). Between you and me: Setting work-nonwork boundaries in the context of workplace relationships. *Academy of Management Journal*, 56(6), 1802–1829.

Watson, N. F., Badr, M. S., Belenky, G., et al. (2015). Recommended amount of sleep for a healthy adult: A joint consensus statement of the American Academy of Sleep Medicine and Sleep Research Society. *Sleep*, 38, 843–844.

Chapter 15) Touchpoint 10: Access to Career Development

Endnotes

1. Bureau of Labor Statistics. (2019). *Number of jobs, labor market experience, and earnings growth: Results from a national longitudinal survey.* (USDL-19–1520). United States Department of Labor. https://www.bls.gov/news.release/pdf/nlsoy.pdf

2. L. A. Mainiero & S. E. Sullivan. (2005). Kaleidoscope careers: An alternate explanation for the "opt-out" revolution. *Academy of Management Perspectives*, 19(1), 106–123.

3. S. E. Sullivan & Y. Baruch. (2009). Advances in career theory and research: A critical review and agenda for future exploration. *Journal of Management*, 35(6), 1542–1571.

4. L. A. Mainiero & D. E. Gibson. (2018). The kaleidoscope career model revisited: How midcareer men and women diverge on authenticity, balance, and challenge. *Journal of Career Development*, 45(4), 361–377.

5. S. Ziegler. (2020). How to let go of working-mom guilt. *Harvard Business Review*. https://hbr.org/2020/09/how-to-let-go-of-working-mom-guilt

6. T. Morrison. (2017). The work you do, the person you are. *The New Yorker*. https://www.newyorker.com/magazine/2017/06/05/the-work-you-do-the-person-you-are

References

Arthur, M. B. (2008). Examining contemporary careers: A call for interdisciplinary inquiry. *Human Relations*, 61(2), 163–186.

Gunz, H. P., & Peiperl, M. (2007). *Handbook of career studies.* SAGE.

Rosenbaum, J. E. (1979). Tournament mobility: Career patterns in a corporation. *Administrative Science Quarterly*, 24(2), 220–241.

Rousseau, D. M. (1989). Psychological and implied contracts in organizations. *Employee Responsibilities and Rights Journal*, 2(2), 121–139.

Chapter 16) Additional Challenges and Resources

Endnotes

1. E. Gould & H. Shierholz. (2020). *Not everybody can work from home: Black and Hispanic workers are much less likely to be able to telework* [Report]. https://www.epi.org/blog/black-and-hispanic-workers-are-much-less-likely-to-be-able-to-work-from-home/
2. S. Sethi, C. Johnson-Staub, & K. G. Robbins. (2020). *An anti-racist approach to supporting child care through COVID-19 and beyond* [Report/Brief] https://www.clasp.org/publications/report/brief/anti-racist-approach-supporting-child-care-through-covid-19-and-beyond
3. B. N. Gaynes, N. Gavin, S. Meltzer-Brody, et al. (2005). *Perinatal depression: Prevalence, screening accuracy, and screening outcomes* [Report]. Agency for Healthcare Research and Quality. https://www.ncbi.nlm.nih.gov/books/NBK37740/
4. J. F. Paulson & S. D. Bazemore. (2010). Prenatal and postpartum depression in fathers and its association with maternal depression: A meta-analysis. *JAMA, 303*(19), 1961–1969.
5. D. Rothert. (2019). *At a loss: Finding your way after miscarriage, stillbirth, or infant death*. Open Air Books.
6. D. L. Davis. (2016). *Empty cradle, broken heart: Surviving the death of your baby*. Fulcrum.
7. New America. (n.d.) A timeline of paid family leave. https://www.newamerica.org/better-life-lab/reports/paid-family-leave-how-much-time-enough/a-timeline-of-paid-family-leave
8. K. H. Kriegsman & S. Palmer. (2013). *Just one of the kids: Raising a resilient family when one of your children has a physical disability*. The Johns Hopkins University Press.
9. J. Sumner. (2020). *Eat, sleep, save the world: Words of encouragement for the special needs parent*. B&H Publishing.

References

Centers for Disease Control Prevention. (2020). *Pregnancy and infant loss*. Department of Health and Human Services. https://www.cdc.gov/ncbddd/stillbirth/features/pregnancy-infant-loss.html

Chidi, E., & Cahill, E. P. (2020). Protecting your birth: A guide for Black mothers. *New York Times*. https://www.nytimes.com/article/black-mothers-birth.html

Dimoff, J., Brady, J., & Gilbert, S. (2021). The painful collision between work life and pregnancy loss. The Conversation. https://theconversation.com/the-painful-collision-between-work-life-and-pregnancy-loss-151196

Hintz-Zambrano, K. (2017). Postpartum care traditions from around the world. MOTHER. https://www.mothermag.com/postpartum-care-traditions/

Oncken, L. (n.d.) Policy recommendation: Paid Family Leave. New America. https://www.newamerica.org/in-depth/care-report/policy-recommendation-paid-family-leave/

Postpartum Support International. (2014). Perinatal mood and anxiety disorders [Fact Sheet]. https://www.postpartum.net/wp-content/uploads/2014/11/PSI-PMD-FACT-SHEET-2015.pdf

Walsh, T. B., Davis, R. N., & Garfield, C. (2020). A call to action: Screening fathers for perinatal depression. Pediatrics, 145(1), 1–3.

Acknowledgments

THIS BOOK WOULD not have been possible without the help and support of many people. Writing a book like this is truly a collaborative process, and we have been blessed beyond measure. Making these acknowledgments feels fraught, as we want to celebrate everyone's support, major and minor! Here goes.

To our core team at the Center for Parental Leave Leadership: Amy Pytlovany, PhD, for excellent research and citation skills; Eric Williams for organizational skills, dad perspective, and deft handling of permissions; Jeff Smith for his patience, generosity, and graphic design expertise for the images in this book and over our many decades; Allison Ellis, PhD, for her beta read and new parent insights; and Alecxix Lopez Tapia for beta reading and jumping in whenever needed.

To our contributors and interviewees, who inspire us with their work to support families: Scott Benson, PhD; Wendy Davis, PhD; Jennifer Goldman-Wetzler, PhD; John Gottman, PhD; Julie Gottman, PhD; Leslie Hammer, PhD; Hermine Hayes-Klein, JD; Ellen Ernst Kossek, PhD; Eve Rodsky, JD; and Jada Shapiro.

Thank you to all the parents who responded to our parental leave transition survey and crowdsourced stories and opinions for this book.

Hugs, deep bows of gratitude, and joyous high-fives to our knife fairy and editing partner Louisa Bennion (Alloy Wordworks) and Kate Beacom for in-the-thick-of-it support and wordsmithing.

Thanks to our wonderful beta readers: Karen Abrams Gerber, EdD; Kate Beacom; Steve Burdick; Deborah Campbell; Meghan Dicklin; Allison Ellis, PhD; Rachel Gupta; Sumeet Gupta; Alecxix Lopez Tapia; Abigail Perry; and Eric Williams. Especially Kisha Edwards-Gandsy, Sharon Ng, and Maryum Tu, who did double duty as cultural sensitivity readers.

Thank you to our editor at Wiley, Mike Campbell, for believing in us and sharing our vision that the world needs this book. Without his advocacy this first book about navigating parental leave would not yet exist.

Special thanks to Microsoft Corporation for their leadership in being the first company in the United States to offer our RETAIN-based employee/manager-aligned parental leave support and training program to their employees. Particularly Teresa McDade for having the vision and strategic acumen to make it happen. Also to Trisha Aldrich and WellSpring EAP for championing this work at every turn and for their visionary and dedicated support of working parents needing parental leave.

Thanks to Sarah Cotton, PhD, of Transitioning Well, LLC for reaching out so many years ago to see if Amy would bring RETAIN to her continent and for the opportunity to pilot RETAIN and train coaches in Australia. Amy will always be grateful for what she learned from their work together.

Thank you to Sam Jeibmann, Tess Whitehead, Ted Helprin, and their team at Supply for their continuing help and support, particularly with our book cover.

Thanks also to Deanna Siegel Senior, PhD; Orla Nic Domhnaill, PhD; Rachael Ellison; Merriah Fairchild; Mary Zamore, PhD; Emily Segal; Vicki Choi; Gemela Foster; and John Bray for extra support and cheerleading.

Thanks to Nancy Schlossberg, PhD, for her trailblazing work in transition theory and development of the 4-S System, in which she graciously allowed us to ground our 6-S System for Parental Leave Transition Success and the Parental Leave Transition Assessment (PLTA).

Thanks to all the movement leaders and female founders who are building companies and solutions to close the egregious gaps in parent support—from policy to practice. The full list would be another book; in the meantime, see Appendix 3 for a small sampling.

And, of course, thanks to our spouses, Mike and Ben, and our children for providing patient, loving support so we could write a book during a pandemic, epic wildfires, ice storms, racial justice awakenings, political insurrection, and the truly unfathomable amount of extenuating circumstances for which 2020–2021 will be forever infamous.

Amy extends special thanks to the following:

David Dotlich, PhD, and Doug Elwood for more than 25 years of support and mentoring for herself and now her children

Karen Abrams Gerber, EdD, for being her soul translator while holding perspective, intention, and heart over the last 20 years from dissertation to new mom to now

Tillie Walton for her unwavering support since they reached double digits (together!); her Brunch Girls for the consistency of their love and life-defining friendship, Kristy Claypoole, Erica Fuson, and Rachel Walchak; and Lisa Nice and Amanda Macklowe Atlas for their ever-present support across all time and distance

Her family: son Luca for the daily walks, special hugs, and you-can-do-it songs; daughter Maggie for the cartwheels, smoothies, and snuggles; dad David, who makes sure she always hears the other side from a loving source; stepmom Mary, who stitches all the quilts to keep everyone warm; mom Peggy who taught her to always notice our gorgeous world; mother-in-love Maureen for constant support; cousin Kate who became the kids' online-school navigator (and best friend!) so pandemic wackiness didn't derail this book (and who also made sure we all ate); cousin Catie who lived her parental leave and shared her insights from it while Amy was writing; and all the aunts, uncles, cousins, and non-blood family who made this possible. Finally, to step-dad Don, who recently left this world and in doing so reminded us of what matters—family; and grandma GG who made sure Amy stayed in school when it counted, gave lifetimes of love, and timed her passing in a way that gave more.

A final thank you to the many client companies and parents we have had the honor to work with over the years. Seeing your success makes the hard work worthwhile.

About the Authors

Amy Beacom, EdD

DR. AMY BEACOM is the founder and CEO of the Center for Parental Leave Leadership, the first consultancy in the United States to focus exclusively on parental leave. Drawing on over 25 years in executive leadership development and coaching, Amy consults with Fortune 100 companies, international organizations, and working parents, transforming the way our companies and our country engage with the parental leave transition. Amy created the first evidence-based parental leave transition coaching model and distilled it into this book, the first of its kind to provide step-by-step guidance for navigating this complex life transition. She has trained and supervised parental leave coaches in the United States and Australia, and the manager-focused training program she created can be found in more than 80 countries around the world. She regularly appears on expert panels, conferences, and podcasts and has been quoted in such publications as the *New York Times*, the *Washington Post*, and *Working Mother*. Amy holds a BA in sociology/anthropology with a minor in gender studies from Lewis and Clark College, an MA in organizational psychology from Columbia University, and a doctorate, also from Columbia University, combining organizational psychology, women's leadership, work/family, and applied anthropology. She lives in Portland, Oregon, with her husband and their son and daughter.

Sue Campbell

Sue Campbell is a writer, author, and coach who has worked with the Center for Parental Leave Leadership since its early days, helping to communicate the transformative impact of their core mission. Her professional background includes 12 years in public service, seven of those as a business systems analyst leading projects and teams to deliver process improvements through technology. Her writing, often focused on issues important to parents, has been published in many outlets, including *Prevention*, *Good Housekeeping*, *Scary Mommy*, and *Mamalode*. She is also the author of *The Cat, the Cat, the Leap, and the List*, a novel for middle-grade readers. Sue lives in Portland, Oregon, with her husband and two children.

Index